Wills, Trusts, and Probate Law for Paralegals

Pamela S. Gibson, J.D.

PEARSON

Prentice
Hall

Upper Saddle River, New Jersey
Columbus, Ohio

Library of Congress Cataloging-in-Publication Data

Gibson, Pamela S.
  Wills, trusts, and probate law for paralegals / Pamela S. Gibson. — 1st ed.
    p. cm.
  ISBN-13: 978-0-13-236982-4
  ISBN-10: 0-13-236982-6
  1. Estate planning—United States. 2. Executors and administrators—United States. 3. Wills—United States. 4. Trusts and trustees—United States.
5. Probate law and practice—United States. 6. Inheritance and succession—United States. 7. Legal assistants—United States—Handbooks,
manuals, etc. I. Title.
  KF750.Z9G53 2009
  346.7305'2—dc22

                                                                                              2007031133

Editor in Chief: Vernon Anthony
Acquisitions Editor: Gary Bauer
Development Editor: Linda Cupp
Project Manager: Jessica Sykes
Senior Operations Supervisor: Pat Tonneman
Art Director: Diane Y. Ernsberger
Cover Designer: Ali Mohrman
Cover art: Corbis
Director, Image Resource Center: Melinda Patelli
Manager, Rights and Permissions: Zina Arabia
Manager, Visual Research: Beth Brenzel
Manager, Cover Visual Research and Permissions: Karen Sanatar
Image Permission Coordinator: Angelique Sharps
Director of Marketing: David Gesell
Marketing Manager: Leigh Ann Sims
Marketing Coordinator: Alicia Dysert

This book was set in Minion by S4Carlisle Publishing Services. It was printed and bound by Edwards Brothers.
The cover was printed by Phoenix Color Corp.

Chapter opener photograph: Rosemary Walker/Stone/Getty Images

Pearson Education Ltd.   Pearson Education Australia Pty. Limited
Pearson Education Singapore Pte. Ltd.   Pearson Education North Asia Ltd
Pearson Education Canada, Ltd.   Pearson Educación de Mexico, S.A. de C.V.
Pearson Education—Japan   Pearson Education Malaysia Pte. Ltd.

10 9 8 7 6
ISBN-13: 978-0-13-236982-4
ISBN-10: 0-13-236982-6

Preface

Planning for the distribution of accumulated wealth and administration of the plan upon death is the focus of *Wills, Trusts, and Probate Law for Paralegals.* The purpose of the book is to familiarize and inform a paralegal student of this specialty area's terminology, its rules of law, and document production. Planning for the preservation of wealth and controlling its distribution is the theme of the textbook. Each chapter begins with a discussion about the importance of planning and then contains the substantive or procedural legal material. This approach fosters a practical development of legal concepts that culminates in an understanding of wills, trusts, and probate. That understanding will be demonstrated by the paralegal student completing an estate planning and administration portfolio. The portfolio approach prepares the student, upon graduation, to meet and even exceed the expectations of an employer.

Objectives

Three primary objectives are met by the material presented. The first objective is to solidify a student's knowledge of wills, trusts, and probate. Regardless of whether a student plans to work in this legal specialty area, this text develops a general appreciation and understanding of the law as it relates to estate planning and administration.

The second objective is a focus on substantive law, procedural law, and ethics related to this specialty area. Thus, a student learns how to function as a valuable estate planning and administration paralegal.

The third and most specific objective is a focus on document production for estate planning and administration. Unlike other texts in the legal area, *Wills, Trusts, and Probate Law for Paralegals* uses a portfolio approach. The text explains to students a step-by-step method of drafting documents and then requires them to draft a variety of documents used in this practice area. These documents, based on two case examples chosen by the student or instructor, may be combined into a portfolio that the student may use as writing samples when interviewing.

Pedagogical Features

The text includes several pedagogical features. Legal terms are set in bold and defined in the margins of the text. Practical examples are included to illustrate more complicated legal concepts. Select case law is summarized to illustrate rules of law. Many sample documents are included to demonstrate proper content and format. An estate administration checklist, interview checklist, summaries of tax schedules, and other similar features make more succinct the concepts discussed in the body of the book.

Assignments and Applications

Assignments encourage a student's development, growth, and knowledge in estate planning and administration. These assignments include practical exercises reviewing information contained in the respective chapter, role-playing activities, legal research, factual investigation, and document drafting. In addition, Chapters 1 through 5 contain "Applying Your Knowledge" features that require students to analyze hypothetical scenarios. All these vehicles allow the instructor to evaluate a student's progress while studying this legal area.

Organization

Wills, Trusts, and Probate Law for Paralegals is organized into two major sections. Part I is Estate Planning, and Part II is Estate Administration. Part I consists of five chapters that focus on planning for how accumulated wealth should be disposed of upon death. Chapter 1 is an overview of the concepts of planning, wealth, and property. Chapter 2 covers intestacy and intestate succession laws. It discusses the disadvantages of failing to plan and emphasizes the need for a plan. Chapter 3 focuses on the substantive law for drafting a will, its revocation, and other basic estate planning documents. Chapter 4 provides a practical, step-by-step approach to drafting a will, the clauses that may be included, how to properly execute the will, and where to store it. Chapter 5 covers the more complicated subject of trusts, the requirements for a trust, different types of trusts, and drafting tips.

Part II, Estate Administration, looks at the procedure used when a person has died and how to transfer wealth from the decedent's estate to its new owners, the heirs or beneficiaries. Chapter 6 is an overview of the procedure. It also introduces the key player: the personal representative. Chapter 7 fleshes out the first step of administration, which is to obtain letters of appointment. It includes a discussion about initial interviews, petitions, and other court documents. Chapter 8 moves the procedure forward with inclusion of inventory preparation, creditor claim notification, and filing of claims. Chapter 9 is a practical approach to tax law, with a focus on the final income tax return of the decedent, estate tax, applicable exclusion amount, inheritance tax, and fiduciary tax. Chapter 10 concludes the procedure with information regarding the final account, receipts, and discharge. It also discusses small estate administration, ancillary administration, and will contests.

This text's thoroughly developed legal content, theme, pedagogical features, and portfolio approach, prepare the student to be employed as a knowledgeable and talented member of a professional legal team.

Additional Resources

The textbook includes an additional tool to help a student succeed:

- Companion Website at **www.prenhall.com/gibson**

Instructors will find the following helpful resources available with this book:

- Instructor's Manual with Companion Website
- PowerPoint Slide Presentation
- Test Generator
- CourseConnect Online: Wills, Trust, and Estates Course

CourseConnect Online: Wills, Trust, and Estates Course

Looking for robust online course content to reinforce and enhance your student learning? We have the solution: CourseConnect! CourseConnect courses contain customizable modules of content mapped to major learning outcomes. Each learning object contains interactive tutorials, rich media, discussion questions, MP3 downloadable lectures, assessments, and interactive activities that address different learning styles. CourseConnect Courses follow a consistent 21-step instructional design process, yet each course is developed individually by instructional designers and instructors who have taught the course online. Test questions, created by assessment professionals, were developed at all levels of Bloom's Taxonomy. When you buy a CourseConnect course, you purchase a complete package that provides you with detailed documentation you can use for your accreditation reviews. CourseConnect courses can be delivered in any commercial platform such as **WebCT, BlackBoard, Angel,** or **eCollege** platforms. For more information, contact your representative or call 800-635-1579.

To access supplementary materials online, instructors need to request an instructor access code. Go to **www.pearsonhighered.com/irc,** click the **Instructor Resource Center** link, and then click **Register Today** for an instructor access code. Within 48 hours after registering you will receive a confirming e-mail including an instructor access code. Once you have received your code, go to the site and log on for full instructions on downloading the materials you wish to use.

ACKNOWLEDGMENTS

Any large project like *Wills, Trusts, and Probate Law for Paralegals* has many people help it come to fruition. I would like to thank the following people for their encouragement, hard work, feedback, and/or faith in me:

- Mom and Dad for believing in my career aspirations and helping them become a reality. Especially my mother, who inspired me to take on life's challenges, to welcome creative endeavors, and to make my dreams come true.
- Carrie Smith for all her hard work, for keeping me organized and on a deadline, for her contributions of research and feedback, and for her encouragement at difficult moments.
- Hillary Cooper for her hard work on this project, her ability to produce charts and graphs that illustrate key points, her organizational abilities and her gentle sense of humor that helped get this project off the ground.
- Sean Collier for his contributions to the chapter about trusts.
- April Cash for her assistance on the ancillary projects.

- Jim Smith for his faith in me and also for his guidance and direction.
- Jim Harsevoort for honoring me by expressing his respect and admiration of my hard work, perseverance, and talents; and especially for the music.
- Richard Colan for all his encouragement and belief in my ability to produce this book, his willingness to celebrate the various milestones of the project, and his ability to always envision its completion, even when not one word had yet been put on paper.
- Jeanne Creekmore for countless hours of listening and support.
- Jessica Sykes and Marianne L'Abbate for their valuable comments and hard work during production.
- Linda Cupp and Gary Bauer for giving me this opportunity and guiding me throughout the journey.

The following reviewers gave valuable feedback and insight during the writing of this textbook:

Ernest Davila, *San Jacinto College North*
Kelly Phillips Erb, *Community College of Philadelphia*
Heidi Getchell-Bastien, *Northern Essex Community College*
Kent D. Kauffman, *Ivy Tech Community College—Northeast*
Sondi A. Lee, *Camden County Community College*
Kurt Stanberry, *University of Houston, Downtown*
Laura Tolsma, *Lansing Community College*
Glenn Yabuno, *San Bernardino Valley College*

About the Author

Attorney Pamela Gibson is the Legal Department Chairperson at Rockford Business College. She maintains her Wisconsin Bar License and does consulting work in the areas of estate planning and administration. A graduate of Carroll College majoring in Business Administration and Communications, with an emphasis in Journalism, she continued on to The Ohio State University to earn her law degree. She started practicing law in a small civil and criminal law firm. Then she turned her attention toward academia, and she has been involved in legal education for eighteen years.

Contents

PART I

ESTATE PLANNING

Chapter **one**

WEALTH, PROPERTY, AND ESTATES

The Need for a Plan

Many of us spend much of our lives focused on acquiring wealth. While chasing after our dreams of acquiring money, property, power, and success, we develop plans and goals of how to achieve these dreams. For the acquisition of money or property, we may plan to work hard and/or enter into a high-paying profession. We analyze the requirements of education to pursue our job careers. We are diligent and disciplined in studying, attending school, or developing physical strength to start on the road to success. Then we put in grueling hours of work to improve our talents, skills, and knowledge in our given occupation. With these plans put into action, we accomplish goals; we acquire money and property.

The concept of wealth can also include desires for the intangible. We want a loving family and faithful friends. We want a degree of influence or power in our workplaces, families, or community. We may desire a strong spiritual connection. All of this wealth is also acquired by beginning with a plan, following through on it, reviewing the plan to make certain our goals are being accomplished, and revising or even completely reforming it as we learn from our mistakes or change our focus on what we desire from the world.

Why then, with so much planning of how our lives need to be ordered, do we forget to plan for what will happen after our death? If we have acquired wealth during our lives, it needs to be distributed properly upon our death. Let's say, for example, we are very wealthy: we have acquired much money and much property, we have a loving family, dedicated friends, hard-working business associates, and influence in our community. We can continue our legacy by leaving

OBJECTIVES

After studying this chapter, you should be able to:

- Explain the need for an estate plan.
- Understand the basic terminology related to wills.
- Recognize and enumerate the purposes for having a will.
- Identify and give an example of different types of property.
- Distinguish among the different types of property ownership in both common law and community property states and determine who receives a deceased tenant's share.
- Understand and identify what property is subject to probate and what property would be exempt from probate.
- Explain the contents of an estate planning and estate administration portfolio and the advantages to preparing one.

careful instructions to be carried out upon our death. An estate plan is just one more plan enabling us to be successful in connection with the wealth we have sought and attained. We decide how this wealth can continue working under new management and benefit the world. If properly thought out and planned, our desires to improve the world can continue even after we are gone. The law applied to our estate plan can accomplish this goal. We should ask ourselves: who needs our property? Who will best use it? Who should receive a symbol of our love? Are there methods we can put into place that allow our dreams to continue? All of these questions can be answered and effectuated with an estate plan. And here are some answers.

Who needs our property? If minor children, a mentally incompetent family member, or a charitable organization is the answer, we can provide for them with a will or trust.

Who will best use the property? If a minor child or another family member who does not wisely spend money needs the property, we can place it into trust. The individual receives the money, but someone else manages it. Maybe we have created a business and need to make certain it will continue successfully after our death. Choosing the beneficiary or providing for a buy-sell agreement in a partnership document may help to secure this goal.

Who should receive a symbol of our love? A beautiful gift of money or property in a will helps those left behind to know they were loved. It may help the survivors to know the decedent will always care for them through the gift.

What methods can be put into place to ensure that our dreams will continue after we are gone? If we were active with a charitable organization, a gift to it in a will or trust perpetuates our desires. If we desire a certain outcome from a family member, a business, or an organization, a trust can be created that funds and yet controls the actions of the designated beneficiary.

Death adds meaning and significance to our precious life. We deepen our respect for ourselves, each other, and the world by planning what will happen to our wealth upon our death. As in life, the first steps for beginning a plan are to gain knowledge, to focus on what can be accomplished, and to learn how to accomplish it. This book contains the first steps. Chapters 1 through 5 contain information so you can learn how an estate plan will help you, your family, your friends, and your clients. Chapter 2 continues the theme of the need for a plan and focuses on the pitfalls of lack of planning. Chapter 3 explains methods to acquire certain results by the use of certain documents. Chapters 4 and 5 discuss the documents to be used to achieve the plan. They focus on the will and the trust and the requirements necessary so the legal formalities are met and the plan can be put into action.

Chapters 6 through 10 show how the courts effectuate the plan: how it is put into action after the individual has died. They include the documents required to make certain the plan is properly instituted and comes to fruition.

Let's take the first step and introduce you to estate planning and property law.

Introduction and Basic Terminology for Wills

estate planning
A method of preparing for the administration of a person's property upon death by using documents and other arrangements usually to reduce the costs of administration and taxes.

Estate planning consists of determining how wealth will be distributed upon our death and how to make certain those we want to receive our wealth get it within the mandates of the law. It includes the laws of wills, trusts, property, insurance, and tax. We will focus on introduction to wills and property law in Chapter 1.

Chapters 3 and 4 contain more on wills. Chapter 5 covers trusts, and Chapter 9 covers taxes. A **will** is a device for distributing wealth. It is typically a written document that contains gifts and directions. The gifts are given to beneficiaries. The person making the will is called a **testator** if male and a **testatrix** if female. The directions in the will include basic items like the nomination of a personal representative, who manages the estate as it goes through court. The procedure of the will being declared valid by the court upon the death of the testator or testatrix is called **probate**. The probate procedure, including the documents filed with the court, comprises the second portion of this textbook. Chapters 6 through 10 explain how to accomplish a probate. The probate proceeding declares whether a will is valid and then ensures the proper distribution of the estate to the beneficiaries. If the court declares a will is not valid or no will was executed, the individual died **intestate**, or without a valid will. Then the probate court applies the statutes of descent and distribution or statutes of intestate succession, which govern the pattern of inheritance if no valid will exists. Those laws are discussed at length in Chapter 2.

This textbook references the **Uniform Probate Code (U.P.C.)**. This is a uniform law that could be adopted by state legislatures to govern wills and probate procedure within a state.

Purposes of a Will

Many people die intestate, or without executing a valid will. Once we understand the purpose of a will, this understanding encourages us to take the time and make the effort to obtain one. Several objectives for executing a will exist. The first is to ensure those individuals whom we want to receive our wealth actually get it. We do not want the government deciding for us who will inherit. We do not want the wealth to be used improperly. We probably don't want the government, rather than our intended beneficiaries, to receive the wealth through the imposition of taxes. Further, we are given the opportunity to nominate who may act on our behalf as a personal representative to ensure that our estate plan is properly carried out. We may also nominate those we trust to care for minor children that we have left behind. Finally, we may save money or costs incurred against the estate. All of these objectives may be accomplished through careful planning.

Summary of the objectives of a will:

1. We choose who receives the estate.
2. We can leave property to individuals or organizations that would not receive it if we died intestate.
3. We could reduce taxes.
4. We could nominate a personal representative to administer the estate.
5. We could nominate a guardian for a minor.
6. We could save money by lowering costs of administering the estate.

The main purposes of a will are to ensure that our goals for our wealth are acted upon and accomplished, and to protect our wealth against waste, improper handling, or being misdirected to the wrong person. A will is our direction or map for how our wealth will continue to benefit society when we are gone.

---

will
A testamentary document that distributes wealth and directs how the estate should be administered.

testator
A man who makes and executes a will.

testatrix
A woman who makes and executes a will.

probate
The process of (a) a court admitting a will as valid, and/or (b) administering a decedent's estate.

intestate
Dying without a valid will.

Uniform Probate Code (U.P.C.)
State legislatures can adopt this body of law relating to all matters in which a probate court has authority.

Definitions and Categories of Property

Although the chapter begins with a definition of wealth that includes more than property, the focus of estate planning is primarily on property. Thus, an understanding of property law is required to grasp estate planning and probate. An introduction to property law is a vital component of understanding how to put together an estate plan.

Two categories of property exist: real property and personal property. **Real property** consists of land and things attached to it. Other names used for real property may be real estate or realty. Real property is tangible; you can touch it, and it is immovable. Things attached to land include **fixtures** or items that become so attached to land that they take on the characteristics of the land and are treated as real property under the law. Examples of fixtures include a furnace, a toilet, or an in-ground swimming pool. Several factors or tests for determining whether an item is a fixture can be used by the court. The court considers how attached the item is to the land. The more securely attached, the more likely the item is a fixture. Could damage be caused to the land if the item is removed? How much damage? If removal of the item would cause much damage to the land, it is likely that the court would declare it a fixture. Does the item increase the value of the land or improve it? If the answer to this question is yes, it is likely a fixture. Finally, how have the parties defined the item? If a contract calls the item a fixture, the court will probably rule that the item is a fixture. Natural vegetation such as trees and shrubbery are also classified as real estate.

Personal property could be called personalty. What distinguishes personal property from real property is that personal property is movable. Personal property is divided into two categories: tangible and intangible. Tangible property consists of items that are touchable. Examples include cars, books, clothing, and so on.

The second category of personal property is intangible items. They are claims represented by bank accounts, promissory notes, stocks, bonds, patents, and so on. They are intangible—you cannot touch them. For example, you have a stock certificate for ABC Corporation. The piece of paper is tangible. However, the stock certificate represents ownership in the corporation. This idea is intangible; you cannot hold onto an item called ownership. That is why it is intangible. Intangible items are movable. You can move the items that represent the concept relatively easily.

Types of Property Ownership

It is important to introduce the law of property in a class about wills. This section provides an overview of the types of property ownership; however, a full understanding of property ownership is recommended to the paralegal who plans on pursuing a career in this legal area. The partnering of a real property class with an estate planning and probate class makes the paralegal more valuable in the workplace.

One person may own the land or have the full bundle of legal rights. This is called ownership in **fee simple** or fee simple absolute. The individual has more than mere possession of the land; he or she also has rights with regard to controlling it, using and enjoying it, excluding others from entering it, disposing of it, mortgaging it, and so on. A fee simple is considered the highest interest in real estate. As previously mentioned, only one person owns the property; therefore, no

real property
Land and items securely attached to it.

fixtures
Personal property that is securely attached to the land so that it takes on the characteristics of real property and is treated as real property under the law.

fee simple
The highest interest in land. One person has full ownership to the land.

one has automatic survivorship rights to it. The owner, upon death, must transfer the real estate to another. This transfer occurs through three methods:

1. Gifting the realty to the beneficiary in a will.
2. Gifting the realty to a trust to be held for the benefit of a beneficiary.
3. Dying intestate and having the statutes of intestate succession prescribe the rightful heir to the land.

This type of ownership is also called ownership by severalty. One person owns the property. Ownership by severalty also applies to personal property.

Sometimes two or more people own the same property—whether it be personal property or real property. This is called concurrent ownership or co-ownership. In most states, three types of concurrent ownership exist:

1. Tenancy in common.
2. Joint tenancy.
3. Tenancy by the entirety.

Tenancy in common is where two or more persons hold a possessory interest in the same piece of property. A tenant in common does not have survivorship rights. In other words, when a tenant in common dies, the tenant's interest passes to heirs (intestate) or beneficiaries (will). For example, Anthony, Marcus, and Thaddeus are tenants in common of a parcel of land. If Anthony dies, his interest goes to his heirs or beneficiaries (see Figure 1-1).

Tenants in common may have this status even if they have not acquired the property at the same time or through the same method (will or deed). Return to the last example. If Thaddeus sells his interest to Greg, Greg becomes a tenant in common with Anthony and Marcus (see Figure 1-2).

Because no survivorship right is created under a tenancy in common, a tenant should plan to dispose of an interest in the property through a will or

tenancy in common
An interest held by two or more persons, each having a possessory right in the same piece of property.

Figure 1-1 Tenants in common

Anthony—dies	Marcus	Thaddeus

Share goes to Anthony's heirs (intestate) or beneficiaries (will).

Figure 1-2 Tenants in common

Anthony	Marcus	Thaddeus—sells to Greg

becomes

Anthony	Marcus	Greg

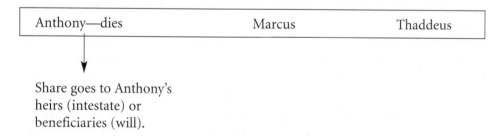

Figure 1-3   Joint tenancy

Anthony	Marcus	Thaddeus

Anthony dies.

Marcus	Thaddeus

Marcus dies.

Thaddeus

a trust. If such a plan is not made, the state's statutes of intestate succession shall be applied.

Traditionally, a way to distinguish among the three types of concurrent ownership is by unities. These are characteristics that demonstrate the differences among the types of co-ownership. A tenancy in common has one unity: the unity of possession. All tenants have the right to possess an undivided interest in the property. Property held in tenancy in common is considered probate property and must be transferred to heirs or beneficiaries in a probate proceeding.

joint tenancy
A single estate in property held by two or more persons created under one instrument at one time.

The second type of concurrent ownership is **joint tenancy**. Joint tenancy is a single estate in property held by two or more people created by one instrument at one time. All of the tenants have an equal right to share in the use and enjoyment of the property. When one joint tenant dies, the interest passes to any surviving joint tenants until one joint tenant owns the property alone or severally. This final surviving joint tenant then passes the property to beneficiaries in a will or to heirs by dying intestate. For example, if Anthony, Marcus, and Thaddeus are joint tenants, they own all of the land together with survivorship rights. If Anthony dies, his interest passes to Marcus and Thaddeus. If Marcus then dies, Thaddeus owns all of the land (see Figure 1-3). Thaddeus now owns the property in fee simple. If Thaddeus dies, the property goes to his heirs (intestate) or beneficiaries (will).

Consider again that Anthony, Marcus, and Thaddeus are joint tenants. Let's say that Thaddeus wants to sell his interest to Greg. Assuming this is accomplished, what is Greg's relationship to Anthony and Marcus? The answer is that he is a tenant in common with them. Review the definition of a joint tenant. It states that the interest must be created at the same time by the same instrument. Greg is purchasing the property at a later time. A different document has been created to purchase his interest in the property than the original document that created the joint tenancy of Anthony, Marcus, and Thaddeus. The new relationship created is shown in Figure 1-4.

Anthony and Marcus are joint tenants. Greg is a tenant in common with Anthony and Marcus.

When Greg dies, his interest would pass to his beneficiaries or heirs. If Anthony dies before Marcus, his interest is inherited by Marcus. If Marcus dies before Anthony, his interest is inherited by Anthony because of the survivorship right created in a joint tenancy. As a result of this concept, property held in joint tenancy is nonprobate property. It does not need to go through a probate proceeding to be

Figure 1-4   Joint tenancy and tenancy in common

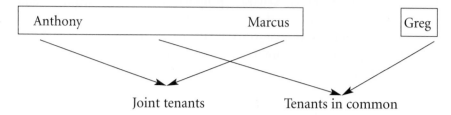

passed on to the next owner, which can be an advantage when it is used as an estate planning device.

A joint tenancy is distinguished from a tenancy in common because of its survivorship right. Another way to distinguish between the two tenancies is the unities that define them. As you recall, a tenancy in common has only one unity: the unity of possession. A joint tenancy consists of four unities: the unities of possession, time, title, and interest. The unity of possession is that each tenant has the right to possess an undivided interest in the property. Time means the tenants acquired possession of the property at the same time. Title means the tenants acquired ownership through the same instrument, a deed or a will. Finally, the unity of interest means the tenants have identical interests in the property with regard to quantity and duration. If Mary and Ann hold property together, but Mary has a fee simple and Ann has a life estate, these interests are not the same. Mary and Ann are not joint tenants.

The third type of concurrent ownership under common law is tenancy by the entirety. A **tenancy by the entirety** is ownership of property by a husband and wife together. For such a tenancy to be created, the man and woman must be married. Fiancées cannot create such an interest. A tenancy by the entirety contains five unities: those of possession, time, title, interest, and person. The fifth unity—person—arises under the common law concept of the doctrine of oneness, where the law presumed that when a man and woman married, they became one person.

A tenancy by the entirety also provides for a right of survivorship. When one spouse dies, the other inherits the property. Thus, property held under tenancy by the entirety is nonprobate property and is not subject to a probate proceeding.

Because of the requirement that the unity of person must exist, some states change the tenancy by the entirety ownership to a tenant in common ownership if the couple divorce. This approach eliminates the right of survivorship requirement. Some states have abolished tenancy by the entirety.

Some states do not follow the common law rules of tenancy by the entirety. They create co-ownership between spouses under community property or marital property. The community property states are Arizona, California, Idaho, Louisiana, Nevada, New Mexico, Texas, and Washington. In 1986, Wisconsin adopted the Uniform Marital Property Act (UMPA) and changed its status from a common law state to a marital property state. Marital property law is similar to community property law.

These states dictate that spouses equally share in their assets. Upon the death of one spouse, the other owns one-half of the property as a survivor. The remaining one-half is subject to estate administration. Community property

tenancy by the entirety
Ownership of property by a husband and wife together.

community property
Property owned by a husband and wife, each having an undivided one-half ownership right because of their marital status.

separate property
Property that one spouse owns exclusively because it was acquired by the individual prior to marriage or through other methods such that the law deems the property as separate.

states divide property into two classifications: **community property** or marital property, and separate property. **Separate property** is property acquired and owned by a man or woman prior to the marriage or acquired during the marriage by gift, will, or inheritance, or it is classified by the parties through agreement or by state statute as separate. Two main tests can be used to help a court determine if property is separate:

1. Time of acquisition.
2. Source of funds used to acquire the item.

The presumption in community property states is that the property is community property. If a spouse wants to protect separate property, the spouse needs to keep it separate from marital property. Tracing the property's use can help to determine if it has lost or retained its separate property classification.

For example, assume that Dave and Beth are married. Beth has inherited $100,000 from her mother. She puts $50,000 of it in a bank account with just her name on it. This account will probably remain separate property. She uses $20,000 of the inheritance to pay off the mortgage on the real estate she and Dave bought together, and it is titled jointly in their names. That $20,000 has been commingled with community property and probably will now be classified as community property. It loses its separate property status. Beth then buys a $30,000 car, which she titles jointly in her name and Dave's. Dave drives the car and uses his paycheck to make repairs on the car and pay for gas. This $30,000 put into a marital asset, coupled with the fact that Dave's community property paycheck maintains it, turns the $30,000 into community property.

Recall Beth's bank account with just her name on it. If Beth allows Dave to deposit money he has earned into her bank account, the bank account may become community property. To protect separate property, a spouse should keep separate property separate. Another method of protecting separate property is to have a spouse sign a written contract agreeing the property is separate. A marital property agreement in Wisconsin helps the court to determine how to classify property. This document can even serve as an estate planning tool. Some spouses may use trust law to protect separate property acquired during a marriage.

APPLYING YOUR KNOWLEDGE

Julia and James are married. During the marriage, James's parents give him $25,000. He takes $5,000 of it and pays for improvements on the house that he and Julia bought during their marriage and have titled jointly in their names. He puts $8,000 of the gift in a stock portfolio that is titled only in his name. Julia signs an agreement saying that she has no claim or right to the portfolio. He uses $12,000 of the money to purchase a car for the family, which he shares with Julia. With regard to the following property, identify whether it is community or separate property. Explain your answers.

a. Repairs to the home.
b. Car.
c. Stock portfolio ($8,000).
d. The amount of $2,000 that the stock portfolio makes during their marriage.

Probate Versus Nonprobate Property

To help in the estate planning process, it is important for a legal professional to be aware of what property is subject to probate and what property passes to another person without being subject to the probate process. Many clients prefer property to pass to their intended recipients outside the probate process. Usually less cost is involved, and the recipient receives the property faster than if it goes through probate. Knowing this information helps the client to plan. Remember, only an attorney can advise a client about probate and nonprobate property. It is unethical for a paralegal to give legal advice.

Nonprobate property consists of several items. One of the main advantages to including life insurance, for example, in an estate plan is that it is nonprobate property. Provided the insurance is left to a designated beneficiary, the gift passes outside the probate proceeding. Generally the insurance proceeds can be received quickly without any major document production. However, if the beneficiary named on the life insurance policy is the estate, then the proceeds are paid into the estate and must go through probate. This might be done if the insured desires the money to be divided among several people; however, it usurps one of the major advantages to acquiring life insurance. The other advantage of life insurance is it provides for a ready estate and may be the only sizable amount of money left to beneficiaries.

Another nonprobate asset is a payable on death bank account, also known as a totten trust. A totten trust provides that the money placed in the account passes to the beneficiaries upon the depositor's death.

A trust created while the individual or grantor is alive also avoids probate. If a living trust or inter vivos trust is created and funded, all money and property placed in it passes to the beneficiaries as the trust vehicle dictates and is not subject to probate. Setting up an inter vivos trust may not provide for cost savings, but it does allow the gifts to remain private. For more information on trusts, see Chapter 5.

As previously discussed, property held in joint tenancy or tenancy by the entirety has survivorship rights. This property passes to the surviving joint tenant or surviving spouse outside probate.

Other nonprobate assets include pensions or 401(k) funds from employment situations that have a designated beneficiary, and U.S. savings bonds that are payable on death to a named beneficiary.

Property that is subject to probate is property gifted by will or through intestate succession. It includes all property held in severalty or as a tenant in common. It also includes life insurance proceeds gifted to the insured's estate and property that passes into a testamentary trust. Any debts owed to the decedent, any gain from the sale of a business, and any damages received from a civil lawsuit are all subject to probate (see Figure 1-5).

The Estate Planning and Estate Administration Portfolio

For many years, professionals have presented to prospective employers portfolios to demonstrate that the job candidates were qualified for the positions. These employment candidates were typically interviewing for jobs in the creative fields such

Figure 1-5   Probate versus nonprobate property

Probate Property	Nonprobate Property
Money and/or property gifted by will or intestate succession when held severally or as a tenant in common.	Money and/or property held with right of survivorship through joint tenancy or tenancy by the entirety.
Life insurance when the estate is the beneficiary.	Life insurance with designated beneficiaries.
Testamentary trusts.	Inter vivos trusts.
Debts owed to the decedent.	Totten trusts.
Gain from the sale of businesses.	Employment pension or 401(k) plans with designated beneficiaries.
Damages awarded in civil lawsuits.	U.S. savings bonds payable on death to named beneficiaries.

as artists, architects, photographers, and so on. The portfolio contained examples of successful artwork, completed projects, and/or writing samples. A prospective employer would peruse the portfolio and determine whether the candidate had a background and a similar vision that the employer desired. The legal field was not traditionally a field where a portfolio was used. However, it was always wise to be able to produce some writing samples for an employer to read.

A portfolio that exhibits document production in the legal practice of wills, trusts, and estate administration can be a very effective learning tool and an impressive interviewing device. If a student produces a variety of estate planning and estate administration documents, many purposes are fulfilled, including:

1. A portfolio provides evidence of application of the law to the facts of a case and demonstrates a student's understanding of legal theory.
2. A portfolio exhibiting quality documents can be reviewed by a potential employer.
3. A portfolio makes a ready and available collection of documents to be referenced by the graduate when required to prepare documents at a new job.

This textbook offers an opportunity to create an estate planning and estate administration portfolio that serves a paralegal upon graduation. It may be used by a teacher to evaluate a student or by a future employer to determine the quality of a job candidate's work. Finally, a completed portfolio is a great accomplishment.

In each chapter, you will find a Build Your Portfolio section. You may be required to complete these documents and others as assigned. You may submit the entire portfolio at the end of a term for a grade. You should then be encouraged to take the portfolio with you during an interview. My experience is that the portfolios are well received by lawyers as evidence of the graduate's ability for document production.

This textbook is divided into two parts: one on estate planning, and the other on estate administration. This chapter contains four estate planning case examples that may be used when preparing the requested documents. Within each case example are five drafting assignments. They are cross-referenced to the chapter that covers that material. Each fact pattern has one additional assignment not found in the Build Your Portfolio section at the end of a chapter. Chapter 6 contains four estate administration case examples that may be used for those documents. It is my hope that you find this evaluation tool helpful and a great learning experience.

ESTATE PLANNING CASE **EXAMPLES**

A. The Richardson Estate

1. Your client is Edward Allen Richardson. He is married and has four children. He wants to leave most of the estate to his wife, Claudia Louise Richardson, if he dies before she does. He wants to leave his 2005 Chevrolet Corvette to his brother Matthew Richardson. If his wife dies before he does, he wants to leave his estate to three of his four children in equal shares: Elizabeth Richardson, age sixteen; Mary Richardson, age twenty-four; and Donald Richardson, age twenty-eight. He wants to disinherit his son Mark Richardson, age thirty-two, because he has not heard from him in ten years. Edward wants any grandchildren to inherit from a parent under per stirpes. A guardian should be nominated for Elizabeth Richardson. Edward desires his wife, Claudia, to be his executrix or Donald to be the successor executor if Claudia cannot so act. Remember to waive bond. Please also include a survivorship provision. Draft a simple will and a self-proving affidavit based on this information (see Chapter 4).

2. Edward has executed his prior will but now desires a couple of minor changes. He has decided he wants his brother to receive his 2005 Harley-Davidson motorcycle, in addition to the 2005 Chevrolet Corvette. He has also determined that he wants to leave his son Mark $5,000 rather than completely disinherit him. (Consider including an in terrorem clause in the codicil.) He wants to change the executor in the document to Beverly Corey, his accountant. Draft a codicil making these changes (see Chapter 4).

3. Edward has determined he wants a general durable power of attorney created. He wants his wife, Claudia, to be his agent. In particular, he wants her to have the power to make decisions regarding bank accounts, investments, real estate, and taxes (see Chapter 3).

4. Edward further determines he wants Claudia to act as his agent for medical decisions. Prepare a power of attorney health care.

5. Edward is going into the hospital for some major surgery. He does not want to be resuscitated if there is a problem. Prepare a living will (see Chapter 3).

B. The Diggle Estate

1. Mae Josephine Diggle is your client. She is widowed and has two children. She wants to leave her best friend, Gloria Wagner, $10,000. She wants to leave her sister, Kelly Foxworth, her bone china tea set, but only if she survives her; otherwise the tea set would go to her niece, Samantha Foxworth. She leaves the remainder of the estate to her two children, Robert Diggle, age forty, and Carolyn Diggle, age thirty, in equal shares. Mae wants any grandchildren to inherit from a parent under per stirpes. Mae wants her two children, Robert and Carolyn, to serve as coexecutors. Waive bond. Draft a simple will with a self-proving affidavit (see Chapter 4).

2. Mae has executed her prior will, but now she wants some small adjustments to be made. She has decided not to leave the $10,000 to Gloria Wagner. They had a falling out, and Gloria is no longer Mae's friend. Mae wants to leave all her cookbooks to the local library. Draft a codicil indicating these changes (see Chapter 4).

3. Mae has decided to travel to Europe for six months and is trying to sell her summer cottage. Prepare a limited power of attorney nominating her son, Robert Diggle, as the agent.

4. Mae wants a general durable power of attorney created. She wants her son, Robert Diggle, to be her agent and to be her guardian if it becomes necessary. She wants Robert to be granted a wide variety of the standard powers that are usually given to an agent for a power of attorney (see Chapter 3).

5. Mae is feeling fine; however, if she becomes terminally ill, she does not want to be resuscitated. She does not want any experimental drugs used, but she does want nutrition and hydration to be continued. Prepare a living will (see Chapter 3).

C. The Weber Estate

1. Your client is Jeanne Morgan Weber. She is very wealthy. She is married to Daryl Vincent Weber. She has a child, Pamela Ann Barker, age twenty-six, from a previous marriage and two children, Martha Suzanne Weber, age twenty, and Kyle Jay Weber, age fourteen, from her marriage to Daryl. Her mother, Miriam Morgan, is still living. Jeanne wants to leave her mother, Miriam Morgan, $50,000 in her will. She also wants to give her horse, Bandit, to her coworker Julie Williams. She wants seventy-five percent (75%) of her estate to go to her husband if he survives her and to her three children in equal shares if he does not. She wants to leave twenty-five percent (25%) of the estate to Pamela, no matter what. If her husband dies before she does, she wants her mother to have guardianship over the person and estate of Kyle. She wants her husband, Daryl, to be the personal representative of the estate or, if he cannot serve, she wants her mother, Miriam, to serve. Bond should be waived. She wants a survivorship provision and a simultaneous death clause to be included because she and Daryl travel a lot together. Prepare a simple will and self-proving affidavit based on this information (see Chapter 4).

2. Several years have passed since Jeanne prepared her will. Her mother, Miriam, passed away; Kyle is now an adult; and her horse has died. Jeanne needs some changes to her will. Remove the gift to her mother. Make Martha the successor executor to the will if Daryl cannot serve. Kyle no longer needs a guardian appointed in the will. Instead of Bandit, give Julie $10,000. No other changes need to be made. Draft a codicil (see Chapter 4).

3. Jeanne wants a durable power of attorney prepared. She wants her husband, Daryl, to be the attorney in fact and to serve as the guardian if she becomes incompetent. In particular, she wants to grant him power to make decisions regarding her investments, bank accounts, real estate holdings, and taxes. Draft the power of attorney (see Chapter 3).

4. Jeanne was injured in a car accident recently and was unconscious for a few days. She wants a living will prepared stating that she wants to be on life support no matter what; keep her alive, whatever it takes, even if she is unconscious or becomes terminally ill (see Chapter 3).

5. Jeanne is very fearful about her health. She wants a power of attorney health care executed naming her husband as the agent.

D. The Ehlers Estate

1. Your client is Marvin Cole Ehlers. He is a widower with two children: Elaine Ehlers Spears and Luke Ehlers. Elaine has two children, Marvin's grandchildren, Amanda Spears and William Spears. Luke Ehlers has one child, Beth Ehlers. All of the grandchildren are minors. Marvin wants to leave his baseball card collection to William Spears. He wants to leave $15,000 to his church, St. John's Catholic Church. He wants the remainder of his estate to be split equally among his two children and his grandchildren to inherit per stirpes. He wants Elaine and Luke to be co-executors of the will and to serve without bond. Prepare a simple will and self-proving affidavit based on this information (see Chapter 4).

2. Marvin wishes to make some changes to his will. He wants to leave his antique gold pocket watch to Luke and a diamond tie clip to Elaine's husband, Mike Spears. He wants to leave $20,000 to his church. Make the indicated changes and prepare a codicil (see Chapter 4).

3. Marvin had a stroke that has left him somewhat incapacitated. He wants you to prepare a general power of attorney naming Luke as his agent. He wants general powers usually given to an agent to be included. Prepare Marvin's power of attorney (see Chapter 3).

4. Marvin needs help leasing a parcel of real estate he owns. It is a rental property. However, he is undergoing some surgery and wants his son, Luke, to have a limited power of attorney to rent to tenants portions of the real estate. Prepare a limited power of attorney.

5. While Marvin is undergoing surgery, he is concerned about having a living will if he ends up in a vegetative state. He does not want to be resuscitated if something goes wrong. Prepare a living will (see Chapter 3).

KEY **TERMS**

community property (p. 10)
estate planning (p. 4)
fee simple (p. 6)
fixtures (p. 6)
intestate (p. 5)
joint tenancy (p. 8)

probate (p. 5)
real property (p. 6)
separate property (p. 10)
tenancy in common (p. 7)
tenancy by the entirety (p. 9)
testator (p. 5)

testatrix (p. 5)
Uniform Probate Code
   (U.P.C.) (p. 5)
will (p. 5)

REVIEW **QUESTIONS**

1. What are the advantages to creating an estate plan?
2. Give an example of each of the following:
   a. Real estate.
   b. Fixture.
   c. Personal property.
   d. Intangible property.
3. What is the Uniform Probate Code?
4. What are the purposes for having a will?
5. What is a fixture? What tests can a court use to determine if an item is a fixture?

6. Distinguish among tenancy in common, joint tenancy, and tenancy by the entirety. Who inherits upon the death of a tenant? What are the unities for each tenancy?
7. Compare and contrast separate property and community property.
8. Name two types of property that must be probated and two types that are not probated.
9. Explain an estate planning and administration portfolio. What does it contain? What are the benefits of preparing one?

ROLE-PLAYING **ACTIVITY**

1. Determine your definition of becoming wealthy. Share your definition with your classmates. Which one does the class like the best?

RESEARCH **ASSIGNMENTS**

1. Find the Uniform Probate Code's definition of a will. What section of the code contains the definition and what is the definition? Find your state statute defining the word *will*. What legislative enactment contains it and what is the definition?
2. Research your state laws with regard to tenancy by the entirety or community property.

3. Interview an estate planning professional. Ask questions regarding the required education and training and the types of projects the individual has responsibility for.

BUILD YOUR **PORTFOLIO**

1. Select the estate planning case example from pages 13–14 that you will use as the basis for drafting your portfolio. Place a copy of it in your portfolio.

Chapter **two**

INTESTATE SUCCESSION

OBJECTIVES

After studying this chapter, you should be able to:

- Identify the disadvantages of failing to have an estate plan.
- Understand the basic terminology related to dying intestate and dying testate.
- Define statute of intestate succession.
- Explain the order of preference for heirs inheriting under a statute of intestate succession and when escheat occurs.
- Explain special rules under statutes of intestate succession for spouses, children, and other heirs.
- Compare and contrast per stirpes and per capita and identify who would inherit and how much under each of these circumstances.

The Consequences of Failing to Plan

Many individuals do not want to face the inevitability of death. Americans face a serious time crunch in their personal lives: working ever-increasing hours, taking care of their families, and having full social calendars; planning their lives is a must. Yet most Americans fail to plan for one of life's inescapable events: death. Dying without a valid will happens more than it should in this country and, as you might expect, adverse consequences can result from lack of estate planning:

1. A person inherits your estate, or a portion of it, whom you do not want to inherit from you. There has been a rift in the relationship, and yet this person receives your money or property.

2. The state or federal government—through income, estate, and fiduciary taxes—receives your money and property rather than your relatives, friends, or a designated organization.

3. The cost of probating the estate is increased because of confusion about your wishes or fighting among your relatives and because you have given no direction about how the court should handle your estate.

In particular, if you fail to make and execute a valid will or die without one, relatives you do not care for may inherit, or relatives or friends that are more in need of your money or property may not receive anything.

Therefore, in most instances, it is important to have at least a will, even if you do no other sophisticated type of estate planning. Usually, a simple will does not cost a lot of money nor does it take a lot of time to obtain. The trouble this document saves your family usually outweighs the expense of having the will prepared.

Intestate Versus Testate: Basic Terminology

One of the basic expressions in this legal area is the term **testamentary**, which means pertaining to a will or testament or derived from, founded on, or appointed by a testament or will. The gift made by the donor passes to the recipient upon the donor's death rather than occurring while the donor is alive.

The term **testate** means dying with a valid will or having a valid will in existence. This is the opposite of dying **intestate,** or dying without a valid will. The maker or executor of a will is called a testator if male or a testatrix if female. The testator or testatrix who dies is called a decedent. Likewise, someone who dies intestate is called a decedent.

If the decedent dies intestate, those persons who inherit under the intestacy law are called **heirs**. Most heirs must be related by consanguinity or by blood. **Lineal heirs** are directly related to the decedent. They could include **issue** or **descendants**, who are children, grandchildren, and so on, working down the family tree. **Ancestors** or ascendants would include parents, grandparents, and so on, climbing up the family tree. Figure 2-1 shows lineal heirs.

The other type of heirs related by blood, **collateral heirs**, are not directly related but have a common ancestor. For example, a brother or sister is a collateral heir to the decedent. The common ancestor is the parent of the decedent and sibling (see Figure 2-2).

testamentary
Pertaining to a will or testament.

testate
Dying with a valid will.

intestate
Dying without a valid will.

heirs
Those persons who inherit from the decedent under the statutes of intestate succession.

lineal heirs
Those relatives who are in a direct line, either ascending or descending from the decedent, such as a decedent's parent or child, respectively.

issue
The stream of progeny of a person, that is, children, grandchildren, etc.

descendants
An ancestor's bloodline. Those relatives that descend as lineal heirs from a person, that is, children, grandchildren, etc.

ancestors
A person's lineal heirs from whom they descend, that is, parent, grandparent, etc.

collateral heirs
People who are not directly related to the decedent, that is, brother, sister, uncle, aunt.

Figure 2-1 Lineal heirs

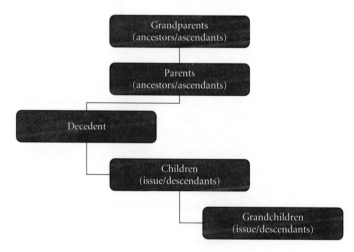

Figure 2-2 Collateral heirs

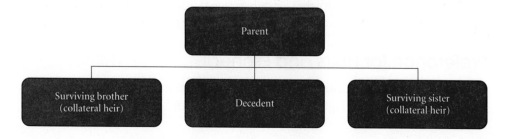

There are two main exceptions to the requirement that an heir be related by blood. First, preference is given to the decedent's spouse, who is related by marriage or affinity. Second, today adopted children are typically entitled to inherit. (See the discussion in the section "Special Considerations for Spouse and Children.") The wisest course of action to determine heirs is to prepare a family tree.

Just because an individual is classified as an heir does not mean he or she will inherit from the decedent. Reasons for not inheriting include the following:

1. The decedent has an insolvent estate. The money and property will be used to pay taxes, funeral expenses, estate costs, or other creditors.

2. The decedent has planned for someone else to inherit by drafting a will naming someone else as the **beneficiary**; by using joint ownership; or by establishing a trust.

3. The decedent has an heir closer in the bloodline who will keep the other heir from inheriting. For example, a child has a higher priority than a grandchild.

Thus, just because you are an heir does not mean you will inherit.

Laws of Intestate Succession

If the decedent has failed to plan, then the laws of the state govern who will inherit. Failing to plan would include, for example:

1. No validly executed will

2. No creation of a trust

3. No jointly held property with survivorship interest.

Intestate law is governed by state law. The laws of the state where a person is domiciled apply with regard to how the decedent's personal property is inherited and how the real estate located in that state will be distributed. A person's **domicile** should be distinguished from his or her residence. Residence means a person is living in a certain area, but domicile includes the concept of intent to make the area a permanent home. A person may have more than one residence but is domiciled only in one locality. Intestate law is based on domicile, not residence. If the decedent's real estate is located in a state other than where the person is domiciled, it will be subject to the laws of the state where it is located.

Statutory law or legislative enactments govern intestate succession. These statutes are most often termed the **statutes of descent and distribution** or statutes of intestate succession. They prescribe the pattern by which heirs, including a surviving spouse, inherit from the decedent. The duration of the relationship doesn't matter; that is, someone on his honeymoon is just as entitled to inherit from his wife as someone who has made it to a golden wedding anniversary. Also, no consideration is given to the friendliness or animosity that exists between the decedent and the heir. The law gives preference strictly based on how close a particular person is in the blood line.

Preference for Heirs and Escheat

Statutes of descent and distribution or statutes of intestate succession have been enacted in all fifty states. Figure 2-3 lists the statute numbers for each state and the District of Columbia.

beneficiary
One who benefits, or inherits property from a will (or one who benefits from a trust or insurance).

domicile
The place where a person makes his or her permanent home and when absent, plans on returning to it.

statutes of descent and distribution
Also called statutes of intestate succession; the statutes that prescribe the pattern of priority to inherit when a person dies intestate.

Figure 2-3   Intestate succession statutes by state

State	Citation
Alabama	Ala. Code § 43-8-41; § 43-8-42
Alaska	Alaska Stat. § 13.12.102; § 13.12.103
Arizona	Ariz. Rev. Stat. Ann. § 14-2102; § 14-2103
Arkansas	Ark. Code Ann. § 28-9-204; § 28-9-205; § 28-9-206; § 28-9-214
California	Cal. Prob. Code § 6401; § 6402; § 6402.5
Colorado	Colo. Rev. Stat. § 15-11-102; § 15-11-103
Connecticut	Conn. Gen. Stat. Ann. § 45a-437; § 45a-438; § 45a-439
Delaware	Del. Code Ann. Tit. 12, § 502; § 503
District of Columbia	D.C. Code Ann. § 19-302; § 19-306 to 19-312; § 19-701
Florida	Fla. Stat. Ann. § 732.102; § 732.103
Georgia	Ga. Code Ann. § 53-2-1
Hawaii	Haw. Rev. Stat. § 560:2-102; § 560:2-103
Idaho	Idaho Code Ann. § 15-2-102; § 15-2-103
Illinois	755 Ill. Comp. Stat. Ann. 5/2-1
Indiana	Ind. Code Ann. § 29-1-2-1
Iowa	Iowa Code Ann. § 633.211; § 633.212; § 633.219
Kansas	Kan. Prob. Code Ann. § 59-504 to 59-508
Kentucky	Ky. Rev. Stat. Ann. § 391.010; § 391.030; § 392.020
Louisiana	La. Civ. Code Ann. Art. 889 to 902; Art. 1493
Maine	Me. Rev. Stat. Ann. Tit. 18-A § 2-102; § 2-103; § 2-106
Maryland	Md. Code Ann., Est. & Trusts § 3-102 to 3-105
Massachusetts	Mass. Gen. Laws Ann. Ch. 189 § 1; Ch. 190 § 1 to 3
Michigan	Mich. Comp. Laws Ann. § 700.2102; § 700.2103; § 700.2105
Minnesota	Minn. Stat. Ann. § 524.2-102; § 524.2-103
Mississippi	Miss. Code Ann. § 91-1-3; § 91-1-7; §91-1-11
Missouri	Mo. Ann. Stat. § 474.010
Montana	Mont. Code Ann. § 72-2-112; § 72-2-113; § 72-2-115
Nebraska	Neb. Rev. Stat. § 30-2302; § 30-2303
Nevada	Nev. Rev. Stat. § 134.040; § 134.050
New Hampshire	N.H. Rev. Stat. Ann. § 561:1
New Jersey	N.J. Stat. Ann. § 3B:5-3; § 3B:5-4
New Mexico	N.M. Stat. Ann. § 45-2-102; § 45-2-103
New York	N.Y. Est. Powers & Trusts Law § 4-1.1
North Carolina	N.C. Gen. Stat. § 29-14; § 29-15
North Dakota	N.D. Cent. Code § 30.1-04-02; § 30.1-04-03
Ohio	Ohio Rev. Code Ann. § 2103.02; § 2105.06
Oklahoma	Okla. Stat. Ann. Tit. 84, § 213
Oregon	Or. Rev. Stat. § 112.025; § 112.045
Pennsylvania	20 Pa. Stat. Ann. § 2102; § 2103
Rhode Island	R.I. Gen. Laws § 33-1-5; § 33-1-6; § 33-1-10; § 33-25-1; § 33-1-1; § 33-1-2

(continued)

State	Citation
South Carolina	S.C. Code Ann. § 62-2-102; § 62-2-103
South Dakota	S.D. Codified Laws § 29A-2-101; § 29A-2-102; § 29A-2-103; § 29A-2-105
Tennessee	Tenn. Code Ann. § 31-2-104
Texas	Tex. Prob. Code Ann. § 38
Utah	Utah Code Ann. § 75-2-102; § 75-2-103; § 75-2-106
Vermont	Vt. Stat. Ann. Tit. 14, § 551
Virginia	Va. Code Ann. § 64.1-1; § 64.1-11
Washington	Wash. Rev. Code Ann. § 11.04.015
West Virginia	W. Va. Code § 42-1-2; § 42-1-3; § 42-1-4
Wisconsin	Wis. Stat. Ann. § 852.01
Wyoming	Wyo. Stat. Ann. § 2-4-101

Figure 2-3   (coninued)

Traditionally the term *descent* meant the pattern of who had preference to the real property owned by the decedent, and *distribution* referred to which heir was preferred to inherit the decedent's personal property. An example of a pattern that has been enacted is found in Figure 2-4. (See the Wisconsin statute in Figure 2-3.)

Most states require that if the decedent dies intestate, with no living heirs, **escheat** occurs, or the state inherits the decedent's estate. The personal property goes to the state where the decedent was domiciled, and the real estate goes to the state where it is situated. Different states require the property to go to different departments. The following Texas case illustrates when dying intestate can create problems for heirs. A portion of the estate could have escheated to Texas.

escheat
The state inherits the decedent's estate.

> In *Kirkpatrick v. Estate of Kane*, 743 S.W.2d 371 (Tex. Ct. App. 1988), Floyd Kane died intestate. He left as his only surviving heir his first cousin, Marion Kirkpatrick. The trial court ruled that Kirkpatrick was entitled under Texas' intestate succession statute to one-half share (maternal moiety) of the estate. Since there were no living heirs to inherit one-half share (the paternal moiety), the trial court ruled that one-half of the estate would escheat to the state of Texas. Kirkpatrick appealed. The issue was the construction of § 38(a) (4) of the Probate Code. The relevant portion of the code states that if the decedent is not survived by his parents, siblings or sibling's issue, the estate should be divided into two moieties (equal shares). One share passes to the decedent's paternal grandparents or descendants and one to his maternal grandparents or descendants. The statute then states if none of the relatives on one side are living, then all of the estate should be given to the grandparents or descendants who are living. The estate of Kane argues that Kirkpatrick should inherit only the maternal moiety. The other half escheats to Texas. Kirkpatrick claims since she is Kane's only living heir that she in entitled to the paternal moiety as well as the maternal moiety since no paternal heirs can be found. The Texas Court of Appeals after reviewing precedent and scholarly authority agreed with Kirkpatrick's argument. Citing as precedent *State v. Estate of Loomis*, 553 S.W.2d 166 (Tex. Ct. App. 1977, writ ref'd) and analyzing the legislature's intent to pass 38(a)(4), the court concluded that the legislature's intention was to pass an intestate decedent's estate entirely to

Figure 2-4 Intestate succession pattern

1	Surviving spouse and children inherit.
2	If no surviving spouse or surviving children, then grandchildren inherit.
3	If no surviving grandchildren, then great-grandchildren inherit.
4	If there are no surviving great-grandchildren, continue with issue moving down the family tree through this line of descendants.
5	If there are no descendants on this line, climb up the family tree to the first set of ancestors or ascendants—the decedent's parents.
6	If there are no surviving parents, work down this line of descendants to siblings or brothers and sisters of the decedent (collateral heirs).
7	If there are no surviving siblings, their children, who are the decedent's nieces and nephews, inherit.
8	If there are no surviving nieces and nephews, continue down this line to grandnieces and grandnephews, and so on.
9	If no descendants on this line survive, climb up the family tree to the decedent's grandparents.
10	If there are no surviving paternal or maternal grandparents, work down both lines of descendants (or collateral heirs) to the decedent's aunts and uncles (grandparent's children).
11	If there are no surviving aunts and uncles, continue down this line to cousins.
12	Preference is given to first cousins, next to cousins once removed, next to second cousins, and so on.
13	Next of kin inherit.
14	The decedent dies intestate with no living heirs; escheat occurs.

his descendants. The Court of Appeals reversed the trial court's decision and held that Kirkpatrick was entitled to inherit both the maternal and paternal moieties, the entire estate.

The statutes of intestate succession vary from state to state. You should consult your state's statute for the particulars. States vary as to how the property is divided between a surviving spouse and children, and community property states may have additional laws to consider. (See Tex. Prob. Code Ann. § 45.) The Uniform Probate Code states that one-half of the estate goes to a surviving spouse and one-half to the child if there is only one child. If there is more than one child, one-third of the estate goes to the surviving spouse and the remaining two-thirds of the estate are divided equally among the children.

Special Considerations for Spouse, Children, and Other Heirs

For purposes of probating an estate, a spouse is considered to be married until a final divorce decree is signed. If Mary files a petition for divorce on May 1, 2006, and her husband dies intestate on May 10, 2006, while the divorce is still pending, she will inherit from him as his surviving spouse.

Today a natural child—a child by birth of a biological mother and father—does not receive preference over an adopted child. An adopted child is not a biological

APPLYING YOUR KNOWLEDGE

Mary and John are married. They have Suzie, a natural child, while they are married. Before they were married, they had Bobby, and they adopted Jenny while they were married. John has a child from his prior marriage, a son named Billy.

1. Mary dies intestate and John is still living. In your state, what are Suzie's, Bobby's, Jenny's, and Billy's inheritance rights under the statute of intestate succession?
2. What if John dies before Mary? How does this change your answer?

posthumous child
A child conceived prior to his or her father's death but born after his or her father's death.

child of the parents but has created a parent-child relationship through the legal process of adoption. (See Del. Code Ann. Tit. 12 § 508.) The law usually makes no distinction between a nonmarital or illegitimate child. All of these children have similar rights. (See Fla. Stat. Ann. § 732.108 and 755 Ill. Comp. Stat. 5/2-2.)

A **posthumous child** is a child conceived prior to his or her father's death but born after the death. Under the Uniform Probate Code and in many states, this child can inherit from the father as other children do. (See 755 Ill. Comp. Stat. 5/2-3.)

As previously outlined in this chapter, states may have a similar line of preference. Yet each state statute should be studied carefully. You will find some variance of treatment of heirs. Here are some examples.

First, in Illinois brothers and sisters have an equal right to inherit as do mothers and fathers. However, if a parent has predeceased the decedent, the living parent receives a double share before the siblings. For example, Robert dies, leaving behind Mom, a widow, and his two brothers, William and Richard. Mom would receive an extra share, which would have been Dad's. Thus, she would get one-half of the estate, William one-fourth, and Richard one-fourth.

Second, other than a surviving spouse or an adopted child, the only people allowed to inherit from an intestate decedent are those within the bloodline of the decedent. Typically, stepchildren cannot inherit from a decedent. Consider, however, the following: "If there are no next of kin, [the estate goes to] stepchildren or their lineal descendants, per stirpes" (Ohio Rev. Code Ann. § 2105.06).

Third, some states may make a distinction between collateral heirs of the whole and half-blood. Texas law provides, "In situations where the inheritance passes to the collateral kindred . . ., if part of such collateral be of the whole blood, and the other part be of the half blood only . . . each of those of half blood shall inherit only half so much as each of those of the whole blood; but if all be of the half blood, they shall have whole portions" (Tex. Prob. Code Ann. § 41(b)).

Per Stirpes Versus per Capita

per stirpes
Also called right of representation. A method of distributing the decedent's estate when the decedent has left behind surviving issue from different generations. A deceased member of one generation who leaves behind surviving issue is represented by them. A living ancestor prevents his issue from inheriting.

per capita
All heirs within a class receive equal shares.

When an individual dies intestate and has descendants in different generations—like children and grandchildren—the statutes of intestate succession specify if the heirs receive through **per stirpes** or **per capita**.

Per stirpes is translated from the Latin, "by roots or by stocks." Today, per stirpes is often called right of representation. Per stirpes is a method of distributing an estate when the decedent has issue in different generations. When a decedent has a

Figure 2-5 Family tree

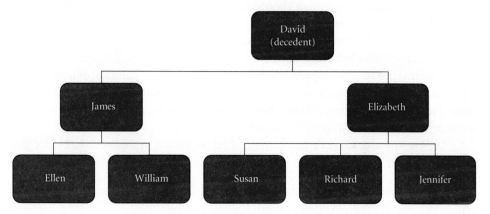

deceased family member in one generation who leaves surviving descendants, his descendants receive his share. However, a living ancestor prevents his heirs from inheriting. Consider the family tree in Figure 2-5. James and Elizabeth are David's (the decedent's) children. Ellen and William, James's children, are David's grandchildren, as are Susan, Richard, and Jennifer, Elizabeth's children. Under the principle of per stirpes, consider the following:

1. All members of this family are living except for David. Who will inherit? The answer is James and Elizabeth only. Because they are living, they preclude Ellen, William, Susan, Richard, and Jennifer from receiving anything. This references the portion of the definition that states a living ancestor prevents his heirs from inheriting. James and Elizabeth would share the estate equally. Each would receive one-half.

2. James dies before David (the decedent), but all other family members are living. Who will inherit? The answer is Elizabeth and Ellen and William. Because James is dead, his children receive his share equally. This references the portion of the definition that states that a deceased member in one generation who leaves surviving descendants allows the surviving descendants to receive his or her share. Elizabeth prevents her children, Susan, Richard, and Jennifer, from inheriting because she is still alive, again referencing the last portion of the per stirpes definition: "a living ancestor prevents his heirs from inheriting." In this example, Elizabeth would still receive her half share. James's half share would be divided equally between his children; Ellen and William would each receive a half share of James's half share, or one-quarter share of the estate.

APPLYING YOUR KNOWLEDGE

Robert is the ancestor who has just died intestate. He had three children: Pam, Fran, and Diana. Pam has no children; Fran has two daughters, Abby and Emily; and Diana has one son, Andrew. Fran has predeceased the decedent, Robert.

1. Draw a family tree diagram.
2. Using per stirpes, who inherits from Robert?
3. What fraction of the estate does each heir receive? Why?

Many statutes of descent and distribution provide for a per stirpes or right of representation distribution. You should read the statutes of your state carefully to determine which law is applied.

The concept of per stirpes is not exclusive to intestate laws. It can be applied if the decedent leaves behind a valid will or dies testate. The will typically specifies if descendants are to receive property by a per stirpes or per capita application. Per capita is Latin for "by heads or polls." It is the concept that all heirs within a class should receive equal shares. All members would share alike, provided they are in the same degree of relationship to the decedent.

Let's reconsider David's family tree which is shown in Figure 2-6. Under the principles of per capita or per stirpes, consider the following:

1. If James and Elizabeth had predeceased David, who would inherit? The answer is Ellen, William, Susan, Richard, and Jennifer.
2. Using per capita, how much would each heir receive? Why? The answer is that each heir would inherit equally. Ellen, William, Susan, Richard, and Jennifer would each receive one-fifth of David's estate. All "heads" receive equal shares (see Figure 2-7).

Figure 2-6   David's family tree

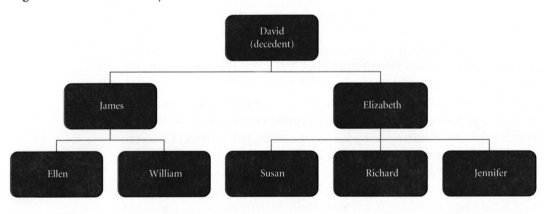

Figure 2-7   Per capita

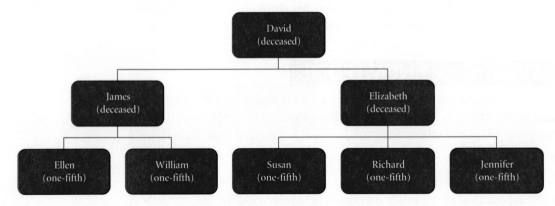

Figure 2-8   Per stirpes

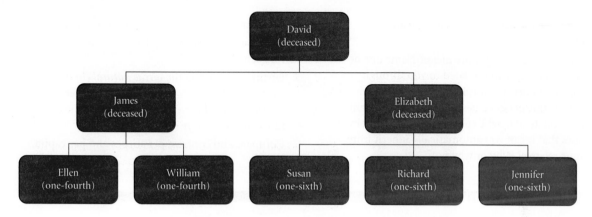

3. Using per stirpes, how much would each heir receive? Why? The answer is that Ellen and William would each receive one-fourth share. They would split evenly James's (their dad's) one-half share. Susan, Richard, and Jennifer would each receive one-sixth share—one-third of Elizabeth's (their mom's) share (see Figure 2-8).

APPLYING YOUR KNOWLEDGE

Jack has died intestate. He has three sons: John, Jeff, and Gary. John has no children. Jeff has two children: Megan and Michael. Gary has three children: Monica, Mark, and Margaret.

1. Draw the family tree.
2. Using per stirpes, if Jeff has predeceased Jack and all other family members are living, who inherits and what fraction of the estate does each receive?
3. If John, Jeff, and Gary have all predeceased the decedent, under per capita who inherits and what fraction of the estate does each receive?

KEY **TERMS**

ancestors (p. 17)
beneficiary (p. 18)
collateral heirs (p. 17)
descendants (p. 17)
domicile (p. 18)
escheat (p. 20)
heirs (p. 17)

intestate (p. 17)
issue (p. 17)
lineal heirs (p. 17)
per capita (p. 22)
per stirpes (p. 22)
posthumous child (p. 22)

statutes of descent and
    distribution (p. 18)
testamentary (p. 17)
testate (p. 17)

REVIEW **QUESTIONS**

1. What are the advantages of having an estate plan?
2. What does consanguinity mean? Name one of your relatives who is related to you through consanguinity. What is his or her relationship to you? Is this person a descendant, an ascendant, or a collateral heir? Explain. If you are an heir, does that mean you automatically inherit from your relative? Why or why not?
3. Compare and contrast domicile versus residence.
4. Define escheat. What requirements are necessary for escheat to occur?
5. Distinguish among the terms *natural child, adopted child,* and *posthumous child*. In general, are they treated the same under the statutes of intestate succession?
6. Compare and contrast per stirpes and per capita.

ROLE-PLAYING **ACTIVITY**

1. Interview a fellow classmate about his or her family. Prepare a family tree labeling the ascendants, descendants, and collateral heirs. If your classmate died intestate, who would be in line to inherit first from him or her?

RESEARCH **ASSIGNMENTS**

1. Obtain a photocopy of your state's statutes of descent and distribution. Write a list describing the order of preference for heirs to inherit. Does your statute prescribe a per capita or per stirpes method of inheriting? Explain.
2. Research your state laws with regard to the rights of a posthumous child to inherit from his or her father.
3. Prepare your family tree. Determine your lineal descendants, ancestors, and collateral heirs.
4. Mary lives in the state in which you are studying. She dies intestate and has no living heirs. Who inherits her house? Who inherits her car?
5. In your state, how is an estate divided among a surviving spouse and children?

BUILD YOUR **PORTFOLIO**

1. Insert your analysis and copy of the statutes of descent and distribution found in Research Assignment 1 into your portfolio.
2. Using the case example you chose in Chapter 1, prepare a family tree labeling the relationships to the decedent. Write a summary of who will inherit first from the decedent if the decedent died intestate, and specify the portion of the estate that will be received.

Chapter **three**

BASIC ESTATE PLANNING

The Advantages of Planning

As with anything in this life, a plan is a good idea. Planning helps to keep us on the right track and achieve typically an advantageous result. This is also true with determining how you want your wealth distributed upon your death. A will might be the *last* plan we make that is implemented. The plan helps to ensure that those people we cherish will be remembered, those charities we hold most dear will receive property, or even that the administration of our estate will be left to those we trust and rely upon.

One simple way to plan for death is to make and execute a last will and testament. This can ensure the following:

1. The people we want to inherit our estate are more likely to receive it.
2. We can leave property to individuals or organizations that would not receive it if we died intestate.
3. We can avoid family quarrels over property by making specific bequests.
4. We can nominate a guardian for a minor or incompetent person.
5. We can nominate a personal representative to administer the estate.
6. We can create a testamentary trust, if we desire, and nominate a trustee to manage the trust.
7. We can save money by waiving bond for the personal representative.

This chapter introduces you to the basic terminology of wills and the requirements for a valid will. It discusses the two goals of a will: to make gifts and state directions. The chapter explains that you can change your mind and revoke or change an existing will. Finally, the chapter explains other basic estate planning devices that can be executed to make you, your family, your friends, and your clients more prepared and protected for difficult decision-making events regarding property, money, and health.

The first step to a great plan is to obtain knowledge. Let's take the first step.

A Will's Content: Gifts

Estate planning has its own specialized vocabulary; you have already been introduced to some of the terms in Chapters 1 and 2. Let us review, in particular, that to die testate means to die with a valid will. What is a will? It is a document by which wealth can be passed to beneficiaries. A beneficiary is the recipient of a gift by will. It could be a person or an organization. (*Note:* The word *beneficiary* is also used in insurance and trust law.) However, the will may also contain directions about how the estate will be managed. Thus, a will contains two types of information: gifts and directions.

The testator's last will and testament should include the gifts he wishes to make. There are several types of gifts that can be included in a will. First, the testator may wish to leave personal property to a beneficiary. The gift by will of personal property is called a **bequest** or **legacy**. Examples include a gift of a car or money in the amount of $10,000. The person making this type of gift is called a **legator**; the person receiving it is the **legatee**. If a legator leaves a gift by will of a particular item of personal property, it is called a **specific bequest**, or specific legacy. A car is a specific bequest. When a legator leaves a sum of money from a specified fund or from the sale of a particular item, this is called a **demonstrative bequest**, or demonstrative legacy. Examples include $1,000 from my checking account at ABC Bank, or $25,000 from the sale of my diamond tiara. When the legator gifts an amount of money to the legatee in the will, it is called a **general bequest**, or general legacy. The earlier example of gifting $10,000 is a general bequest. Finally, when the legator leaves the rest of his or her remaining personal property to a beneficiary, it is called a **residuary bequest**, or residuary legacy. A residuary clause should be included in the will and typically reads:

> I give the rest and remainder of my personal property to James.

The inclusion of this clause protects the property not listed in the will from being inherited by heirs under the statutes of intestate succession.

Real property may be gifted by will. This traditionally is called a **devise**. Today this term may be used interchangeably with *bequest*. (See UPC § 1-201 (10).) Thus, the language reading, "I give you my house," is traditionally called a devise.

How Gifts Fail

Just because you are named as a beneficiary in a will does not mean you receive the gifted property. Under certain circumstances, the beneficiary does not receive the gift or may receive only a portion of it. The failure of a gift by will can occur under abatement, ademption, or lapse.

---

bequest
A gift by will of personal property.

legacy
A gift by will of personal property.

legator
A person who makes a gift by will of personal property.

legatee
A party who receives a gift by will of personal property.

specific bequest
A gift by will of a particular item of personal property.

demonstrative bequest
A gift by will of a sum of money from a specified fund or from the sale of a particular item.

general bequest
A gift by will of an amount of money.

residuary bequest
A gift by will of all the remaining property owned by the decedent that has not been gifted in another clause.

devise
A gift by will of real property. Today, under the U.P.C., also known as a bequest.

APPLYING YOUR KNOWLEDGE

Barbara dies testate. She leaves her furniture to Jennifer, her ranch to Ben, her dance shoes to Marty, $100 to Rebecca, $2,500 in a savings account at Billionaire Bank to Millicent, and the rest and remainder of her estate to Guary. Discuss the following:

1. What would you call Barbara?
2. What would you call Ben?
3. What would you call Guary?
4. What type of gift is:
   a. The furniture?
   b. The ranch?
   c. The dance shoes?
   d. The $100?
   e. The $2,500 from the savings account at Billionaire Bank?
   f. The rest and remainder of the estate?

In an **abatement** situation, the decedent has debts that must be paid to creditors. All creditors have the right to receive payment of the debt from the estate before anyone may inherit (see Chapter 8). Thus, if the testator has more liabilities than assets, a beneficiary does not receive anything. Abatement is the proportional reduction of gifts because the estate lacks sufficient funds to pay the debts. For example, if Tina owes creditors $5,000 and leaves an estate valued at $5,000, all of the $5,000 pays her debts and none of the money is inherited by her beneficiaries. Sometimes, however, only a portion of the gifts abate. Tina owes $3,000 and has an estate valued at $5,000. Her beneficiaries inherit $2,000 of the estate's money and property. If only a portion of the gifts abate, three questions must be answered: Who does not inherit from the estate? Who does inherit from it? and How much of the estate does an inheriting beneficiary receive?

abatement
A proportional reduction of gifts to beneficiaries because the estate lacks sufficient funds to pay the decedent's debts.

The answers depend upon the type of gift that was given to the beneficiary. There is an order of abatement; in general, it is as follows:

1. Any intestate property not gifted in the will abates first.
2. Residuary bequests and devises abate.
3. General bequests abate.
4. Demonstrative bequests abate.
5. Specific bequests and devises abate last.

Here is an example of the order of abatement. Michael leaves his house to Danielle, $10,000 to Emily, his car to Dave, his $2,000 in a checking account at North State Bank to Richard, and the rest and remainder of his estate to Pam. Pam will lose her gift first (residuary bequest and devise); then Emily (general bequest); then Richard (demonstrative bequest); and finally, Danielle (specific devise) and Dave (specific bequest) last. Therefore, although Pam may be excited that she is getting most of Michael's estate, she also is the first to lose her gift. Danielle and Dave would be the most protected and likely to inherit.

APPLYING YOUR KNOWLEDGE

Recall from the first Applying Your Knowledge in Chapter 3 that Barbara died testate. She left her furniture to Jennifer, her ranch to Ben, her dance shoes to Marty, $100 to Rebecca, $2,500 in a savings account at Billionaire Bank to Millicent, and the rest and remainder of her estate to Guary.

Which gift abates first? Which gift abates second? Which gift abates third? Which gift abates fourth and last?

State statutes disagree on the treatment of real property and personal property in an abatement situation. Some states require personal property to be sold and used to pay debt before real property is liquidated and applied to debt. Other states make no distinction between the two types of property. Real property and personal property are treated the same, provided they are in the same "gift" category.

> [D]evises shall abate equally and ratably and without preference or priority as between real and personal property (Fla. Stat. § 733.805 (2)).

ademption
A gift by will fails because it is no longer owned by the testator or it is no longer in existence.

Another way a gift can fail is by **ademption**. Ademption occurs when a gift by will fails because it is no longer owned by the testator. This concept affects specific bequests. Therefore, if Mary leaves her diamond engagement ring to Susan in her will, and later Mary loses the ring but does not change her will, Susan does not receive the ring upon Mary's death. Similarly, if Mary sells the ring prior to her death, Susan does not receive it.

Lapse is another way a gift by will can fail. With ademption, the gift failed because of a problem with the item. With lapse, the gift fails because of a complication with the beneficiary. **Lapse** is a gift by will that fails because the beneficiary has predeceased the testator/decedent, or the beneficiary is unwilling to take the item. If Rachel leaves her ugly red elephant clock lamp with a green shade to Fred and he does not take the item, a lapse occurs.

lapse
A gift by will fails because the beneficiary predeceased the decedent or the beneficiary is unwilling to take the item.

More commonly, lapse occurs because the beneficiary has predeceased the decedent. If Jennifer leaves her television set to Jack, but he died a year before she did, he cannot receive the item. The gift becomes part of the residuary estate. For example, Tracy leaves her doll collection to Nancy and the rest and remainder of her estate to Martha. If Nancy predeceased Tracy, the doll collection is inherited by Martha. This is the general rule unless:

1. The testatrix designates someone else to receive the gift; Tracy "leaves her doll collection to Nancy or to Martha, if Nancy does not survive me." In this situation, Martha inherits the doll collection.

2. The state has an **anti-lapse statute**. An anti-lapse statute provides the gift will not shift to the residuary beneficiary. The anti-lapse statute passes the item to the deceased beneficiary's children or other heirs. Under the anti-lapse statute, some states restrict the gift to just the children. Others expand it to other heirs. If Tracy's will states: "I leave my doll collection to Nancy and the rest and remainder of my estate to Martha" and Nancy predeceases Tracy, the doll collection will be inherited by Nancy's children or other heirs provided the state has an anti-lapse statute.

anti-lapse statute
A legislative enactment that passes the gift of property to a deceased beneficiary's heirs rather than through the will's residuary clause or intestate succession statute.

The anti-lapse statute is not applied to a probate when the testatrix has written certain language in her will. The key language is "if she shall survive me." If Tracy's will reads, "I leave my doll collection to Nancy if she shall survive me and the rest and remainder of my estate to Martha," the anti-lapse statute would not be applied and the gift would pass to Martha under the residuary clause.

One additional method in which a gift can fail is if the state has a **slayer's rule** or **slayer's statute**. These laws apply both in testate and intestate situations. Case law or statutes state that an heir or beneficiary does not inherit if he or she intentionally or unjustifiably killed the decedent. Some states treat the heir or beneficiary as having predeceased the decedent. Under UPC § 2-803, an intentional killing revokes the person's interest in inheriting. The Illinois statute reads:

slayer's rule or slayer's statute
An heir or beneficiary does not inherit from the decedent if the heir or beneficiary killed the decedent.

> A person who intentionally and unjustifiably causes the death of another shall not receive any property, benefit, or other interest by reason of the death, whether as heir, legatee, beneficiary, . . . The property, benefit, or other interest shall pass as if the person causing the death died before the decedent . . . (755 Ill. Comp. Stat. § 5/2-6).

Typically the legal requirement is an intentional causing of the death, not negligence (see *Miller v. Kramarczyk*, 306 Ill. App. 3d 731, 714 N.E. 2d 613, 239 Ill. Dec. 694 (1999)). Illinois has held that the heirs of the killer beneficiary could not inherit either. For example, Bob kills his mother-in-law Beatrice. Beatrice's will reads, "the estate passes to Bob and then to his children, Sally and James." Sally and James are not related by blood to Beatrice. They are step-grandchildren. They do not inherit because of the court's application of the slayer's rule to the case (see *In re Mueller's Estate*, 275 Ill. App. 3d 128, 655 N.E. 2d 1040, 211 Ill. Dec. 657 (1995)).

A Will's Content: Directions

Different directions may be contained in a will. Directions guide the **personal representative** or court about managing and administering the estate; they include nominating the **executor** or personal representative, nominating a trustee if a testamentary trust is created, nominating a guardian for minor children or incompetent persons, and waiving bond. Another direction often included is that the executor pay all legally enforceable debts, funeral expenses, and costs of administering the estate from the funds of the estate. Direction clauses are discussed more fully in Chapter 4.

personal representative
Also known as administrator or executor; a legal representative appointed by the court to administer the decedent's estate.

executor
A person nominated in the will to carry out the directions and the distribution of gifts contained in the will.

Requirements for a Valid Will

For a will or codicil to be valid, two essential requirements must be met. First, the testator must have the requisite intent or desire to make a valid will. Second, he must have testamentary capacity. Other formalities may exist. The formalities can include whether the will must be written, the special requirements for the testator's signature, and rules regarding witnesses' signatures. Individual state laws should be consulted for will requirements and formalities.

Intent

The maker of a will must have the requisite intent or desire to create a will. *Animus testandi* is Latin for "intent to create a will." If the maker desires some other type of document or has another goal to accomplish, this intent element is not met. Therefore, the maker would not have a valid will. Most wills drafted by attorneys include statements saying, "Last Will and Testament of . . ." thus indicating the intention. Further, most introductory or exordium clauses (see Chapter 4) contain language stating the testator voluntarily and with intent is executing his last will and testament. A Pennsylvania case explores the meaning of intent.

> In *In re Good Estate*, 34 Pa. D. & C. 2d 14 (1963), the decedent left behind a will, meeting all legal requirements, dated February 12, 1947, and a writing on a piece of cardboard that read: "My Will: My farms, etc., I leave to those who can take them. . . . If I may have inspired anyone to cherish the good earth during my lifetime, we take this with us." This handwritten document was signed by the decedent and dated February 15, 1961. The 1961 document was admitted to probate and the appeal ensued. The appellate court considered whether the decedent had the requisite intention to make his last will. Referencing other legal authority, the court stated, "In ascertaining that intention it is not our province to consider what he possibly intended, but only his intention as expressed in the language used. . . It is where the intention is ambiguously expressed that problems arise. If it is so indefinite and uncertain as to be incapable of intelligent interpretation and enforcement, it is void. . . *Id*. at 16. The court went on to conclude that the document only superficially resembled a will and " that whatever may have been in the testator's mind, his intention is so vaguely and obscurely stated in the 1961 document as to be void for uncertainty." *Id*. at 17. The cardboard document dated February 1961 was set aside and the probate register was directed to probate the will dated February 1947.

Testamentary Capacity

The testator must have testamentary capacity to execute a valid will. Testamentary capacity consists of two elements:

1. Of legal age—Legal age is met if the person is eighteen years of age or older. Therefore, a minor cannot execute a valid will. There are some exceptions to this general rule. The exceptions include if the minor is emancipated, married, or in the armed forces. The laws of your state should be consulted if a client raises one of these issues.

2. Of sound mind or mentally competent—This criterion is more difficult to prove or disprove than the age requirement. Generally, the law states that a person has the mental capacity to make or revoke a will if he or she understands four items:

    a. That he or she is making a will—The person needs to realize that a will is being prepared and executed, that gifts are being made and directions are stated to take effect upon death.

    b. The person must know essentially what he or she owns and the amount of property available to be distributed—For example, if an individual has $10,000 in a bank account and no other major assets, a gift of "$8,000,000 to my best friend" would indicate a problem with the sound mind requirement.

    c. The person must know the individuals who are the "natural objects of his or her bounty"—The will maker needs to be aware of which family members, friends, or organizations he or she has affection for and who would typically receive the property. The person does not need to leave his or her property to any of them, but the person must know who they are.

d. The person must be able to formulate a plan—The person must be able to decide to whom he or she wants the property to go and to understand the effect of the plan.

An individual may be essentially mentally incompetent but have a **lucid interval**. During a lucid interval, the person can execute a valid will. If there is a question with regard to a person's mental state, it is often wise to have a health care professional serve as a witness. After execution, ask the health care professional his or her opinion about the maker's mental capacity. If the professional is confident that he or she could testify to the probate court that the maker was of sound mind, the will should be valid. If the professional doubts the sanity of the maker, the will may not be upheld as valid. This element of sound mind is one of the most well-known grounds for a will contest.

lucid interval
A temporary return to mental capacity.

Other Formalities

Certain other requirements may exist for a state to declare that a will is valid, including:

1. A writing.
2. Testator's signature.
3. Witnesses' signatures.

1. A Writing

Generally, a will must be written to be valid. Some states recognize **nuncupative wills** as valid. A nuncupative will is also known as a deathbed will. It is an oral declaration made in the presence of witnesses and later put in writing. The law requires that the maker is anticipating death in the near future and may gift only personal property. Most states do not recognize nuncupative wills. Another type of will is a **holographic will**. It is done in the handwriting of the testator or testatrix. By definition, it generally is not witnessed. States vary as to the treatment of holographic wills. Some states recognize holographic wills as valid. Other states declare them invalid. Still other states may recognize a holographic will if the witness requirement is met. These states do not have a straightforward approach to the validity of a holographic will.

nuncupative will
An oral will made by the testator in anticipation of death gifting personal property and made in the presence of witnesses.

holographic will
A will written entirely in the testator's handwriting and not witnessed.

To meet the writing requirement, the best approach is to have the will typed or computer-generated. These wills are less likely to be scrutinized by the court with regard to being in proper written form.

2. Testator's Signature

Courts require the testator to sign the will. Most do not require the signature to be at the end of the document, but it is good practice to have it placed there. New York requires the signature to be at the end of the document. Courts prefer that the testator sign his name in full or write his formal name. However, most statutes allow the testator to make any mark with intent to execute the will or allow for a proxy signature.

A proxy signature requires the testator to direct another person to sign the testator's name on his behalf. Wis. Stat. § 853.03(1) states:

> [The will] must be signed by the testator, by the testator with assistance of another person with the testator's consent or in the testator's name by another person at the testator's direction and in the testator's conscious presence.

If a proxy signature method or a mark other than the formal signature is being used, research should be conducted as to changes in language for both the testimonium and attestation clauses of the will (see Chapter 4).

3. Witnesses' Signatures

All states require at least two witnesses to the will. Vermont requires three. Each witness verifies that the will is genuine and signs his or her name to it. It is recommended that the witnesses use the same pen as the testator. The laws vary as to whether the witnesses and testator must all sign at the same time. It is wise to have all individuals sign at the same time. The laws of the governing state should be consulted prior to the will being executed. (See Chapter 4 regarding execution.) In an Alabama case, the court determined that the will lacked the number of witnesses required by law.

> *Rucker v. Morgan*, 702 So. 2d 452 (Ala. Civ. App. 1996), two issues were raised. One was whether the writing was a deed or a will. The second was if the document was a will, did it meet the legal formalities required for witnessing. The decedent left behind a widow who argued the document was a deed transferring to her full ownership of a parcel of real estate while the decedent was living. The decedent's daughter from a previous marriage argued the document was a will, and an invalid one because of the missing witnesses' signatures. The court of Civil Appeals determined the document which was entitled "Last Will" on a standard bill of sale form was intended to be a will. However, the document lacked the requisite number of witnesses' signatures required under Alabama law. In Alabama two witnesses are required. The court stated, "[T]he purpose of requiring the attestation of two witnesses is to remove uncertainty regarding the execution of wills and to safeguard testators from the possibility of frauds and impositions." *Id.* at 454. As a result of the document being ruled an invalid will and not a deed, the real estate in question passed through Alabama's intestate succession statute and half was inherited by the decedent's widow and half by his daughter from a previous marriage.
>
> Of interest, the case was appealed by the widow to the Supreme Court of Alabama under *Ex parte Rucker*, 702 So. 2d 456 (Ala. 1997). The Supreme Court reversed the Court of Appeals decision and ruled the document was a deed since the document was executed on a bill of sale form and the husband's signature was notarized. The husband then delivered the document to his wife and she recorded it. Thus, the parcel of real estate was owned outright by the wife prior to the decedent's death.

supernumerary witness
An extra witness to a will beyond the statutorily required number.

If an extra witness signs, beyond the statutorily required number, this person is called a **supernumerary witness**. Why might you have an extra witness? If there is a concern with the testator's capacity or one of your other witnesses is older or infirm, the extra witness may be needed to testify at the probate hearing. A witness must be mentally competent at the time the will is signed. Usually, personnel at the law firm serve as the witnesses. However, an interested person should not sign as a witness. Interested persons include anyone who is a beneficiary to the will. Although the law does not disqualify the person named as personal representative or trustee to act as a witness, practically, he or she should not act as a witness. If an interested person acts as a witness, a will contest ground of undue influence may be successfully asserted.

Some states allow a will to be proved in court without the testimony of the witnesses. These states have enacted a **self-proving will** statute. In these states, the testator and witnesses sign the will, and a self-proving affidavit is prepared and signed by a **notary public**. The notary acknowledges the testator's and witnesses' signatures as genuine. The notary signs in an area called the **jurat** (see Figure 3-1).

Changing or Revoking Wills

A will is an **ambulatory** instrument, meaning that it can be changed. It also is a testamentary document, meaning that the gifts will not be given until the testator dies. As a result, wills can be amended, changed, or destroyed at any time while the testator is living, provided, of course, that the testator is of sound mind. There are three methods for revoking a will:

1. By physical act.
2. By later instrument.
3. By operation of law due to changed circumstances.

self-proving will
As prescribed by statute, a will that removes some of the requirements of proof to be admitted to probate. Usually a self-proving affidavit is used.

notary public
A public officer who administers oaths and certifies signatures as genuine.

jurat
A clause that states where, when, and whom the notary public is that is certifying the signature.

ambulatory
Subject to change.

Figure 3-1 Self-proving affidavit clause

STATE OF WISCONSIN

COUNTY OF _____

We, _____, _____, and _____,

The testatrix and the witnesses, respectively, whose names are signed to the foregoing instrument, being first duly sworn, do hereby declare that the testatrix signed the instrument as her will in the presence of the witnesses; and that she signed voluntarily and that each of the witnesses, in the presence of the testatrix, at her request, and in the presence of each other, signed the will as a witness; and that to the best of the knowledge of each witness the testatrix was at that time eighteen (18) years of age or more, of sound mind, and acting under no constraint or undue influence.

_____
Testatrix

Witnesses:

_____

_____

Signed and sworn to before me on _____, 20 ____
By _____, _____,
and _____

_____
Notary Public, State of Wisconsin

My Commission expires: _____

1. By Physical Act

A will can be revoked by physical act. The testator rips up, tears, obliterates, burns, or in some other method destroys the physical writing. He must "desire or have intent" to revoke the will, in Latin called *animus revocandi*. If the will is accidentally destroyed, it is not revoked. For example, Claudia is cold one winter day and accidentally uses her will to start a fire in the fireplace. She lacks the requisite *animus revocandi* or intent to revoke; therefore, the will is still in existence.

A concern arises about how the law treats the possibility that the will was innocently misplaced or lost rather than intentionally revoked by the testator. States differ on how lost wills are treated. However, one should not automatically reach the conclusion that a lost will has been revoked. If an individual argues the will is lost, the burden of proof is on the person to prove it was not revoked (*In re Wise's Estate*, 9 Ill. App. 3d 20, 291 N.E. 2d 292 (1972)). Although Illinois law has a presumption in favor of a lost will being revoked, it is a rebuttable presumption (*In re Maximiuk's Estate*, 29 Ill. App. 2d 144, 172 N.E.2d 524 (1961)). Various evidence can be used to override the presumption. For example, in *Matter of Estate of Babcock*, 119 Ill. App. 3d 482, 456 N.E. 2d 671, 74 Ill. Dec. 950, *aff'd*, 105 Ill. 2d 267, 473 N.E. 2d 1316, 85 Ill. Dec. 511 (1983), the court determined there was sufficient evidence to overcome the presumption. In this case, a conformed copy of the will was found. Statements by the deceased that she liked the will, correspondence written by her that demonstrated her continued love and affection for the beneficiaries of a farm, and testimony of others was also used. The precedent stated that future court analysis of similar cases should be made on a case-by-case basis.

2. By Later Instrument

A newly executed valid last will and testament replaces or revokes an old will. The use of a revocation clause that reads "this will revokes all prior wills and codicils" is common language found in wills. In fact, it is a drafting recommendation to include this language in all wills. A **codicil**, an amendment to a will, which is also a testamentary document, may revoke a portion of a will. A codicil does not completely alter an existing will or replace it; however, it can add to, delete, or change portions of an existing will.

codicil
A testamentary document that amends a will.

The codicil certainly served a valuable purpose when typewriters were used. Rather than retype a twenty-page document for one small change, it was much easier to make the change in a codicil and execute that document. With the advent of the computer, codicils are rarely used today. Rather than drafting a codicil, it is just as easy to insert the new language or change into an old will and have the client execute a new will. During the probate proceeding, the court must read a codicil and incorporate its provisions into those found in the will. More possibility for ambiguity or confusion exists if the will and codicil contradict each other or if the codicil is not clearly drafted. Drafting recommendations contained in Chapter 4 regarding a will also apply for a codicil (see Figure 3-2).

Often the prior will is destroyed. In some cases, retention of an earlier will may be recommended. If the lawyer is concerned about the testator's capacity or voluntariness in executing the new will, the old will may be retained. If the court determines the new will does not meet the requirements of a valid will, the old will may be revived and probated. In some states, this is prohibited.

Figure 3-2   First codicil to Richard Gordon's last will and testament

I, Richard Gordon, of Rockford, Winnebago County, State of Illinois, do make, publish, and declare this to be the first codicil to my last will and testament, executed August 6, 2005.

First: Whereas in Article III in my said last will and testament, I gave my pocket watch to my son, James Gordon, I hereby give my baseball card collection; in addition to my pocket watch, to my son, James Gordon, if he shall survive me.

Second: Whereas in Article II, I gave my estate to my wife, Claudia S. Gordon, if she survives me; in addition, I would like to give a gift of $5,000 to The National Lung Association.

Third: Whereas in Article VIII, I named my daughter, Jennifer Gordon, as successor executor of my last will and testament; I no longer wish to have Jennifer Gordon as successor executor, and name Harold Mogenson as successor executor to my last will and testament and to serve without bond.

Fourth: Except as modified by this codicil, in all other respects, I ratify, confirm, and republish all of the provisions of my said last will and testament dated August 6, 2005.

IN WITNESS WHEREOF, I have hereunto set my hand to this, the first codicil to my Last Will and Testament, dated this _____ day of _____, 20 ___, consisting of one (1) typewritten page including this page.

Richard Gordon

_____
Address

THIS INSTRUMENT, bearing the signature of the above-named Testator, was by him on the date thereof willingly signed, published, and declared by him to be the first codicil to his last will and testament, in our presence, and in the presence of each other, we believing him to be of sound mind and under no constraint or undue influence, have hereunto subscribed our names as attesting witnesses.

_____   _____
_____   _____
(Witness)   (Witness)

3. By Operation of Law Due to Changed Circumstances

Traditionally, major life-changing events or certain circumstances could terminate a will. Two examples are if the testator married or divorced. Statutory law now provides whether an existing will is terminated under either of these circumstances. Under UPC § 2-804, the will is terminated upon divorce. Under UPC § 2-508, the law that a single person's will is terminated upon marriage is rejected. Jurisdictions vary as to revoking the will upon divorce; some may not, some may revoke the entire will, and some may revoke only the portion of the will leaving property to the spouse. For example in Illinois, dissolution of marriage does not revoke the entire will, but does "... revoke every legacy or interest or power of appointment given to or nomination to fiduciary office of the testator's former spouse in a will executed [before the divorce judgment]" (755 Ill. Comp. Stat. § 5/4-7).

The UPC also provides that the slayer's rule operates to revoke a gift by will (see UPC § 2-803).

Other Basic Estate Planning Documents

Certain other basic estate planning documents may be prepared by the law firm to meet the client's needs. Some may be done in addition to the will, or they can be prepared independently of it. These documents include the codicil, power of attorney, living will, and power of attorney health care.

1. Codicil

The codicil was previously discussed in this chapter. See Figure 3-2.

2. Power of Attorney

power of attorney
A document that authorizes one person (the agent or attorney-in-fact) to act on behalf of another person (the principal).

A **power of attorney** is a document that authorizes one person (the agent or attorney-in-fact) to act on behalf of the other person (the principal). Typically, the document is notarized and contains a jurat. A power of attorney can be general or special. A general power of attorney grants broad powers to the agent, including, but not limited to, the power to manage bank accounts, securities, investments, real estate, taxes; to make decisions about hiring accountants or attorneys; and so on. A special or limited power of attorney, as its name suggests, is more narrow and may authorize only one type of activity for the agent to pursue. For example, if John is moving to England and still needs to sell his home located in Colorado, he may execute a power of attorney appointing Claude as his agent. Claude can perform only those activities with regard to the sale of the real estate. He is not directed to manage any other part of John's estate.

Although the agent may be called an attorney-in-fact, the individual does not have to be a lawyer. In estate planning situations, typically a spouse or other family member is appointed as the agent. A corporation, bank, or trust company can also be an agent.

durable general power of attorney
A power of attorney that does not terminate upon the principal becoming mentally incompetent.

In estate planning, a **durable general power of attorney** is executed. A power of attorney terminates upon a principal's death or incompetence. However, a durable power of attorney continues in existence if the principal becomes mentally incompetent. Special language is included in the durable power of attorney. Normally the document nominates the attorney-in-fact as the guardian over the principal if the principal becomes incompetent. In the estate planning area, often a spouse is nominated as an agent for another spouse who is ailing or facing surgery. An adult child may be selected to be an agent for a parent who is ill or physically unable to conduct business. Agency law should also be consulted with regard to

APPLYING YOUR KNOWLEDGE

Martha executes a power of attorney. She owns some stock in AT&T. She is not certain when to sell the shares and is going to the hospital for major surgery. She directs Beverly to sell the shares when they reach a price of $200 per share. What type of power of attorney has been created? What is Martha called? What is Beverly called?

powers of attorney. When drafting a general durable power of attorney, inclusion of certain types of information should be considered:

1. The name and address of the principal.
2. The name and address of the agent or attorney-in-fact.
3. What powers are granted:
   a. To buy or sell securities?
   b. To open, continue, or close various bank accounts?
   c. To sell or buy real or personal property?
   d. To bring litigation or sue for collection?
   e. To represent the principal before taxing authorities?
   f. To access or remove items from a safe deposit box?
   g. To act on behalf of the principal before the Social Security Administration?
   h. To employ or dismiss agents, attorneys, or accountants?
4. The compensation to be paid to the agent.
5. Limitations placed on the agent:
   a. To act only on behalf of the principal.
   b. To not change beneficiary names on life insurance, individual retirement accounts (IRAs), and so on.
   c. To not amend a trust.
6. Nomination of a guardian (if durable power of attorney).
7. Name the effective date.
8. Include a severability provision that would read, "The invalidity of a provision of this power of attorney shall not affect another provision."
9. The date of execution of the document and the principal's signature.
10. A jurat if required.

See Figure 3-3.

Power of Attorney Health Care

A specialized power of attorney is the **power of attorney health care**. It can also be called an advanced care directive or medical power of attorney. The principal gives authority to the agent to make health care decisions as the principal would direct. If the principal cannot advise, the agent makes decisions based on the best interests of the principal. The principal has discussed with the agent what health care is desired. This document and the powers it gives to the agent are much broader than the health care directives contained in the living will, which is discussed in the next section. Under certain circumstances, a power of attorney health care may be preferred over a living will because it allows the agent to react to changing circumstances and is broader in its coverage than the living will. The power of attorney health care grants powers including decisions about whether the principal wants a do-not-resuscitate order or no-code-blue order, about whether the principal wants experimental drugs used or experimental treatments tried and under what circumstances, and so on. It also deals with decisions regarding whether the principal would ever want to be admitted to a nursing home or whether homeopathic or chiropractic medical treatments can be used (see Figure 3-4). In general, it includes information regarding withholding and withdrawing health care.

power of attorney health care
A specialized power of attorney where the agent has authority to make health care decisions for the principal.

Figure 3-3   General durable power of attorney

I, Jack Gordon, of Winnebago County, Illinois, appoint Lisa Gordon of Winnebago County, Illinois, as my agent. My agent may perform for me and in my name and on my behalf any act in the management, supervision, and care of my estate and affairs that I personally have authority to perform. My agent may exercise for me and in my name and on my behalf the powers enumerated below, which are intended to illustrate, and not to limit, the scope of this power.

I. Securities

My agent may buy, sell, pledge, exchange, assign, option, or otherwise transfer any securities of any kind (including without limitation flower bonds); deal with any broker, banker, or other agent; receive all dividends and interest payments now or hereafter due or payable to me from any security or other indebtedness or investment; vote stock and otherwise represent me at all meetings of shareholders or companies or corporations in which I have an interest; sign proxies or other instruments; tender my resignation as director or officer; and subscribe to shares of stock.

II. Accounts

My agent may open, continue, maintain, change, or close any account, including without limitation any checking or savings account, certificate of deposit, share account, and other like arrangement with any bank, trust company, savings bank, building and loan association, savings and loan association, credit union, or other financial institution; make deposits and withdrawals by check, draft, or otherwise; and endorse checks, notes, and drafts for deposit, collection, or otherwise.

III. Other Property, Including Real Estate

My agent may sell, exchange, option, and convey my real and personal property, wherever located; execute and deliver deeds of general warranty, with the customary covenants for such property; manage and control my real and personal property, wherever located; negotiate, execute, and deliver any leases of my property; demand and collect rents; buy every kind of property, real or personal; arrange for appropriate disposition, use, insurance, and safekeeping of all my property; and settle, compromise, and adjust insurance claims.

IV. Collection and Litigation

My agent may demand and collect all property, real or personal, now or hereafter due, payable, or belonging to me; contest, compromise, settle, or abandon claims in my favor or against me; give receipts, releases, and discharges; commence, pursue, or oppose any action, suit, or legal proceeding relating to any matter in which I am or may hereafter be interested; and compromise, settle, or submit to judgment any such action or proceeding.

V. Taxes

My agent may represent me before any office of the Internal Revenue Service or the Treasury Department of the United States and before the tax department of any state, county, or municipality with regard to any tax with which I am concerned. In particular without limitation, my agent may represent me in connection with any federal income tax return and any Illinois income tax returns. My agent may perform all acts that I can perform with respect to any tax matters without limitation. My agent may prepare, sign, and file any tax return; receive originals of all notices and other written communications; negotiate and make compromises; file claims; receive, endorse, and collect checks; receive and examine confidential information; and take appeals, file protest, and execute waivers and closing agreements.

VI. Social Security

My agent may represent and act for me before the Social Security Administration of the United States, and any similar agency of a state or local government; collect all Social Security benefits due me; and make such arrangements in connection with Social Security benefits including without limitation Medicaid and Medicare as will facilitate their application to my care and support.

(continued)

Figure 3-3 (continued)

VII. Employment of Agents

My agent may employ and dismiss agents, attorneys, investment advisers, accountants, housekeepers, and other persons, and terminate any agency that I may have created at any time.

VIII. Compensation

My agent is not entitled to compensation for services rendered.

IX. Limitations

My agent shall not exercise this power in favor of my agent, my agent's estate, my agent's creditors, or the creditors of my agent's estate. My agent shall have no power to change any beneficiary designation for any life insurance policy, qualified plan, or IRA, and my agent shall have no power to amend, alter, or revoke any trust of which I am a grantor. Nothing in this instrument shall be construed to delegate any right or power that I may hold in a fiduciary capacity.

X. Nomination of Guardian

In accordance with Illinois Compiled Statutes, I nominate my agent to serve as my guardian, conservator, or in any similar capacity.

XI. Effective Date

This durable power of attorney becomes effective when signed by the principal.

XII. Photocopies

Photocopies of this power of attorney shall have the same effect as an original.

XIII. Severability

The individuality of a provision of this power of attorney shall not affect another provision. This is a durable power of attorney under Illinois Compiled Statutes and shall not be affected by my subsequent disability, incapacity, or incompetency.

No effect is to be given to article headings.
The following information is current.

	Principal	Agent
Address:	1232 Jim Lane	1232 Jim Lane
	Rockford, Il. 61103	Rockford, Il 61103
Phone:	815-555-1111	815-555-1111
SSN #	000-00-0000	002-00-2000

Dated this _____ day of _____, 20_____.

_____
(Principal)
In the presence of:

_____

_____

State of Illinois
County of Winnebago

    Personally came before me, this _____ day of _____, 20—., the above-named _____, to me known to be the person who executed the foregoing instrument and acknowledged the same.

_____
Notary Public, State of Illinois
My commision expires:_____

Figure 3-4 Illinois statutory power of attorney health care

ESTATES (755 ILCS 45/) Illinois Power of Attorney Act

"ILLINOIS STATUTORY SHORT FORM POWER OF ATTORNEY FOR HEALTH CARE

(NOTICE: THE PURPOSE OF THIS POWER OF ATTORNEY IS TO GIVE THE PERSON YOU DESIGNATE (YOUR "AGENT") BROAD POWERS TO MAKE HEALTH CARE DECISIONS FOR YOU, INCLUDING POWER TO REQUIRE, CONSENT TO OR WITHDRAW ANY TYPE OF PERSONAL CARE OR MEDICAL TREATMENT FOR ANY PHYSICAL OR MENTAL CONDITION AND TO ADMIT YOU TO OR DISCHARGE YOU FROM ANY HOSPITAL, HOME OR OTHER INSTITUTION. THIS FORM DOES NOT IMPOSE A DUTY ON YOUR AGENT TO EXERCISE GRANTED POWERS; BUT WHEN POWERS ARE EXERCISED, YOUR AGENT WILL HAVE TO USE DUE CARE TO ACT FOR YOUR BENEFIT AND IN ACCORDANCE WITH THIS FORM AND KEEP A RECORD OF RECEIPTS, DISBURSEMENTS AND SIGNIFICANT ACTIONS TAKEN AS AGENT. A COURT CAN TAKE AWAY THE POWERS OF YOUR AGENT IF IT FINDS THE AGENT IS NOT ACTING PROPERLY. YOU MAY NAME SUCCESSOR AGENTS UNDER THIS FORM BUT NOT CO-AGENTS, AND NO HEALTH CARE PROVIDER MAY BE NAMED. UNLESS YOU EXPRESSLY LIMIT THE DURATION OF THIS POWER IN THE MANNER PROVIDED BELOW, UNTIL YOU REVOKE THIS POWER OR A COURT ACTING ON YOUR BEHALF TERMINATES IT, YOUR AGENT MAY EXERCISE THE POWERS GIVEN HERE THROUGHOUT YOUR LIFETIME, EVEN AFTER YOU BECOME DISABLED. THE POWERS YOU GIVE YOUR AGENT, YOUR RIGHT TO REVOKE THOSE POWERS AND THE PENALTIES FOR VIOLATING THE LAW ARE EXPLAINED MORE FULLY IN SECTIONS 4–5, 4-6, 4-9 AND 4-10(b) OF THE ILLINOIS "POWERS OF ATTORNEY FOR HEALTH CARE LAW" OF WHICH THIS FORM IS A PART (SEE THE BACK OF THIS FORM). THAT LAW EXPRESSLY PERMITS THE USE OF ANY DIFFERENT FORM OF POWER OF ATTORNEY YOU MAY DESIRE. IF THERE IS ANYTHING ABOUT THIS FORM THAT YOU DO NOT UNDERSTAND, YOU SHOULD ASK A LAWYER TO EXPLAIN IT TO YOU.)

POWER OF ATTORNEY made this . . . . day of

. . . .

(month) (year)

1. I, ... ,

(insert name and address of principal)

hereby appoint:

. . . .

(insert name and address of agent)

as my attorney-in-fact (my "agent") to act for me and in my name (in any way I could act in person) to make any and all decisions for me concerning my personal care, medical treatment, hospitalization and health care and to require, withhold or withdraw any type of medical treatment or procedure, even though my death may ensue. My agent shall have the same access to my medical records that I have, including the right to disclose the contents to others. My agent shall also have full power to authorize an autopsy and direct the disposition of my remains. Effective upon my death, my agent has the full power to make an anatomical gift of the following (initial one):

. . . Any organs, tissues, or eyes suitable for transplantation or used for research or education.

. . . Specific organs: . . . .

(THE ABOVE GRANT OF POWER IS INTENDED TO BE AS BROAD AS POSSIBLE SO THAT YOUR AGENT WILL HAVE AUTHORITY TO MAKE ANY DECISION YOU COULD MAKE TO OBTAIN OR TERMINATE ANY TYPE OF HEALTH CARE, INCLUDING WITHDRAWAL OF FOOD AND WATER AND OTHER LIFE-SUSTAINING MEASURES, IF YOUR AGENT BELIEVES SUCH ACTION WOULD BE CONSISTENT WITH YOUR INTENT AND DESIRES. IF YOU WISH TO LIMIT THE SCOPE OF YOUR AGENT'S POWERS OR PRESCRIBE SPECIAL RULES OR LIMIT THE POWER TO MAKE AN ANATOMICAL GIFT, AUTHORIZE AUTOPSY OR DISPOSE OF REMAINS, YOU MAY DO SO IN THE FOLLOWING PARAGRAPHS.)

2. The powers granted above shall not include the following powers or shall be subject to the following rules or limitations (here you may include any specific limitations you deem appropriate, such as: your own definition of when life-sustaining measures should be withheld; a direction to continue food and fluids or life-sustaining treatment in all events; or instructions to refuse any specific types of treatment that are inconsistent with your religious beliefs or unacceptable to you for any other reason, such as blood transfusion, electro-convulsive therapy, amputation, psychosurgery, voluntary admission to a mental institution, etc.):

. . . .

. . . .

. . . .

. . . .

. . . .

(THE SUBJECT OF LIFE-SUSTAINING TREATMENT IS OF PARTICULAR IMPORTANCE. FOR YOUR CONVENIENCE IN DEALING WITH THAT SUBJECT, SOME GENERAL STATEMENTS CONCERNING THE WITHHOLDING OR REMOVAL OF LIFE-SUSTAINING TREATMENT ARE SET FORTH BELOW. IF YOU AGREE WITH ONE OF THESE STATEMENTS, YOU MAY INITIAL THAT STATEMENT; BUT DO NOT INITIAL MORE THAN ONE):

I do not want my life to be prolonged nor do I want life-sustaining treatment to be provided or continued if my agent believes the burdens of the treatment outweigh the expected benefits. I want my agent to consider the relief of suffering, the expense involved and the quality as well as the possible extension of my life in making decisions concerning life-sustaining treatment.

Initialed . . . .

I want my life to be prolonged and I want life-sustaining treatment to be provided or continued unless I am in a coma which my attending physician believes to be irreversible, in accordance with reasonable medical standards at the time of reference. If and when I have suffered irreversible coma, I want life-sustaining treatment to be withheld or discontinued.

Initialed . . . .

I want my life to be prolonged to the greatest extent possible without regard to my condition, the chances I have for recovery or the cost of the procedures.

Initialed . . . .

(THIS POWER OF ATTORNEY MAY BE AMENDED OR REVOKED BY YOU IN THE MANNER PROVIDED IN SECTION 4–6 OF THE ILLINOIS "POWERS OF ATTORNEY FOR HEALTH CARE LAW"(SEE THE BACK OF THIS FORM). ABSENT AMENDMENT OR REVOCATION, THE AUTHORITY GRANTED IN THIS POWER OF ATTORNEY WILL BECOME EFFECTIVE AT THE TIME THIS POWER IS SIGNED AND WILL CONTINUE UNTIL YOUR DEATH, AND BEYOND IF ANATOMICAL GIFT, AUTOPSY OR DISPOSITION OF REMAINS IS AUTHORIZED, UNLESS A LIMITATION ON THE BEGINNING DATE OR DURATION IS MADE BY INITIALING AND COMPLETING EITHER OR BOTH OF THE FOLLOWING:)

(continued)

Figure 3-4   (continued)

3. ( ) This power of attorney shall become effective on. . . . .
. . . .
. . . .
(insert a future date or event during your lifetime, such as court determination of your disability, when you want this power to first take effect)

4. ( ) This power of attorney shall terminate on . . . .
. . . .
(insert a future date or event, such as court determination of your disability, when you want this power to terminate prior to your death)

(IF YOU WISH TO NAME SUCCESSOR AGENTS, INSERT THE NAMES AND ADDRESSES OF SUCH SUCCESSORS IN THE FOLLOWING PARAGRAPH.)

5. If any agent named by me shall die, become incompetent, resign, refuse to accept the office of agent or be unavailable, I name the following (each to act alone and successively, in the order named) as successors to such agent:

. . . .
. . . .

For purposes of this paragraph 5, a person shall be considered to be incompetent if and while the person is a minor or an adjudicated incompetent or disabled person or the person is unable to give prompt and intelligent consideration to health care matters, as certified by a licensed physician. (IF YOU WISH TO NAME YOUR AGENT AS GUARDIAN OF YOUR PERSON, IN THE EVENT A COURT DECIDES THAT ONE SHOULD BE APPOINTED, YOU MAY, BUT ARE NOT REQUIRED TO, DO SO BY RETAINING THE FOLLOWING PARAGRAPH. THE COURT WILL APPOINT YOUR AGENT IF THE COURT FINDS THAT SUCH APPOINTMENT WILL SERVE YOUR BEST INTERESTS AND WELFARE. STRIKE OUT PARAGRAPH 6 IF YOU DO NOT WANT YOUR AGENT TO ACT AS GUARDIAN.)

6. If a guardian of my person is to be appointed, I nominate the agent acting under this power of attorney as such guardian, to serve without bond or security.

7. I am fully informed as to all the contents of this form and understand the full import of this grant of powers to my agent.

Signed . . . .
                                                             (principal)

The principal has had an opportunity to read the above form and has signed the form or acknowledged his or her signature or mark on the form in my presence.

. . . . Residing at . . . .
     (witness)

(YOU MAY, BUT ARE NOT REQUIRED TO, REQUEST YOUR AGENT AND SUCCESSOR AGENTS TO PROVIDE SPECIMEN SIGNATURES BELOW. IF YOU INCLUDE SPECIMEN SIGNATURES IN THIS POWER OF ATTORNEY, YOU MUST COMPLETE THE CERTIFICATION OPPOSITE THE SIGNATURES OF THE AGENTS.)

Specimen signatures of agent (and successors).

. . . .
        (agent)

. . . .
   (successor agent)

. . . .
   (successor agent)

I certify that the signatures of my agent (and successors) are correct.

. . . .
       (principal)

. . . .
       (principal)

. . . .
       (principal)"

Living Will

The final simple estate planning document is the **living will**. A living will might also be called a directive to physicians. Unlike the last will and testament, the living will does not gift property. It discusses the health care wishes of the signer. The signer may direct that no artificial measures be employed to postpone his or her death. The signer sets forth his or her wishes regarding the withholding or withdrawing of health care. The living will may provide for a no-code-blue or do-not-resuscitate order to take effect when the person is in a constant vegetative state or has a terminal condition and there is no hope of recovery. The document may also state whether experimental drugs should be used. It often contains language relieving the medical provider of liability, even if the decisions in the living will are adverse to the family's wishes. The document must be witnessed. There are usually limits as to who can serve as a witness. State laws should be consulted, but typically relatives of the signer, health care providers of the signer, and creditors of the signer cannot serve as witnesses (see Figure 3-5).

living will
A document where the signer may direct that no artificial measures be employed to postpone his or her death.

Figure 3-5   Living will

I, John Currie Gordon, revoke all prior living wills and all prior declarations to physicians and other interested persons, if any, and declare this to be my last living will and declaration to take effect immediately.

I wish to live and enjoy life as long as possible. However, I do not wish to receive medical treatment or health care that will only postpone the moment of my death from an incurable and terminal condition or that will only prolong my life if I have a permanent loss of consciousness. For purposes of this document, terminal condition means a condition that is reasonably expected to result in my death within twelve months regardless of the treatment that I may receive, and permanent loss of consciousness means a loss of consciousness from which there is no reasonable possibility that I will return to a cognitive and sapient life, and includes, but is not limited to, a persistent vegetative state.

Therefore, if two licensed and qualified physicians (neither of whom is related to me by blood, marriage, or adoption) have personally examined me, are familiar with my condition, and have diagnosed and noted in my medical records either (1) that I have a terminal condition as defined above and that I am unable to receive and evaluate information effectively or to communicate decisions to such an extent that I lack the capacity to manage my health care decisions, or (2) that I have a permanent loss of consciousness as defined above, then:

1. I direct that treatment or procedures that will only postpone the moment of death if I have a terminal condition, or that will only prolong my life if I have a permanent loss of consciousness, not be instituted or, if previously instituted, direct that they be discontinued.
2. I direct that procedures used to provide me with nutrition and hydration (including, for example, but not limited to, misting and all forms of intravenous, parenteral, rectal, and tube feeding) be instituted and continue to be provided in the amount and kind determined by my physicians as to be necessary to prevent stressful dehydration, particularly of the mouth and skin, so as to maximize my life.
3. I direct that my physician or health care provider issue a "No Code" or "Do Not Resuscitate" order if I am diagnosed with a terminal illness or permanent loss of consciousness as described above.
4. I direct that my physician or health care provider order whatever is appropriate to keep me as comfortable and free of pain as is reasonably possible, including the administration of pain-relieving drugs of any kind or other surgical or medical procedures calculated to relieve my pain, including unconventional pain-relief therapies that my physician or health care provider believes may be helpful, even though such drugs or procedures may have adverse side effects including permanent physical damage, may cause addiction, or may hasten the moment of (but not intentionally cause) my death.

I request that my directions and wishes as expressed in this instrument be carried out despite any contrary feelings, beliefs, or opinions of my family members, relatives, friends, conservator, or guardian.

For the purpose of inducing any person or entity ("person"), including, but not limited to, any health care facility or health care provider to act in accordance with the directions given in this instrument, I represent, warrant, and agree that, except as provided below, I release and forever discharge any person who is or may be claimed to be liable to me, my estate, or my heirs, successors, or assigns, from all claims, demands, damages, actions, or suits of any kind, on account of all injuries or damages both to person and property that arises from that person's acting in accordance with my directions as given in this instrument. I do not release or discharge any person from liability for negligence in the performance of acts performed in accordance with my directions as given in this instrument.

If any portion of this instrument is invalid or unenforceable under application of law, I direct that the balance of this instrument shall not be affected and shall continue in full force and effect.

(continued)

Figure 3-5   (continued)

I voluntarily have executed this instrument this _____ day of _____, 20_____.

_____

STATEMENT OF WITNESSES

I know the person signing this document ("the declarant"), and I believe the declarant to be of sound mind. I believe the declarant's execution of this document is voluntary. I am at least eighteen years of age, and I am not re-lated to the declarant by blood, marriage, or adoption. To the best of my knowledge, I am not entitled to and do not have a claim on any portion of the declarant's estate. I am not directly financially responsible for the declarant's health care. I am not a health care provider who is involved in the declarant's health care at this time. I am not an employee, other than a chaplain or social worker, of an inpatient health care facility in which the declarant is a patient.

_____ of _____
_____ of _____

KEY **TERMS**

abatement (p. 29)
ademption (p. 30)
ambulatory (p. 35)
anti-lapse statute (p. 30)
bequest (p. 28)
codicil (p. 36)
demonstrative bequest (p. 28)
devise (p. 28)
durable general power of
   attorney (p. 38)

executor (p. 31)
general bequest (p. 28)
holographic will (p. 33)
jurat (p. 35)
lapse (p. 30)
legacy (p. 28)
legatee (p. 28)
legator (p. 28)
living will (p. 43)
lucid interval (p. 33)

notary public (p. 35)
nuncupative will (p. 33)
personal representative (p. 31)
power of attorney (p. 38)
power of attorney health care (p. 39)
residuary bequest (p. 28)
self-proving will (p. 35)
slayer's rule or slayer's statute (p. 31)
specific bequest (p. 28)
supernumerary witness (p. 34)

REVIEW **QUESTIONS**

1. Name two advantages to estate planning.
2. Give an example of:
   a. Devise.
   b. Specific legacy.
   c. Residuary legacy.
   d. Demonstrative legacy.
   e. General bequest.
3. What is the difference between ademption and lapse?
4. What types of directions may be included in a will?
5. The maker of a will must be mentally competent.
   a. Explain the four factors used to judge if a person is mentally competent to execute a will.
   b. If you doubt the mental competency of the testator when he is executing the will, what precautions should you take?

6. Compare and contrast a nuncupative will and a holographic will.
7. List and explain the options available for the requirement of a testator's signature on the will.
8. Why isn't it a good idea to have an interested person serve as a witness on the will? What could happen?
9. What does revocation mean? List and explain three methods of revoking a will.
10. Distinguish among the following:
   a. Limited power of attorney.
   b. General power of attorney.
   c. Durable power of attorney.
   d. Power of attorney health care.
   e. Living will.

ROLE-PLAYING **ACTIVITIES**

1. Choose a partner. One student should be the lawyer and the other the potential client. Research the law regarding lost wills in your state. Explain that the client's deceased relative may have revoked or lost his will. Discuss the state's law regarding the lost will and the likelihood that the will would be accepted in probate.

2. With a classmate, pretend you wish to effectuate an estate plan. Discuss the advantages of estate planning, the types of documents available, and which documents should be used.

RESEARCH **ASSIGNMENTS**

1. Find your state's statute on abatement. What is the order of abatement? Does the statute treat real property and personal property the same or differently in an abatement situation?

2. Does your state have an anti-lapse statute? What are its provisions?

3. How does your state's slayer's rule operate?

4. Does your state recognize holographic wills or nuncupative wills as valid? Explain.

5. Research and determine if your state has a self-proving will statute. If it does, what does it require?

6. Does your state allow an old will to be revived? Under what circumstances?

7. Research your state's law regarding a living will and a power of attorney health care. Do you have statutory forms for the documents?

BUILD YOUR **PORTFOLIO**

1. Using the case example you chose in Chapter 1, draft a general durable power of attorney.

2. Using the case example you chose in Chapter 1, draft a living will.

Chapter **four**

DRAFTING A BASIC WILL

Implementing the Client's Plan

Now that you realize the value of a plan, you must know that the same plan does not work for every person. This is where the art of estate planning comes into play. As you create your own life and goals, you obtain different resources and have different desires for who shall receive those resources upon your death. Different estate plans are created to meet the needs and desires of different clients. First, this chapter focuses on learning the client's current status and desires for an estate plan. Second, the chapter discusses the science of how to translate those goals into a constructive written plan. Narrowed down to basic estate planning, the chapter focuses on drafting a simple will. The word *simple* is a misnomer because to adequately understand and accomplish a client's estate plan should never be called *simple*. It is truly magical to capture the intent of a person in a written document. Drafting a will is a simpler project compared to the typically longer and more complex nature of a trust. Chapter 5 discusses trusts.

Initial Client Conference

How do we determine the client's current financial and family status and determine his or her future goals? The typical method is through the initial client conference. With regard to the estate planning and probate areas, most law firms ask the paralegal to play a role in the interviewing process. In some law firms, the paralegal is present to take notes and plays a passive role. The attorney asks the questions and explains the procedures. In other firms, the paralegal may be the only interviewer. In these situations, you must remember *not* to give legal advice nor to discuss the fee arrangements with the potential

OBJECTIVES

After studying this chapter, you should be able to:

- Understand why each client's estate plan differs.
- Understand how to effectively conduct an initial client interview and gather the important estate planning information from the client.
- Explain, determine under what circumstances to include, and draft various sections of a will.
- Understand the implications of disinheriting an heir, draft a disinheritance clause, and draft an "in terrorem" clause.
- Explain why a spouse cannot be completely disinherited under spousal election or community property law.
- Understand the need for a survivorship clause and draft one.
- Explain a simultaneous death clause, determine under what circumstances it should be included in a will, and draft one.
- Draft a clause naming the personal representative.

- Define guardian and draft a clause nominating a guardian.
- Understand the importance of a testimonium clause and draft one.
- Explain the requirements of a testator's signature.
- Define an attestation clause and draft one.
- Explain the requirements of witnesses' signatures.
- Recall additional drafting tips.
- Describe the procedure for executing a will.
- List and know the advantages and disadvantages of the four storage places for wills.

client. A paralegal discussing this information violates the ethical rule of the unauthorized practice of law. Only a licensed attorney can give legal advice and make fee arrangements with a client. During the interview, make it very clear that you are a paralegal and explain to the client that the attorney must respond to those types of inquiries. The third option requires the paralegal to record statistical information about the client, the family names, phone numbers, financial items, assets, liabilities, and so on. Then the attorney gives legal advice and recommends the best documents, explains how they are drafted, and sets the fee schedule.

No matter which interview style is used, having an interview checklist promotes a well-organized, efficient, and effective interaction with a client. Many form books and law firms have already prepared an interview checklist. If you are conducting many interviews, you may want to draft your own or revise the one provided by the law firm. Some law firms give a questionnaire to the client when he or she arrives at the firm. The receptionist asks the client to complete the form while awaiting the interview. The extensiveness of this form varies from one office to the next. Often the first step in the interview process is to review the information requested in the form.

The ability to interact well with people is vital during the interview. One should possess a pleasant and professional demeanor when meeting with the client. Remember, this may be the client's first impression of the law firm. Listening is a key component to the interview process. You are working to get the client's story, not trying to tell yours. Asking open-ended questions is a good idea. However, knowing when to ask for clarification or to focus on detail is important. This is the art of performing estate planning and other legal work.

Information gathering for estate planning can be grouped into three areas. See Figure 4-1.

1. *The client's and client's family's statistical information:* You need to learn about the client, including details like his or her name, address, phone number, email address, and employment. You should also determine the client's family, in particular, those closest in the bloodline to the client. It might be wise to prepare a family tree at this time. You should learn and record the spouse's name, the children's name(s), addresses, phone numbers, ages, and so on.

2. *The client's financial status:* You must determine the assets and liabilities of the client. Determine bounty, or what the estate contains. This information includes bank accounts, investments, real estate holdings, salary, collections, life insurance, retirement plans, and so on. It also includes gathering information on liabilities, mortgages, liens, and credit card debt. You need to learn where the items are located and approximate values or amounts.

3. *The client's plan:* What does the client want? The closer you can come to giving the client what he or she desires, the better the professional relationship. This, of course, is not always possible; sometimes the client wants conflicting or impractical results or wants something that is illegal. The attorney will need to judge and explain to the client if any of these problems arise.

In the first interview, you must determine what the client wants and what type of estate planning is the most beneficial for the client's financial prosperity and family. Tax law should also be consulted (see Chapter 9). After the client conference is

Figure 4-1 Estate planning interview checklist

Date: _____

A. Client's and client's family's statistical information

1. *Client:*
   Name:
   Address:
   Phone numbers:
   Social security number:
   Date of birth:
   Employer/income:

2. *Spouse:*
   Name:
   Address:
   Phone numbers:
   Social security number:
   Date of birth:
   Employer/income:
   Date of marriage:

3. *Children* (obtain statistical information for all children):
   Name:
   Address:
   Date of birth:
   Children who are married:
   Grandchildren:
   Children who are not children of the current spouse:
   a. Who is the other parent?
   b. Are there any children who have died?
   c. Did they have any children?
   d. Do you have any stepchildren?

4. *Other relatives:*
   a. Parents (if appropriate):
      Name:
      Address:
      Relationship:
   b. Siblings:
      Name:
      Address:
      Relationship:
   c. Others (if appropriate):
      Name:
      Address:
      Relationship:

5. *Prior marriage:*
   Name:
   Date marriage ended:
   How marriage ended:

(continued)

Figure 4-1 (continued)

6. *Miscellaneous personal background:*
   a. Relatives:
      (1) Minors?
      (2) Disabled? How?
      (3) Disinherited? Why?
   b. Documents:
      (1) Prior will? Date?
      (2) Trust?
      (3) Prenuptial agreement?
   c. Client:
      (1) Health?
      (2) Mental competence?
      (3) Voluntarily acting?

B. Financial information
   1. *Assets:*
      a. Home:
         Value:
         Mortgage/liens:
         Title:
      b. Other real estate:
         Address:
         Value:
         Mortgage/liens:
         Title:
      c. Bank accounts:
         Type:
         Where:
         Value:
         Title:
      d. Securities:
         Type:
         Where:
         Value:
         Title:
      e. Automobiles:
         Make:
         Model:
         Value:
         Title:
      f. Receipt of or anticipated substantial gift or inheritance?
         From whom?
         Value:
      g. Collectibles, artwork, antiques:
         Type:
         Where located:
         Value:
         Title:

(continued)

Figure 4-1   (continued)

---

      h. Other personal property:
          Type:
          Where located:
          Value:
          Title:
      i.   Life insurance:
          Name of company:
          Type of policy:
          Title:
          Beneficiary:
          Insured's name:
          Value:
      j.   Retirement plans:
          Type:
          Where located (company):
          Beneficiary:
          Value:
   2. *Debts:*
      Creditors:
      Secured by party?
      Amount:
C. Client's plan
   1. *Will?*
   2. *Codicil?*
   3. *Trust?*
   4. *Power of attorney?*
   5. *Power of attorney health care?*
   6. *Living will?*
   7. *To make gifts while living?*

---

completed, a memorandum to the file is often prepared and any notes taken are placed in the file.

Sections of a Will

Now that you have gathered the requisite client information, you can turn your attention to drafting the will. Language for a will can be found in form books or you can look through other wills the law firm has done. Although these sample documents and this section can serve as valuable guidelines, each will must be tailored to the specific client. For an example of a will, see Figure 4-2. The will consists of several sections:

1. Title

The title of the will is its heading. It states the "Last Will and Testament of ———." The testator's or testatrix's name is then inserted in the document. Many law firms have specially embossed stationery for the first page of the will and "Last Will and

Figure 4-2   Last will and testament of Richard L. Gordon

LAST WILL AND TESTAMENT
OF
RICHARD L. GORDON

I, Richard L. Gordon, residing at 1144 Oaks Street, City of Rockford, County of Winnebago, State of Illinois, being of sound and disposing mind and memory, and not acting under undue influence of any person whomsoever, make, publish, and declare this document to be my last will and testament, and expressly revoke any prior wills and codicils, made by me.

ARTICLE I

I direct my personal representative hereinafter named, to pay all my legally enforceable debts, and expenses of my last illness, funeral, burial, and estate administration out of the residue of my estate. I further direct my personal representative to pay out of my residuary estate all estate, income, and inheritance taxes assessed against my taxable estate or the recipients thereof, whether passing by this will or by other means, without contribution or reimbursement from any person.

ARTICLE II

I have intentionally not provided in this will for my son, William Gordon, and this omission is not caused by accident or mistake.

ARTICLE III

I give my pocket watch, which I own, to my son, James Gordon, if he survives me.

ARTICLE IV

I give the rest and remainder of my estate, real, personal, or mixed, of whatever kind and wherever located, after the payment of debts, expenses, and taxes, as mentioned in Article I, subject to the laws, to my wife, Claudia S. Gordon, if she survives me. If she does not survive me, I give said residue to my children, Jennifer Gordon, and James Gordon in equal shares.

ARTICLE V

I nominate and appoint as personal guardian of my minor son, James Gordon, Jennifer Gordon, my daughter. I nominate and appoint as property guardian of my minor son, James Gordon, Charles Gordon, my brother. If either guardian becomes disabled or declines to serve, I nominate the other to serve in the former's capacity as well as the capacity in which he/she is presently serving.
I direct that bond be required of neither of said guardians for the performance of the duties of their respective offices.

ARTICLE VI

In the event that my wife, Claudia S. Gordon, and I die under such circumstances that it is difficult or impossible to determine who died first, it shall be presumed that my wife predeceased me. If my said wife dies within a period of six (6) months after the date of my death, my said wife shall be deemed to have predeceased me, and all provisions contained herein for her benefit shall be cancelled and my estate shall be administered and the assets of my estate distributed as though I had died immediately after the death of my said wife.

ARTICLE VII

I nominate and appoint my wife, Claudia S. Gordon, to be personal representative of this will, and to serve without bond.
If Claudia S. Gordon does not survive me or does not qualify as personal representative, I nominate Jennifer Gordon, my daughter, to be successor personal representative of this will and to serve without bond.
My personal representative shall have the power to sell publicly or privately all or part of the residue of my property in the event that such sale will become necessary for the payment of debts, taxes, or expenses, until the testamentary dispositions thereof are complete; and to settle all valid claims against my estate.

(continued)

Figure 4-2   (continued)

ARTICLE VIII

I freely and willingly subscribe my name to this will consisting of two pages, including this page, on this _____ of _____, 20__, in the presence of these witnesses: John Doe and Jane Doe, each of whom I have requested to subscribe their names in my presence and in the presence of all others.

Richard L. Gordon

On the last date shown above, Richard L. Gordon, known to us to be the person whose signature appears at the end of this will, declared to us, the undersigned, that the foregoing instrument was his will. He then signed the will in our presence; at his request, we now sign our names in his presence and the presence of each other.

Names	Addresses

/S/
(Witness)
/S/
(Witness)

Testament of" is preprinted on it. The maker's name should be a formal name and clearly indicate to whom the will belongs. The use of a middle name or initial is preferred. If the person had another name, especially one that was used on other legal documents demonstrating ownership of real estate or investments, that name should also appear in the title. Use aka or "also known as." A full title might read:

Last Will and Testament
Of
Elizabeth Ann Smith
aka
Bettina Smith

2. Exordium Clause

The **exordium** or introductory clause is contained in the first paragraph of the will. It is often referred to as a publication clause. It identifies the maker and where he or she lives, states that the document is the last will and testament, and demonstrates the individual has intent and capacity to make a will. An example of such a clause would read:

> I, Elizabeth Ann Smith, residing at 1234 Ferncreek Street, Chicago, Illinois, being of sound mind and memory do hereby voluntarily make and publish this document as my Last Will and Testament.

exordium clause
The introductory clause to a will or codicil.

3. Revocation Clause

The **revocation clause** also appears within the first paragraph. As you recall from Chapter 3, one method of revoking or canceling an already existing will is by later instrument or executing a new will. This clause is standard language and should be

revocation clause
The clause in the will that cancels an already existing will.

included even if the client has not previously executed a will. It safeguards the validity of the document. It typically reads:

> I do hereby revoke my former Wills and Codicils and declare this to be my last Will.

4. Direction to Pay Debts and Taxes

Most wills contain language instructing the personal representative to pay debts, taxes, and funeral expenses from the estate assets. Remember, all liabilities are paid before any heir or beneficiary inherits anything. You should recall the discussion on abatement from Chapter 3, which covers how creditors are paid when the estate is probated. More information on creditor's claims is also found in Chapter 8. Although this is often **boilerplate** language, be careful about the wording of the clause. In some states, recent case law has held the expression "legal debt" or "just debt" revives the testator's old debt that had become unenforceable under the statute of limitations. Preferred language now is "legally enforceable debts." This clause often reads:

> I direct the payment of my funeral expenses, administration expenses, taxes, and legally enforceable debts as provided by law.

5. Instructions for Funeral

The client may want funeral instructions to be included in the will. This information would include burial versus cremation, organ donation, where the funeral would be held, where the internment would be, and other details. Although sometimes included in a will, this information should be contained elsewhere for the best results. The law firm may prepare a letter of instructions containing information about the testator's preferences for funeral and burial plans and organ donation. The letter could be more thorough and contain information about the estate to help the personal representative locate documents necessary for the estate administration. The letter should be placed with the attorney, nominated personal representative, and primary beneficiaries. The will may be found after arrangements have been made, and if organ donation is desired, after the organs could be effectively harvested and transplanted. Some states provide that organ donations be indicated on the back of a driver's license.

Funeral instructions and organ donations may be contained in the will. However, I would discourage drafting such information into the will. Remember though, only an attorney can give this type of advice. It would be unethical for a paralegal to discuss this information with a client.

6. Dispositive Provisions

One major goal of a last will and testament is to make gifts. You may want to review the section that covers gifts, found in Chapter 3. Recall the differences among specific bequests, demonstrative bequests, general bequests, residuary bequests, and devises. Today the term "give" is usually the verb used rather than "bequeath or devise." This section is relatively easy to draft provided you have a clear understanding of the client's desires. Try to be organized in the drafting. My preference is to begin with any devises, then specific bequests, then demonstrative bequests, then general legacies, and finally end with the residuary clause. For example: James wants to leave his car to his son, Michael Moore; $1,000 to his daughter, Meghan Moore; and his house to his wife, Mary Moore. The will would read:

> First: I hereby give my home located at 787 Mockingbird Lane, Milwaukee, Wisconsin, to my beloved wife, Mary Moore.
>
> Second, I give my 2000 Chevrolet Impala to my beloved son, Michael Moore.
>
> Third, I give $1,000 to my beloved daughter, Meghan Moore.

7. Residuary Clause

The **residuary clause** is a vital component of the will. If it is not included, any property not gifted in the will would pass to heirs as designated under the statutes of intestate succession. This would complicate the probate of the estate. The clause should always be included. It gives the remainder of the estate to whomever the testatrix desires. Some examples:

residuary clause
A provision in a will that leaves to a designated beneficiary all remaining property not previously gifted.

> I hereby give the rest and remainder of my estate to my husband, Ryan Jones.
>
> I hereby give the rest and remainder of my estate to my three children: Lauren Jones, Zachary Jones, and Melissa Jones in equal shares.
>
> I hereby give the rest and remainder of my estate to the American Red Cross.

A Tennessee court was required to interpret the meaning of a residuary clause.

> In *In re Estate of Jackson*, 793 SW. 2d 259 (Tenn. App. 1990), the Tennessee Court of Appeals grappled with whether the will created a residuary clause for a certificate of deposit to be inherited by the Eastminster Presbyterian Church or if it should pass to the decedent's heirs through intestate succession. The pertinent portion of the will read, "I direct that my Executor shall allow the members of my family to select such item or items from my clothing, jewelry, household goods, personal effects and all other tangible personal property not otherwise specifically bequeathed, except securities and cash on hand or on deposit, as each of them may desire . . ." *Id*. at 260. The will continued that if there remained any personal property the Executor was to sell it and the proceeds would be paid to the church. The appellate court analyzed the will and determined that the certificate of deposit was part of the "securities and cash on hand or deposit" category and the certificate of deposit was expressly excluded from the grant of remaining personal property to the church. Thus, the decedent's heirs were entitled to inherit the certificate of deposit through intestate succession.

APPLYING YOUR KNOWLEDGE

Richard Collingsworth has hired your law firm to draft his will. He wants his Colorado ranch to be left to his son, Jeff Collingsworth; he wants to leave his gun collection to his son, Cody Collingsworth, if he survives him, otherwise to Jeff. He wants to leave $10,000 to his daughter, Alyssa Collingsworth, and the rest and remainder of his estate to his three children: Jeff, Cody, and Alyssa in equal shares. Draft the dispositive provisions section of this will.

8. Disinheritance

A testator may disinherit almost any heir from inheriting. However, a deceased spouse cannot completely disinherit a surviving spouse. The law has created special protections for spouses. In common law states, it is called spousal election, and it is called community property in non-common-law states. These concepts are discussed later in this chapter. Usually, the maker of the will desires to disinherit children or grandchildren. If this is the maker's desire, the will should contain language specifically communicating the intention. If a child is merely not mentioned in the will, sometimes the child can convince the court it was an oversight of the maker, and the child should inherit anyway.

pretermitted heir
A child or other relative, whether living or not yet born, of the decedent who has been omitted from the will.

A **pretermitted heir** is not living at the date of execution of the will or is a later-born heir. This heir can argue to the court that he or she is entitled to inherit from the decedent. States may have a statute allowing the child to inherit from the decedent. See 755 Ill. Comp. Stat § 5/4-10, which provides that a child born after the will is executed can inherit an intestate share.

Typically, a disinheritance clause should appear before any gifts are made. The testator can include the reason the disinheritance is occurring; however, if it is for a sensitive, personal reason, the maker may not want the reason given. If the intent to disinherit is clearly communicated, that is enough. Two sample disinheritance clauses follow:

> It is my intention to purposely disinherit my son, James Johnson, for reasons he is well aware.

> It is my intention to purposely disinherit my son, James Johnson, because I have not had any contact with him for the past five years.

An older method of disinheriting an heir was to leave one dollar ($1) to him or her. Although this obviates the argument that the heir was accidentally left out of the will, it has resulted in additional problems or delays in probate. The heir then must receive the one dollar ($1) and sign a receipt that it was accepted. The angry disinherited heir may be reluctant to sign the receipt and thus slow down the closing of the estate. The Tennessee case mentioned earlier in this chapter also faced the issue of whether the heirs were disinherited. The pertinent portion of the will read:

> I have not made a devise or bequest to any of my relatives in this will because they are all financially secure in their own right and do not need any little thing I have to offer, therefore, they are not to try to change or break this will at any time or in any way . . ." *Id.* at 260.

The appellate court ruled this language did not create disinheritance. It stated:

> A testator can disinherit his heirs only by giving his property to others and mere words excluding the heirs, without an affirmative disposition to others, will not suffice to disinherit them; for the right of a person to disinherit his heirs exists, not as a distinctive or abstract substantive power, but merely as a consequence of the power to leave his estate to others, and while a testator may make or revoke his will, he can neither make nor unmake a law of the state." *In re Estate of Jackson*, 793 S.W. 2d 259, 261-262 (Tenn. App. 1990).

It is more likely for the disinherited heir to bring a will contest than an heir named as a beneficiary. (Will contests are discussed in Chapter 10.) The testator may include an **"in terrorem" clause** or penalty clause for contest to discourage a will contest. An "in terrorem" clause states the person does not receive the gift under the will upon contesting the will. More specifically, the clause would read,

> In the event that a beneficiary contests this Will or any part of it, the gift given to such beneficiary is hereby revoked, and the gift will be distributed as part of my residuary estate.

For example, Caitlin, as a daughter, would probably inherit $50,000 from her mother, but instead her mother leaves her $10,000. Her mother also includes an "in terrorem" clause in her will. Caitlin will have to decide if she desires to contest the will. If she wins the will contest, she gets $50,000; however, if she loses, she will inherit nothing. She loses her inheritance of $10,000 as designated in the will. This is another clever way to limit an heir's share. Different states treat "in terrorem" clauses differently. Some enforce them, and some do not recognize them. You should be familiar with your state's treatment of an "in terrorem" clause. See, for example, PaCSA § 2521, which states the clause is unenforceable if probable cause exists.

"in terrorem" clause
A provision in a will that states a beneficiary will not receive his or her gift if he or she contests the will.

9. Spousal Election/Community Property

Special protections exist for a spouse's right to property belonging to a decedent. If a spouse attempts to disinherit the surviving spouse, the law steps in and provides that the surviving spouse receives certain property. This protection differs depending on whether your state is a common law state or a community property state. Traditionally, in common law states, this was called dower or curtesy. Dower protected the surviving wife from receiving nothing from her deceased husband's estate. Curtesy protected the surviving husband from receiving nothing from his deceased wife's estate. Under old common law, the law usually granted the surviving spouse one-third to one-half of a life estate in the deceased spouse's estate. This has changed to a fee simple interest or full ownership right to one-third up to one-half of the deceased spouse's estate.

Today, common law states have typically enacted spousal election statutes. These usually allow for a one-half interest in fee simple in the deceased spouse's estate.

In community property states, the surviving spouse owns one-half of the estate outright. Because both spouses contribute to property obtained during the marriage, the spouses share equally in the ownership of it. Therefore, upon the death of a spouse, the husband and wife share equally in the division of the community property. This automatically offers protection to the surviving spouse.

10. Survivorship Requirement

Suppose that a husband and wife are in a car accident together. The husband is immediately killed, and the wife lingers for one week in the hospital before she dies. In this case, the husband has predeceased the wife. Assume the spouses had no issue. They executed similar valid wills. The husband left his property to the wife and then to his parents, Mr. and Mrs. Cooper, in equal shares. The wife's will left her property to her husband and then to her parents, Mr. and Mrs. Smart, in equal shares. Who would inherit? The answer is the husband's estate would pass to the wife under his will. Then the wife's estate would be probated and her parents, Mr. and Mrs. Smart, would receive the couple's property and money. Remember, the wife outlived her husband by only one week. This may not be what the spouses had intended as an end result. Furthermore, the husband's estate must be probated first. All the property passed through his estate and then went through the wife's probate. The property went through two sets of taxes and administration costs, which causes delay. A method exists to get a more fair result and avoid delay and unnecessary duplication of costs and taxes. A clause can be added to a will to obtain the fairer result. It is often called a **survivorship clause** or **delay clause**, which reads:

> If any beneficiary dies prior to the entry of an order, decree, or judgment in my estate, distributing the property in question, or within six months after the date of my death, whichever is earlier, any interest which would have passed to said beneficiary under other provisions of the will are to be disposed of according to the plan of distribution which would have been effective under this will if such beneficiary had predeceased me.

The time frame stated in the clause can vary. However, state law should be consulted before determining the length of time specified.

survivorship clause or delay clause
A provision of a will that requires a beneficiary to outlive the decedent by a certain specified period of time for the gift to pass to him or her.

11. Simultaneous Death Clause

Consider again the example of the husband and wife in a car accident, discussed in the prior section about a survivorship requirement. The couple was found a few hours after the accident, and experts cannot adequately determine who died first. You may still have the same problems as discussed in the earlier section, for example, additional costs, unfairness in inheritance, and so on. Many states have enacted the Uniform Simultaneous Death Act. The act sets forth the rule that if it is unclear who died first, and the order of the deaths is an important factor in the probate, the decedent whose estate is being probated has survived the other decedent. In other words, because of the wording of the couple's wills, the husband is presumed to have outlived his wife when the court is probating his estate and the wife is presumed to have outlived the husband when the court is probating her estate. UPC § 2-702 (a) states:

> An individual who is not established by clear and convincing evidence to have survived an event, including the death of another individual, by 120 hours is deemed to have predeceased the event.

simultaneous death clause
A provision in a will that provides that another person predeceased the decedent if it is unclear who died first.

A **simultaneous death clause** would be a recommended provision in wills for spouses or others who are closely related and leave property to one person and then on to someone else. These clauses typically read:

> If my wife, Joanne Baker, and I die under circumstances where it is difficult to determine who died first, it is my intention that the court shall presume my wife predeceased me.

12. Nomination of Personal Representative

The will should contain language nominating an executor or personal representative to administer the probate of the estate. Recall in Chapter 3 that certain directions are contained in the will. The court may then appoint the nominated executor to go forward with the probate. Chapter 7 discusses the procedure for appointment, and Chapter 6 discusses the personal representative's rights and duties. The testator wants someone trustworthy to manage the estate, someone who has enough business or common sense to make intelligent, informed choices about the management of the estate. The testator should nominate an adult who is in good health so the work can be performed. Often the testator chooses a family member, a spouse or adult child, a trusted friend, or a business colleague to serve in this capacity. The personal representative has a **fiduciary** duty to be fair and honest when administering the estate.

Although the attorney drafting the will could be nominated, this may not be a wise choice. Unless it can be shown there is a close relationship to the testator, an ethical issue may arise. Usually, it is best to name someone other than the attorney responsible for writing the will.

The testator's first choice for personal representative may not be the person who is appointed by the court. This person may be ineligible, dead, or unwilling to work as the executor. Usually a successor executor is also named in the event the first person cannot act. It is also possible to name two personal representatives or co-executors. For example, a parent may name two of his or her children to perform the duties. A sample clause reads:

> I hereby nominate Dwight Carter Personal Representative of this Will. If Dwight Carter cannot so act, I nominate Linda Carter as my successor Personal Representative. No bond shall be required of any Personal Representative or Successor.

Note the last sentence waives bond. Because bond is an additional cost to the estate, the testator typically does not want another bill to reduce the amount of money available for inheritance by beneficiaries. The testator prefers that beneficiaries inherit as much as possible. This clause states that the court should not require bond to be posted for this executor. The testator trusts the individual and would not nominate someone who would embezzle from the estate. This is just another advantage of having a will and planning rather than dying intestate, with no plan.

The will could also include language specifying the powers and duties of the personal representative. These are discussed in more detail in Chapter 6. However, the powers and duties are usually typical and need not be spelled out. The main duties are to manage the assets of the estate, pay creditors, and make certain all distributions are properly made to designated beneficiaries.

13. Direction Nominating Guardian

If the maker of a will has a minor child or a mentally incompetent child, a direction nominating a **guardian** should be included in the document. A guardian oversees the person of the minor child or mentally incompetent person and/or the estate of the minor or mentally incompetent person. If the other parent is still living, such a clause may not be included; it is often recommended, however, in case both parents die at the same time.

A guardian over the person makes decisions regarding schooling, health care, shelter, food, and so on. A guardian over the property or estate manages investments, bank accounts, and other finances. Usually, the same person is guardian over the person and property. However, if the minor or mentally incompetent person has a great deal of money or is inheriting a large amount, a separate guardian over the estate may be nominated. This guardian may be a corporate entity, like a bank or trust company. The court will finalize the nomination by confirming and appointing the guardian. A standard clause would read:

> I hereby nominate Dolores Doeffler as the guardian over my son's, Jeremy Jones, person and property. No bond shall be required of any guardian.

fiduciary
One who acts on behalf of another with trust and confidence.

guardian
A person who has legal authority and a duty to act on behalf of a minor or mentally incompetent person.

The testatrix could include additional language in the will outlining the powers and rights of the guardian. Note that the last sentence of the sample clause waives bond. As with the nomination of a personal representative, the testatrix nominates someone she trusts, and bond would just be an added expense. With this language, the court is persuaded not to incur the additional cost of bond against the estate. This is another example of the benefits of having a plan.

On occasion, a single parent may ask that someone other than the surviving parent be nominated as the guardian of the child. The law favors a surviving parent over any other individual nominated. Under these circumstances, I explain to the client that the surviving parent receives custody unless the parent does not want to raise the child, is imprisoned, or has been held by a court to be an unfit parent. We can include a clause nominating someone else as guardian, but the surviving parent most likely will obtain custody of the child. However, this clause can help the court in determining who should be the guardian if a legal battle ensues, and it does let the court know the desires of the deceased parent.

For example, Cindy wants her mother, Audrey, to be the guardian of her daughter, Tammy, rather than her ex-husband and Tammy's father, Tim, having guardianship. She states this in her will. If Tim is alive and is deemed fit and willing to take Tammy, the court will give him his child. If the court determines he is unfit, Audrey probably will receive guardianship. However, let's say that Tim's mother, Rebecca wants guardianship. A legal battle ensues between the two grandmothers. Because of the language contained in the will, the court has been instructed as to the mother's, Cindy's, preference of who should be appointed guardian of her daughter.

14. Testimonium Clause

After the direction sections of the will, we see the concluding clauses. Remember from Chapter 3 that the will must contain the signature of the testator or testatrix. The clause that appears above this signature is called the **testimonium clause**. The testatrix states that she is acting voluntarily and is intending this document to be her last will. It often contains language specifying the length of the will.

testimonium clause
The provision in a will stating that the testator is signing and dating the document.

> I freely and willingly sign my name to this will consisting of two typewritten pages, including this page, on the _____ day of _____, 20____, in the presence of these witnesses, each of whom I have requested to sign their names in my presence and in the presence of all others.

The date would be handwritten into the clause by the testator or testatrix. Remember, a proxy signature or any mark intended to serve as a signature can be used by the maker of the will. If either of these methods are used, the testimonium clause language should be adjusted to reflect the method of signing that was used.

15. Testator's Signature

The maker of the will must sign and date the document. A blank line for the signature should follow the testimonium clause. Under the line, the typewritten name of the maker should appear. For example:

_____

John Taylor

This line may be adjusted if a proxy signature is used.

16. Attestation Clause

The final clause in the will is the **attestation clause**. It appears after the testator's signature but before the witnesses' signatures. Remember, all states but one require two witnesses to the will; Vermont requires three. The witnesses attest or verify that the testator or testatrix signed the will and that the signature is genuine. The witnesses then subscribe their names to the last will and testament. A sample attestation clause would read:

> The foregoing instrument, consisting of two typewritten pages, including this page, was signed and published by said John Taylor as his Last Will in the presence of us, who at his request, in his presence and in the presence of each other, have hereunto subscribed our names as witnesses. We each certify that at the time of the execution of the Will, said John Taylor was mentally competent and acting voluntarily.

Again, an adjustment in language might be required if a proxy signature is used.

17. Witnesses' Signatures

The two witnesses (or three if you are in Vermont) then sign their names on designated lines appearing below the attestation clause. They should also indicate their addresses.

Name: Address:

_____   _____

_____   _____

_____   _____

_____   _____

An Alabama case illustrates the importance of a witness properly attesting to a will.

> In *Dawkins v. Dawkins*, 179 Ala. 666, 60 So. 289 (1912), the Supreme Court of Alabama had to determine if the witnesses had properly attested to and subscribed the will. The testatrix was unable to write her name, so her attorney held the pen and she made her mark. The attorney then signed his name as a witness. The second witness was not able to write his name well so he practiced on a separate sheet of paper. When he attempted to sign his name, the attorney ended up holding the pen with him and helped him sign. The Alabama statute at the time read, ". . . where the testator or grantor cannot write, but subscribes by making his mark, the attesting witnesses must write their names. A mark in such case is insufficient." *Id.* at 290. In this case, the testatrix could not sign her name so both attesting witnesses were required by law to sign their full names. Since one witness could not properly sign, the court held the will was not attested to and subscribed as the law required.

Remember, a self-proving affidavit with a notary witnessing the will may be included (see Chapter 3).

A sample will incorporating a variety of the aforementioned clauses appears in Figure 4-2 (please note that the codicil contained in Chapter 3 amends this will).

Drafting Tips

We have completed a discussion on the clauses and information contained in a will. Some additional recommendations should be considered when drafting a will:

1. Number the pages of the will. Make certain all pages are included when finalizing the will and putting it into proper storage.

2. Do not include interlineations or cross-outs on the will. If a change must be made, draft a new will or codicil. State laws differ on how to treat any interlineations or deletions of a portion of the will. Consider 755 Ill. Comp. Stat. § 5/4-9, which states, "Interlineations . . . of any part of a will which does not constitute a revocation of a will is of no effect . . ."

3. Do not leave large blank spaces between sections or paragraphs. This protects against additional, unauthorized clauses being added.

Execution of the Will

execution
The completion of all actions to make a document valid.

Once you have completed drafting the last will and testament, the client should review it. If the client determines the will meets the requisite expectations specifying the client's plan and approves it, the final will is executed. Proper **execution** of the will can vary from state to state, so current law must be researched and applied. Typically the client comes to the law firm and reads through the will. The attorney should answer any questions the client has and explain the procedure to the client. Provided the client is comfortable and understands the procedure, the attorney asks the witnesses to enter the room. Often the witnesses are employees of the law firm. It is common for a paralegal to serve as a witness to a will. After introductions, the attorney may question the client briefly about the will. This allows the witnesses to determine if the client is of sound mind and acting voluntarily. The attorney may ask the client if this plan is the way the client wants the property distributed. If concerned about the client's competency, the attorney may ask several questions of the client to give the witnesses more time and information to reach a conclusion.

Then the client is asked to sign and date the will. It is recommended that—and some states require—the testator and attesting witnesses all watch each other sign the will. The testator then hands the pen to the first witness and he or she signs while the others watch. The next witness signs and the others watch. If a self-proving affidavit is being executed, the notary public will be present and this document is completed.

The witnesses may be called to court to testify regarding the validity of the will. This procedure is covered in more detail in Chapter 7. However, proper selection of witnesses is required at the time the will is executed. The witnesses must be mentally competent when they witness the execution of the will. If a witness becomes mentally incompetent after the will's execution, it does not invalidate the will. The witness does not have to be an adult; however, an adult would always be recommended. The age of the witness should not be too advanced, and often it is a good idea to have someone younger than the testator serve as a witness. Ideally, the witness will outlive the testator and be available to testify at the probate hearing. Finally, the witness should not be an interested person, an individual who is going to inherit from the testator. In some states, an interested person serving as a witness does not receive the gift, and in other states, the entire will is declared invalid. It is important to note that a paralegal may not ethically oversee the execution of a will. The paralegal's role is to assist the attorney in proper will execution.

Typically, the attorney who drafted the will does not serve as a witness to the will. Ethically, this situation presents a conflict of interest. If the attorney serves as a witness to the will and the will is contested, the attorney may be prevented from probating the estate.

Proper Will Storage

Once the will is properly executed, the original will must be placed somewhere that is safe yet accessible upon the testator's death. Therefore, the original will is given to the client, who determines where it is stored. The law firm places a copy of the executed will in the client's file. However, the general rule is that only an original will can be probated. Usually a will is stored in one of four places:

1. A safety deposit box at a financial institution.
2. The attorney's office, provided it has a fireproof safe or vault.
3. The register of probate's office or other court office that offers this service.
4. A fireproof safe or box in the testator's home.

1. The Safety Deposit Box at a Financial Institution

A safety deposit box at a financial institution protects the document and ensures that it is safe; however, accessibility can be difficult upon the testator's death. Some states allow for a search of the box just to determine the existence of the will. Others may not allow the box to be opened until the personal representative has been issued the letters testamentary from the court.

2. The Attorney's Office

Provided the attorney has a fireproof safe and vault, this is a safe spot. Accessibility is good, but some ethical issues are raised. Does this create undue influence on the decedent's family to hire that attorney to probate the estate? Some attorneys frown on the practice of storing original wills at an attorney's office.

3. The Courthouse

Will storage at the courthouse is basically safe and accessible. A fee may be charged. If the will is changed, an additional fee may not be charged.

4. Fireproof Safe or Box

A fireproof safe or box is safe as long as the box is not stolen or lost. The will is accessible if others know where the box or safe is located in the decedent's home.

It is vital that the testator not keep the location of the original will a secret from family members or friends. Although the contents of the will are private, its location should be known by a few people. A will may never be located if the decedent has not told anyone where it was placed. You may recall from Chapter 3 that states vary on their treatment of lost wills and revocation of them.

KEY **TERMS**

attestation clause (p. 61)
boilerplate (p. 54)
execution (p. 62)
exordium clause (p. 53)
fiduciary (p. 59)

guardian (p. 59)
"in terrorem" clause (p. 57)
pretermitted heir (p. 56)
residuary clause (p. 55)
revocation clause (p. 53)

simultaneous death clause (p. 58)
survivorship clause or delay
clause (p. 58)
testimonium clause (p. 60)

REVIEW **QUESTIONS**

1. During an initial estate planning interview:
   a. What types of information should be learned from the client?
   b. What ethical considerations must a paralegal keep in mind?
   c. What are some practical tips about interviewing that you should remember?
   d. What would you do if the client started crying during the interview?
2. a. Explain and draft an example of each of the following: exordium clause, revocation clause, "in terrorem" clause, survivorship or delay clause, simultaneous death clause, testimonium clause, attestation clause.
   b. Which of the clauses mentioned in Review Question 2a are vital to include in a will?
   c. Which clauses might be omitted without calling the will's validity into question? Under what circumstances could such clauses be easily omitted?
3. What is meant by boilerplate language? Give an example. What are the advantages and disadvantages to using it?
4. Can the maker of a will completely disinherit his or her spouse? Explain.
5. What is the difference between a co-executor and successor executor?
6. Distinguish between a guardian over the person and a guardian over the estate.
7. What is an interlineation? Would interlineations be considered a good method for changing a portion of the will?
8. What is the general procedure for executing a will?
9. Discuss the advantages and disadvantages of the four storage places for wills.

ROLE-PLAYING **ACTIVITY**

1. With a classmate, create an estate planning interview checklist. Enact an interview where one of you is the client and the other is the interviewer. Complete the checklist during the interview.

RESEARCH **ASSIGNMENTS**

1. Determine your state laws with regard to organ donation.
2. Research your state's "in terrorem" clause law.
3. Find your state's spousal election statute. If a husband tried to disinherit a wife, how much would she be able to receive under spousal election?
4. Find a community property state. How does that state treat a surviving spouse's rights to property?
5. Has your state enacted the Uniform Simultaneous Death Act? What is your state's legal treatment of estates when spouses die during the same event?
6. Research the general rules regarding an agent's fiduciary duty to a principal. In estate planning and probate, identify relationships where a fiduciary duty is created.
7. What is your state's legal treatment of cross-outs and interlineations that appear on an otherwise properly executed will?
8. Research state law on proper execution of a will. Locally, what is the method most law firms employ during execution?
9. Check your state's law about what happens to the will and the particular gift bequeathed to the individual if an interested person signs as a witness to the will.
10. What court office in your county stores wills? Is there a fee? If so, how much is it?

BUILD YOUR **PORTFOLIO**

1. Create an estate planning interview checklist for your portfolio.
2. Using the case example you chose in Chapter 1, draft a will, including a self-proving affidavit. Draft a codicil.

Chapter **five**

TRUSTS

Complicated Planning

So far, we have focused on preparing an estate plan for our client. In Chapters 3 and and 4, we learned about basic estate planning documents and how to effectuate a solid plan for the client. In some instances, however, a will may not be an adequate document to meet the client's need. Sometimes a more complicated written vehicle is required because the client has special circumstances. In these situations, a trust may be just the answer. In particular, a trust should be considered if:

1. The client is wealthy.
2. The client wishes to preserve privacy and keep the gifts quiet and out of the public's eye.
3. The client needs or wants more complicated tax planning done in connection with the gratuitous transfer.
4. The client is protecting or caring for a minor child or mentally incompetent individual.
5. The client needs to protect the beneficiary's gift from being attached by creditors.

The drafting of a trust poses additional challenges that do not exist when drafting a will. This chapter looks at basic terminology for a trust and then different types of trusts. Which type of trust is drafted depends upon the particular circumstances of the client. The chapter then discusses drafting tips for trusts and for a pour-over will.

- Compare and contrast a private trust and a public trust, identify the elements of a public trust, and define cy-pres doctrine.
- Compare and contrast an inter vivos trust and a testamentary trust.
- Explain the differences between a revocable trust and an irrevocable trust.
- Name some miscellaneous trusts and explain a spendthrift trust and tot-ten trust.
- Describe under what circumstances a trust terminates.
- Identify the sections of a trust agreement and recall drafting tips.

trust
Property placed in the care of one person (trustee) for the benefit of another (beneficiary).

beneficiary
The person who receives the benefit of the property placed in a trust.

trustee
The party who manages and oversees the property placed in trust.

settlor
The creator of the trust who originally owned the property and transferred it to the trust.

cestui que trust
The beneficiary of a trust.

equitable title
The interest a beneficiary has in property contained in a trust. The rights to benefit from the property but not manage it.

The Requirements of a Trust

With regard to estate planning, a **trust** is property placed in the care of one person (trustee) for the benefit of another (beneficiary). Although many different trusts can be created for different purposes, let's look at a standard example. Monica is very wealthy and wants to gift money to Chad. However, she does not want to give the money to him outright; she wants another person to manage the money for him. This person is Doris. Monica could create a trust. She puts the money in a trust fund for the benefit of Chad. Chad is the **beneficiary** of the trust. He receives the benefit of the money. Doris is the manager of the trust; she oversees how the money is invested and how it is distributed to Chad. Doris is the **trustee** of the trust. Monica is the creator of the trust and would be called the **settlor**, grantor, or trustor of the trust.

According to *City Bank Farmer's Trust Co. v. Charity Organization Soc. of City of New York*, 238 App. Div. 720, 265 N.Y.S. 267 (1993), four essential elements are required to establish a trust:

1. A designated beneficiary.
2. A designated trustee.
3. A fund sufficiently identified to enable title to pass to the trustee.
4. Actual delivery by the settlor to the trustee with the intention of passing title.

To determine if the four elements are met, we need to have a more thorough understanding of their meaning.

1. A Designated Beneficiary

As previously mentioned, a beneficiary ultimately receives the money or property that was placed in trust for his or her benefit. Other terms for the beneficiary of a trust are *cestui que trust* or *cestui que use*. These French terms are loosely translated as "he for whose benefit certain property in trust is held." For a trust to be created, a beneficiary must be designated. A beneficiary can be any legal entity that has the right to own property and includes a person; a class of persons; a charitable organization or foundation; or a business entity, like a sole proprietorship, partnership, or corporation.

If a natural person is selected as the beneficiary, he or she does not have to meet the requirements of legal capacity. The beneficiary does not have to be of legal age nor of sound mind. In fact, trusts are often created to protect minors or mentally incapacitated individuals. Planning for the needs of a loved one who lacks capacity is one purpose for creating a trust.

The beneficiary is said to have **equitable title** or ownership to the trust. Title equals the concept of ownership. Usually when someone has title to property, he or she owns it and has both legal and equitable title. Under the law of trusts, however, this two-prong concept of ownership is divided. Equitable title means the beneficiary receives the benefits of the property but does not have the right to manage the trust. The trust document coupled with a trustee's discretionary power determines how much and under what circumstances the beneficiary receives income, property, or principal from the trust.

2. A Designated Trustee

The trustee has **legal title** to the trust. This person or entity manages or oversees the trust. It's commonplace for the settlor or grantor to nominate the trustee in the trust agreement. If the settlor chooses an individual, the nominated trustee must have legal capacity. As discussed in Chapter 3, legal capacity consists of two requirements:

1. Legal age.
2. Sound mind or mentally competent.

Thus, a child or mentally incompetent individual cannot serve as a trustee. Another option available to the settlor is to nominate a corporate trustee, such as a trust company or trust department of a bank. It is wise for the settlor to choose a trustee with high integrity who can effectively manage the trust assets. If more than one beneficiary is included in the trust, the trustee nominated should also be fair in distributing the trust property to the different beneficiaries and not demonstrate a preference.

A nominated trustee does not have to accept the position. The trustee may renounce the nomination. The trust will not fail as a result. The court appoints another qualified individual or entity. Further, the court could hold that a nominated trustee was ineligible (not of sound mind or legal age) and deny confirming the appointment. The trust appointment could also be terminated through resignation, removal, or death of the trustee. The trustee could determine that he or she no longer wished to act and the court could accept the resignation and appoint a new trustee. Another possibility is that the trustee is acting improperly: not performing the duties or abiding by the requirements of the fiduciary relationship that has been created. The court has the authority to remove the trustee from his or her position. If the trustee dies, the court must appoint a replacement.

With regard to a testamentary trust in Wisconsin, once the trustee is appointed, a document called **letters of trust** is executed by the court. This is the formal document granting the powers and duties to the trustee to act on behalf of the trust (see Figure 5-1).

The settlor could decide to nominate co-trustees of the trust. If this is done, the co-trustees must work with each other and engage in a cooperative relationship.

A trustee owes a fiduciary duty to the beneficiary, which means that the trustee will act on behalf of the beneficiary for the beneficiary's best interest with trust and confidence. The Restatement of Trusts outlines the fiduciary duties the trustee owes a beneficiary:

1. Duty to administer the trust (Restatement (Second) of Trusts § 169).
2. Duty of loyalty (Restatement (Third) of Trusts § 170).
3. Duty to not delegate duties that the trustee can reasonably be required to personally perform (Restatement (Second) of Trusts § 171).
4. Duty of accounting (Restatement (Second) of Trusts § 172).
5. Duty to provide information (Restatement (Second) of Trusts § 173).
6. Duty to use ordinary, reasonable skill in administration of the trust (Restatement (Second) of Trusts § 174).
7. Duty to take possession of and control trust property (Restatement (Second) of Trusts § 175).

legal title
The interest a trustee has in the property contained in a trust. The rights to manage the trust but not benefit from it.

letters of trust
A document issued by the court confirming the appointment of a trustee to a trust.

Figure 5-1   Letters of trust

	For Official Use
STATE OF WISCONSIN, CIRCUIT COURT, <u>DANE</u>_____ COUNTY	

IN THE MATTER OF THE ESTATE OF

<u>Sean Collier</u>
For the following trust:

<u>Collier Family Trust</u>

Letters of Trust
(Issued under Formal Administration)

Case No. <u>01PR145T</u>

To: Madison E. Collier
       400 W. Sycamore Ln.
       Madison, WI, 53562

The decedent, whose date of birth was <u>March 22nd, 1945</u> and date of death was <u>August 13th, 2001</u>,

died domiciled in <u>Dane</u> County, State of <u>Wisconsin</u>.

The decedent's will has been admitted to probate. Based upon your appointment and qualification to act as trustee, you are granted Letters of Trust with the general powers and duties of trustee. You are authorized to administer the trust as required by law.

BY THE COURT:

Seal

_____
Circuit Judge/Court Commissioner

<u>Daniel P. Jenkins</u>
Name Printed or Typed

<u>November 11th, 2001</u>
Date

Name of Attorney
Justin Sorvino
Address
1312 Main St.
Madison, WI 53562
Telephone Number
(608) 404-1322

PR-1931, 10/00 Letters of Trust (Issued under Formal Administration)   §§701.16 and 856.29, Wisconsin Statutes
This form shall not be modified. It may be supplemented with additional material.

Source: For the most current version of this form, visit www.wicourts.gov.

8. Duty to preserve the trust property (Restatement (Second) of Trusts § 176).

9. Duty to enforce claim (Restatement (Second) of Trusts § 177).

10. Duty to defend against lawsuits (Restatement (Second) of Trusts § 178).

11. Duty to separate trust property from trustee's individual property (Restatement (Second) of Trusts § 179).

12. Duty with regard to bank deposits (Restatement (Second) of Trusts § 180).

13. Duty to make trust property productive (Restatement (Second) of Trusts § 181).

14. Duty to pay trust income to beneficiary (Restatement (Second) of Trusts § 182).

15. Duty to impartially deal with two or more beneficiaries of a trust (Restatement (Second) of Trusts § 183).

16. Duty to participate and work with co-trustees of the trust (Restatement (Second) of Trusts § 184).

17. Duty to act in compliance with a person who holds power of control (Restatement (Second) of Trusts § 185).

Source: Copyright 2009 by the American Law Institute. All rights reserved. Reprinted with permission.

The trustee has a lot of duties to perform. Let's look more closely at three of the duties. One major duty is the duty of loyalty. The trustee must act on behalf of the beneficiaries and no one else. Any actions taken must be for the best interest of the beneficiary. The trustee should not make decisions where the main benefit is to the trustee or the trustee's friend, family member, or business. This is the rule against self-dealing that is created in fiduciary relationships. The trustee should not sell property to himself, nor compete against a beneficiary in business, nor profit at the expense of the beneficiary.

Another duty is the trustee's requirement to use reasonable skill in performance. From tort law, the rule is to act as a reasonable person would act under the same or similar circumstances. If the trustee has extra knowledge or skill, the standard may be increased. For example, if a stockbroker is the trustee, his or her standard of care in investment decisions would be increased to what a reasonable stockbroker would do under the same or similar circumstances.

Finally, the trustee must provide an accounting to the beneficiaries indicating the financial dealings of the trust. The trustee needs to diligently keep accurate

APPLYING YOUR KNOWLEDGE

George Billingsworth is the trustee of the Wendt Trust, which was created to benefit Amy, Peter, and Charles Wendt. The Wendt Trust includes a rental property that generates a substantial amount of rental income. The beneficiaries want the property sold. George Billingsworth is a stockholder in a close corporation—ABC Rental, Incorporated. He owns ninety percent (90%) of the stock. He sells the rental property for fair market value to ABC Rental. Does this violate the duty of loyalty? What if he owns only one percent (1%) of the stock of ABC Rental? Explain your answers.

APPLYING YOUR KNOWLEDGE

Richard is a certified public accountant and named as the trustee to a trust. The trust requires he submit a detailed financial accounting every year. For the last two years, he has failed to submit the report. What fiduciary duties has he violated? What standard of care would be used?

financial records of the income and distributions of the trust. The account should detail the type and amount of trust property and how it is being administered. This accounting should be provided to the beneficiaries on a regular basis or as requested by the beneficiaries.

Many states require the trustee to submit the account at designated times to the proper court for approval. If these duties are violated, the trustee could be removed from the appointment or may be subject to personal liability.

The flip side of the trustee's duties are the powers that are granted to the trustee. The trust agreement should be carefully drafted and specify the powers given to the trustee. Once the trustee is appointed, he or she should carefully study the agreement to determine the powers granted. Examples of trustee powers include the following:

1. To buy or sell real property or personal property.
2. To open, continue, or close bank accounts.
3. To lease or rent real property or personal property.
4. To lend or borrow money and to use property as collateral to secure a loan.
5. To oversee and continue operation of a business.
6. To vote stock either directly or by proxy vote.
7. To collect or litigate on behalf of trust property.
8. To hire and fire business professionals, such as bankers, stockbrokers, lawyers, or accountants.
9. To settle claims.
10. To purchase life or other types of insurance.
11. To build or demolish structures.
12. To make tax decisions with the goal of minimizing taxes.
13. To accept additions of any kind to the trust.
14. To distribute property to a guardian for the benefit of a minor under the Uniform Transfer to Minors Act, or similar law.
15. To exercise the same powers any property owner exercises over his or her property.

State law should be consulted because it may specify certain powers or place limits or restrictions on the powers. See Figure 5-2, which is a chart summarizing the Illinois Trust and Trustees Act: 760 Ill. Comp. Stat. § 5/4.01–5/4.25 for trustee powers in Illinois.

Figure 5-2 Chart summarizing powers of trustee in Illinois

Powers of Trustee Illinois Trusts and Trustees Act 760 Ill. Comp. Stat. § 5/4.01–5/4.24	
Statute	**Summary of Certain Trustee's Power**
5/4.01	. . . to sell, contract, grant options, purchase any or all of trust estate at public or private sale.
5/4.01	. . . to exchange any or all of trust estate for other property.
5/4.02	. . . to enter into leases.
5/4.03	. . . to borrow money, mortgage, pledge, encumber the trust estate.
5/4.04	. . . to grant easements, subdivide, and improve real estate.
5/4.06	. . . to enter into agreements with regard to bank accounts.
5/4.07	. . . to exercise powers with regard to stocks, bonds, or other securities.
5/4.08	. . . to pay taxes and reasonable expenses incurred in administering trust estate.
5/4.09	. . . to appoint attorneys, auditors, financial advisors, and other agents . . .
5/4.11	. . . to compromise, contest, prosecute, or abandon claims in favor or against estate.
5/4.12	. . . to execute contracts, notes . . . containing covenants and warranties binding upon the trust estate.
5/4.13	. . . to receive and administer additional property as part of the trust estate.
5/4.14	. . . to invest in or hold individual interests in property.
5/4.16	. . . to make equitable division or distribution in cash . . .
5/4.19	. . . to purchase and keep in force insurance for the protection of the estate.
5/4.20	. . . to distribute income/principal . . . to beneficiary(ies).
5/4.21	. . . to plant and harvest crops; breed, raise, purchase, and sell all livestock . . .
5/4.22	. . . to drill, mine, or otherwise operate land for development of oil, gas, and other minerals . . .
5/4.23	. . . to continue an unincorporated business and participate in management.
5/4.24	. . . to continue a partnership and participate in its management . . .

The trustee may be compensated for his or her work. The trust agreement typically specifies the amount. If the document is silent, however, usually a state statute specifies the figure. According to Nevada law:

[T]he court shall allow the trustee his proper expenses and such compensation for services as the court may deem just and reasonable. Nev. Admin. Code § 153.070 (2005).

In Georgia, the statute reads:

(a) Trustee(s) shall be compensated in accordance with either the trust instrument or any separate agreement . . . (b) If the trustee's compensation is not specified in the trust instrument or any separate written agreement, the trustee, for services rendered, shall be entitled to the same compensation as guardians receive for similar services. Ga. Code Ann. § 53-12-173 (2005).

In Idaho:

When a declaration of trust is silent upon the subject of compensation, the trustee is entitled to the same compensation as an executor. If it specifies the amount of his compensation, he is entitled to the amount thus specified and no more. Idaho Code Ann. § 68-103 (2005).

The court may set the fee if the agreement is silent or there is no state statute in existence. Finally, if a family member serves as trustee, a refusal to accept the fee often occurs. Under these circumstances, the trustee's goal is for the beneficiary to receive the money or property.

3. A Fund Sufficiently Identified to Enable Title to Pass to the Trustee

A trust fund has many different names. It is also called trust corpus, trust res, and trust principal. These names refer to the property that has been placed into the trust and is managed by the trustee for the benefit of the beneficiary. Any property that has a transferable interest may be placed into a trust. Such property includes real estate, money, bank accounts, investments, patents, copyrights, and other personal property. Any property that has restrictions on its transferability may not be used to fund a trust. An example of nontransferable property is a government pension. The statute of frauds requires that certain transfers of property must be in writing and signed to be enforceable. The main concern is with a transfer of real estate. If the trust fund contains land, the trust must be in writing to satisfy the state's statute of frauds. Of course, even if personal property funds the trust, it is wisest to execute a written trust agreement.

4. Actual Delivery by the Settlor to the Trustee with the Intent of Passing Title

The settlor is the original owner of the property or money that is put into trust. He or she creates the trust. The settlor is also called the grantor, trustor, or donor. A settlor can be an individual or any legal entity.

The settlor must actually deliver the property to the trustee with the intent of passing title. The settlor must relinquish full ownership of the property or money to the trustee. The settlor cannot retain both prongs of title, equitable and legal, once the trust is created. The settlor can name him- or herself as trustee and have legal title, the right to manage or oversee the trust, or can name him- or herself as beneficiary and keep equitable title, the right to receive the benefits of the trust fund. However, the settlor cannot have both legal and equitable title. This situation would create a merger of interests and terminate the trust. For a trust to remain in existence, these two titles must be vested in two different legal entities.

Finally, the settlor must actually move the property into the trust. If the settlor writes and executes a trust agreement, the trust has not been fully created until it is funded.

APPLYING YOUR KNOWLEDGE

Martha transfers $1,000,000 into a trust for the benefit of Thomas. She names Alan as the person to manage or oversee the trust. Who is the settlor? Who is the beneficiary? Who is the trustee? Who is the *cestui que trust*? Once the trust is funded, who has legal title to the $1,000,000? Once the trust is funded, who has equitable title to the $1,000,000? What are three names for the $1,000,000?

Types of Trusts

Many varieties of trusts can be created. They can be created through direct communication or circumstance, for the benefit of individuals or charitable organizations, while the settlor is living or upon death, to be altered or unchangeable, and for other reasons. We will focus on some of the choices available, including:

1. Express versus implied trusts.
2. Private versus public trusts.
3. Inter vivos versus testamentary trusts.
4. Revocable versus irrevocable trusts.
5. Other miscellaneous trusts.

1. Express Versus Implied Trusts

An **express trust** is one that is explicitly communicated either by oral declaration or by a written document. Although the document or declaration must specify its purpose, the term *trust* does not have to be used to create one. If real estate is used to fund the trust, it must be in writing to meet the statute of frauds. Sample trust agreements are found later in this chapter, and drafting guidelines are discussed. Most trusts fall under the broad heading of express trusts.

The opposite of an express trust is an **implied trust**. An implied trust is not overtly communicated but is created if (1) the circumstances indicate the parties intended to create a trust, by analyzing the behavior of the parties; or (2) if the court determines a trust must be created to avoid unjust enrichment or fraud.

If the trust is created by the court after analyzing the parties' conduct and determining an implied trust has been created, this is called a **resulting trust**. One person possesses the property for the benefit of another. No unjust enrichment or fraud is occurring. The court may hold such a trust was created if one of the essential elements of a trust is missing.

If the implied trust comes into existence because the court is ruling one party acted fraudulently or unjust enrichment may result, then a **constructive trust** has been created. For example, an elderly widower named Paul owns some real estate. Paul begins dating Leslie. Leslie convinces Paul that he will save on the real estate taxes if he transfers the deed to her. He transfers the deed to her. Leslie then tries to get Paul kicked off the property. The court may hold that a constructive trust was created with Leslie as the trustee, and Paul as the beneficiary.

express trust
A trust that is communicated, usually in written terms, and not inferred by the conduct of the parties or by the court to prevent unjust enrichment.

implied trust
A trust not expressly communicated but implied based on the conduct of the parties or to prevent unjust enrichment.

resulting trust
An implied trust based on the circumstances or conduct of the parties.

constructive trust
An implied trust created by law to prevent fraud or unjust enrichment.

2. Private Versus Public Trusts

Another distinction between trusts is whether they are private or public. A **private trust** is created to benefit a single beneficiary or several beneficiaries, but it is not created for a charitable purpose. If I create a trust and name my daughter, Karen, as the beneficiary, this is a private trust. The opposite is a **public trust**, also known as a charitable trust or eleemosynary trust. It is created for a charitable purpose: to benefit a church, school, Red Cross, the United Way, and so on. For a public trust to be so classified, certain criteria must be met. First, the settlor must intend to make a public trust and expressly designate the trust as such. His or her goal should be that a charitable organization would benefit from the trust. Second, the general public

private trust
A trust created to benefit a designated individual or definite class of individuals.

public trust
Also known as a charitable trust; a trust created to benefit the public at large.

APPLYING YOUR KNOWLEDGE

Donna creates a trust and designates the purpose as follows: "to provide financial assistance to any qualified individual needing cancer treatment and living in Minnesota." She nominates Dr. Frank to manage and oversee the trust. Who is the trustee? Who is the settlor? Who is the beneficiary? Is this an express trust? Why or why not? Is this a public trust? Are all three requirements for a public trust met?

Consider that a trust is created in the same manner as the trust that Donna created, except that its purpose is "to provide financial assistance to any of my living relatives who are diagnosed with cancer." Is this a public trust? How does it differ from the earlier trust created by Donna?

cy-pres doctrine
As near as possible. If the settlor's intention for a trust cannot be carried out because it would be illegal or impractical, the court will order that the trust provisions be carried as near as possible to the settlor's initial intention.

must be benefited. Perhaps the trust helps victims of a disaster, promotes medical research or treatment, provides education or help to the less fortunate, or funds a church; these are all examples of benefiting the general public. The third requirement is that the beneficiaries must consist of an indefinite class, members of which the settlor may not personally know. If I create a trust for my grandchildren, a definite class of persons, I have created a private trust. If my trust is created to benefit all the victims of Hurricane Katrina, this is an indefinite class. This trust also meets the second criterion of benefitting the public. It would be considered a public trust.

Sometimes the settlor creates a charitable trust with a purpose that cannot be carried out because it is illegal, impossible, or impractical. In this situation, the trust does not automatically fail. The courts will apply the **cy-pres doctrine**, a term that is derived from the French expression *cy-pres comme possible*, or "as near as possible." The doctrine means that the court examines the intended purpose of the trust and attempts to have it administered as nearly as possible to its stated purpose. For example, David puts money into a trust to create and build a beautiful church library for his church, EverGlen. Before the trust comes into existence, EverGlen builds a brand new library. David never changes the trust's purpose. The trust comes into existence. Rather than terminate the trust, the court may determine that the money be used to acquire more books for the library or upgrade or outfit the library with computer equipment. This would be a use of the cy-pres doctrine.

In *Quinn v. People's Trust and Savings Co.*, 223 Ind. 317, 60 N.E. 2d 281 (1944), the court ruled that the settlor created a testamentary trust that left her estate to a friend and also promoted college or university education of children of the Pennsylvania Railroad Company employees living in Fort Wayne, Indiana. Heirs of the settlor/decedent brought suit claiming they were entitled to the estate rather than the railroad employees' children. One argument raised was that the trust was illegal because of the rule against perpetuities and that the trust fund would not be distributed quickly enough. The court ruled that the cy-pres doctrine could be implemented to administer the estate quickly enough so the trust purposes would not be illegal.

However, consider *Simmons v. Parson's College*, 256 N.W. 2d 225 (Iowa 1977), where the cy-pres doctrine was not applied. The testator created a testamentary trust leaving money to Parson's College and Drake College for education of needy students. Parson's College became bankrupt, and Drake College claimed that the amount for Parson's should be distributed to Drake College students. The will read, "If either or both of said institutions should fail . . . then said trust . . . shall fail . . . and the principal thereof I will . . . to my legal heirs at law . . ." *Id.* at 226. The court ruled cy-pres was not applicable because the testator had anticipated the failure of the trust and made alternative disposition to his heirs.

3. Inter Vivos Versus Testamentary Trusts

Next, we should examine the distinction between inter vivos and testamentary trusts. An **inter vivos trust**, or living trust, becomes effective while the settlor is still alive. The settlor typically creates the inter vivos trust to effectuate a purpose that the settlor wishes to see carried out. The settlor wants to witness the trust in action. Rather than gift the money outright to the beneficiary, the settlor has someone else manage the property. For example, Dawn has an adult child, Tom, who is mentally impaired. Dawn would like to gift Tom money, but she realizes he may not spend it properly. She places it into trust for his benefit and has Sandy oversee the trust. By doing this Dawn can observe how the trust operates while she is still living. If she makes it a revocable trust (see the next section), she can make changes to it or cancel it while she is alive. An inter vivos trust can avoid probate and keeps the gift private. The trust is not placed in a court record and cannot be read by the public.

inter vivos trust
Also known as a living trust; a trust created to take effect while the person is living, not upon the death of a person.

A **testamentary trust**, on the other hand, takes effect upon the death of the settlor. It is included in the will. The testamentary trust becomes a portion of the probate record and the public can view it. Instead of the money or property passing directly to individuals under the will, the money or property is placed into a trust to be administered by the trustee for the benefit of the specifically designated trust beneficiaries. This type of trust is useful if the money would otherwise go to minors, incompetent persons, or those who would mismanage the gift.

testamentary trust
A trust created to take effect upon the death of a person.

4. Revocable Versus Irrevocable Trusts

A **revocable trust** is one that can be changed, amended, or cancelled. The settlor retains the right to get rid of it or terminate it at any time. Most settlors prefer to keep this power when they create a trust. They can retain an amount of control that the irrevocable trust does not afford. An **irrevocable trust** is one that the settlor may not change or terminate. All control is relinquished.

revocable trust
A trust that can be terminated or changed by the settlor.

irrevocable trust
A trust that cannot be terminated or changed by the settlor.

5. Other Miscellaneous Trusts

The previous sections have covered the main types of trusts. However, many more exist, including but not limited to, accumulation trusts, clifford trusts, crummey

APPLYING YOUR KNOWLEDGE

Donald creates a trust through an explicit trust agreement that names the Red Cross as the beneficiary. He puts William in charge of administering the trust. Donald creates and funds the trust while he is alive and retains the right to terminate the trust. Who is the *cestui que trust*? Who is the trustee? Is this a public or private trust? Explain your answer. Is this an inter vivos or testamentary trust? Explain your answer. What other types of trust(s) have been created?

trusts, fixed trusts, liquidation trusts, precatory trusts, spendthrift trusts, sprinkling trusts, and totten trusts. Research should be done if a particular type of trust would best suit the needs of the client. Two additional trusts, the spendthrift trust and the totten trust, will be discussed here.

spendthrift trust
A trust created to protect the beneficiary from his own inability to spend wisely. The property cannot be reached by creditors.

A **spendthrift trust** may be created when the beneficiary is unable to manage finances properly because of incapacity or unwise choices in spending. For example, Mark wants to give Ivy $1,000,000, but he knows she will waste the money and spend it all at the racetrack. By placing the money in trust, Mark could designate someone else to manage and distribute it for Ivy's education or other purchases. A spendthrift trust may be created to protect minors or young adults who are not yet good at making choices about personal spending. The settlor may choose an age at which time the child is old enough to properly handle personal finances. However, the settlor may not create a spendthrift trust and name himself the beneficiary.

Another benefit of a spendthrift trust is that it cannot be attached by creditors. According to Restatement of Trusts (Third) §58(1):

> [I]f the terms of a trust provide that a beneficial interest shall not be transferable by the beneficiary or subject to the claims of the beneficiary's creditors, the restraint on voluntary and involuntary alienation of the interest is valid.

This concept is more fully explained in the official comments of the section stating that the income and principal of the trust are protected against the creditors' claims as long as they remain in the trust. The money or property cannot be attached by judgment creditors nor does it become part of the beneficiary's bankruptcy estate.

These protections are very appealing to many parents who create trusts for children. A spendthrift clause should be inserted in the trust. Usually the requirement is that the provision demonstrate intent to create a spendthrift trust. Sample language for a spendthrift clause would include:

> "[T]his trust is to be a spendthrift trust."

> ". . . payments to Mr. Johnstone for life not to be anticipated by him or subject to interference by others."

Certainly, state laws should be consulted when drafting a spendthrift trust. An Illinois case determined that a testamentary trust created to pay some trust income to the grandson, Ronald, created a spendthrift trust. The grandson petitioned the court to receive the principal of the trust, and the appellate court ruled that granting the petition would violate the intent of the settlor, who used language to create a spendthrift trust. The appellate court stated:

> The language employed in the instant will expresses the clearest intention on the part of the testator that neither Arthur nor Ronald should have or enjoy during his lifetime, more than the net income of the trust estate. See *Tree v. Continental Ill. National Bank and Trust Company*, 347 Ill. App. 358, 106 N.E. 2d 870 (1952).

totten trust
A trust created by one person depositing money (in a bank) in his or her name, which becomes payable to another upon the depositor's death.

Illinois law further states that a spendthrift trust is generally exempt from invasion to satisfy judgments; however, it does allow the trust to be invaded to provide for the collection of child support. 735 Ill. Comp. Stat. § 5/2-1403 (2005).

The second miscellaneous trust is the **totten trust**. The totten trust was established in *Matter of Totten*, 179 N.Y. 112, 71 N.E. 748 (1904). It provides that if money is deposited in a bank by one person for the benefit of another, a tentative trust is created. If the depositor dies, the money is paid to the person named on the account. State law should be consulted. Consider the Oklahoma statute that reads:

> Whenever any deposit shall be made in a bank by any person which is in form in trust for another, and no other or further notice of the existence and terms of a legal and valid trust shall have been given in writing to the bank, in the event of the death of the trustee, the same, or any part thereof, together with the interest thereon, may be paid to the person or persons for whom the deposit was made. A deposit held in this form shall be deemed to constitute a totten trust. Okla. Stat. tit. 6 § 902.

Termination of Trusts

A trust may be terminated under several circumstances. If terminated, it is no longer in existence. The Restatement (Second) of Trusts lists the methods available. We will explore some of those methods here:

1. Revocation of the trust by the settlor.
2. Rescission or reformation of the trust.
3. Expiration of the period for which the trust was created.
4. The purposes of the trust become impossible or illegal to perform.
5. Merger.

1. Revocation of the Trust by the Settlor

This method is discussed in the Restatement of Trusts (Second) § 330. The settlor may revoke or cancel the trust if such a power was reserved or intended by the settlor in the trust agreement. If the agreement is in writing, it must explicitly state that such a power was reserved. If a mistake was made in inserting the provision, the settlor may change the trust and include the clause. (See Restatement of Trusts (Second) § 332.) If the trust was created under fraud, duress, or undue influence, the settlor may terminate it. (See Restatement of Trusts (Second) § 333.)

If the trust is an oral declaration, the inference is that the trust is irrevocable. However, if circumstances infer that the settlor intended to create the trust, the courts may determine the settlor has this power.

2. Rescission or Reformation of the Trust

> A trust can be rescinded or reformed upon the same grounds as those upon which a transfer of property not in trust can be rescinded or reformed. Restatement of Trusts (Second) § 333.

Rescission means completely terminating the trust and putting all parties back to their original positions before the trust was created. Reformation means the trust agreement must be rewritten or redefined to make it fairer to all parties. This section of the Restatement of Trusts provides for several situations where the trust can be terminated, including:

1. Undue influence: Undue influence occurs when someone is pressured into an agreement against his or her normal intention. It usually happens when a close relationship is involved. If undue influence is used against the settlor and pressure is exerted on him or her to create the trust, the trust may be rescinded.

2. Fraud: Fraud is when a person uses deceit or misrepresentation to connive someone into a certain situation. For example, you learn the settlor wants to name another person as beneficiary to a trust and so you lie about the moral character of the person, thus convincing the settlor to create a trust naming you as the beneficiary. In this case, fraud is committed. The trust could be rescinded.

3. Duress: Duress is the use of force or violence or the threat of it to convince the settlor to create a trust. This, too, would be valid grounds to terminate the trust.

4. Mistake: If the settlor created the trust and received nothing in return for it (no consideration), the trust may be rescinded under the grounds of material mistake. If the settlor received consideration for creating the trust, contract law would govern and may limit the ability of the settlor to terminate the trust.

3. Expiration of the Period for Which the Trust Was Created

Under the Restatement of Trusts (Second) § 334, if the terms of the trust specify a time in which the trust is terminated, the trust will no longer be in existence when that time occurs. Termination can happen in several ways: the trust may terminate on a specified date, such as August 20, 2010; upon the death of a designated person; or upon the happening of a designated terminating event, for example, Jill graduates from law school.

4. The Purposes of the Trust Become Impossible or Illegal to Perform

The Restatement of Trusts (Second) § 355 provides termination if the purposes of the trust become impossible or illegal. Impossibility would occur, for example, if money is placed into the trust to take care of my pet cat, Fluffy. Upon Fluffy's death, the money is no longer needed. The destruction of the subject matter has made it impossible for the trust purpose to continue. If it becomes illegal to carry out the purposes of the trust, the court will provide for the termination of the trust. If the trust provides for a corporation to make a legal prescription drug that subsequently becomes illegal, the trust will end.

5. Merger

Recall that, to create a trust and keep it in existence, the equitable interest and legal interest must be held by two distinct parties. The beneficiary has equitable interest, and the trustee has legal interest. The Restatement of Trusts (Second) § 341 provides that if one party has both interests, the trust is terminated. The person who has both interests now has full ownership, and a trust can no longer remain in existence. For example, if a beneficiary dies and his interest in the trust passes to the trustee, the legal interest and equitable interest now become merged, and the trustee has full ownership rights to the trust property. The trust is terminated.

Note, however, that if there are three beneficiaries, one dies, and the trustee inherits his interest, the trust will not terminate. For example, Bill is the sole trustee. Julie, Annette, and Gwen are the beneficiaries. Gwen dies, leaving her interest in the trust to Bill. He is not the sole beneficiary. Two other beneficiaries of the trust are

APPLYING YOUR KNOWLEDGE

Identify if the following trusts terminate, and under what grounds.

1. A trust is created and its purpose is to fund Duke's ranch. A tornado destroys the property. Has the trust terminated? Why or why not?
2. Duke's ranch land becomes rezoned as residential only. Does the trust terminate? Why or why not?
3. April is the settlor of a revocable inter vivos trust. She has reserved the power to terminate the trust in her written trust agreement. Can she terminate the trust? Under what reason?
4. Dwight holds a gun to Richard's head and forces him to create a trust. Richard does so. Can the trust be terminated? Why or why not?
5. Claudia creates a trust naming Meghan and Linda as the cotrustees and Pam, Jennifer, and Jim as the co-beneficiaries. If Jennifer dies leaving her interest in the trust to Meghan, does the trust terminate? Why or why not?

still living. The trust would not terminate. Likewise, if the sole beneficiary becomes one of several trustees, the trust would not terminate.

Source: Copyright 2009 American Law Institute. All rights reserved. Reprinted with permission.

Drafting Tips and Sample Trust Agreements

In this section, we will focus on the drafting of two different types of trusts. The first is the revocable inter vivos trust. With this type of trust, it is vital that the power to revoke be described in some detail. The trust should explain the manner in which the revocation may be accomplished and whether revocation of the entire trust is allowed or only a portion of it. Several component parts are contained in this type of trust. The following discussion matches the order in which the sample revocable inter vivos trust in Figure 5-3 is written.

1. Name of Trust and Introductory Information

The top section of the trust contains its name and an introductory section naming the settlor and nominating the trustee.

2. Section One: Trust Estate

This section lists the property being transferred to the trust. It also meets one of the four essential elements of a trust: actual delivery from the settlor to the trustee with the intent of passing title.

3. Section Two: Revocation and Amendment

A provision reserving the power to revoke and amend should be included in the trust if the settlor wants to retain the right of revocation. This clause provides the trustee with power to revoke and amend all or a portion of the trust.

Figure 5-3 Revocable inter vivos trust

STEWART REVOCABLE TRUST

Trust agreement made on June 14th, 2005, between Jonathon K. Stewart, of 1255 N. Main St., Madison, of Dane County, Wisconsin, ("settlor"), and Walter Stewart, of 1313 Mockingbird Lane, Madison, of Dane County, Wisconsin ("trustee").

SECTION ONE

TRUST ESTATE

Settlor assigns, transfers, and conveys to trustee the property described in the attached Exhibit A, which is incorporated by reference, and the receipt of which property is acknowledged by trustee. The property shall be held by trustee in trust on the terms and conditions set forth below.

SECTION TWO

REVOCATION AND AMENDMENT

Settlor reserves the right at any time, by an instrument in writing delivered to trustee, to revoke or amend this trust in whole or in part. The duties and liabilities of trustee shall under no circumstances be substantially increased by any amendment of this agreement except with his written consent.

SECTION THREE

ADDITIONS TO TRUST ESTATE

Settlor reserves the right for himself or any other person to increase this trust by delivering property to trustee, by having the proceeds of insurance policies made payable to trustee, or by bequest or devise by will. Settlor will notify trustee in writing of any policies made payable to it or will deliver the policies to trustee as custodian. Trustee's duties and liabilities under this agreement shall under no circumstances be substantially increased by any such additions, except with his written consent.

SECTION FOUR

DISPOSITION OF INCOME

After paying the necessary expenses incurred in the management and investment of the trust estate, including compensation of trustee for his own services, trustee shall pay the net income of the trust in the following manner: to settlor, Jonathon K. Stewart's, two children, Vanessa Stewart, of 1000 E. State Boulevard, Madison, Dane County, Wisconsin, and Philip Stewart, of 622 Melrose Place, Madison, Dane County, Wisconsin, in equal shares until the youngest reaches the age of thirty-five (35).

SECTION FIVE

INVASION OF PRINCIPAL FOR SPOUSE AND DESCENDANTS

After settlor's death, trustee may apply so much of the principal of the trust for the use of settlor's wife, Abigail Stewart, and settlor's descendants, or any of them, at such time or times as in trustee's discretion it may deem advisable for their proper education, care, or support. The provisions of this section are intended primarily as a means of affording financial assistance to settlor's wife and children in the event of their serious illness, misfortune, or other emergency or unusual condition, and also to assist his descendants during the period of their education or setting up in business or at the time of their marriage. This enumeration is to serve only as

(continued)

Figure 5-3   (continued)

a guide and shall not be construed to restrict the discretionary powers so conferred on trustee. Any amounts so applied to the use of settlor's wife or any descendant shall be charged against, or deducted from, the principal of any share then, or later, set apart for such wife or descendant.

SECTION SIX

POWERS OF TRUSTEE

A. Delegation of Powers. In addition to the powers granted by law and those customarily exercised by fiduciaries, I grant to the trustee the following powers:

1. To retain original investments and to invest and reinvest in the trustee's discretion, irrespective of statutes or rules of law governing the investment of trust funds, including the right to invest in common trust funds.
2. To retain any part or all of the original assets constituting this trust, as well as any assets into which the original assets may be converted by reason of corporate merger, exchange of stock, reorganization, or similar conversion.
3. To sell any property at fair values, for cash or on credit, at public or private sale; to exchange any property for other property; and to grant options to purchase or acquire any property.
4. To operate, maintain, repair, rehabilitate, alter, improve, or remove any improvements on real estate; to make leases and subleases for terms of any length, even though the terms may extend beyond the termination of a trust; to subdivide real estate; to grant easements, give consents, and make contracts relating to real estate or its use; and to release or dedicate any interest in real estate.
5. To borrow money on such terms and conditions as the trustee may deem proper and to pledge or mortgage estate or trust assets as security therefore, including authority to a personal representative to borrow from the trustee, the trustee to borrow from a personal representative, and a corporate personal representative and trustee (or either) to borrow from itself in its corporate capacity.
6. To purchase property at its fair market value as determined by the trustee, from my probate estate or from the trust created under this agreement.
7. To lend money to any person, including my probate estate, provided any such loan shall be adequately secure and shall bear a reasonable rate of interest.
8. To allocate in the trustee's discretion all charges and credits as between principal and income or partly to each, where uncertainty exists as to allocations of charges and credits under the applicable law, whenever the trustee considers these other allocations to be more reasonable and equitable under the circumstances.
9. To take any action with respect to conserving or realizing upon the value of any property and with respect to foreclosures, reorganizations, mergers, or other changes affecting the trust property; to collect, pay, contest, compromise, or abandon demands of or against the property wherever situated; and to execute contracts and other instruments, including instruments containing covenants, representations, and warranties binding upon and creating a charge against the property and containing provisions excluding personal liability.
10. To purchase casualty, health, and liability insurance as the trustee believes to be desirable.
11. To hire such agents, attorneys, and employees as the trustee deems appropriate, including persons to attend to my maintenance, comfort, companionship, enjoyment, and medical care.
12. To exercise any power or discretion without qualifying before, being appointed by, or obtaining the order or approval of any court.
13. To do all other acts to accomplish the proper management, investment, and distribution of the trust.

(continued)

Figure 5-3 (continued)

B. Additional Trustee Provisions.

1. If a trustee is serving as trustee for more than one trust created under this agreement, the trustee shall have the power to commingle trusts; the trustee need not physically segregate or divide the various trusts except when segregation or division is required because one of the trusts terminates, but the trustee shall keep separate accounts for the different trusts.

2. In the exercise of the trustee's powers, the trustee shall use the judgment and care a prudent person would use if the prudent person were the owner of the trust assets.

3. The trustee may rely on any notice, certificate, affidavit, letter, telegram, or other paper or document believed to be genuine, or on any evidence deemed by the trustee to be sufficient, in making any payment or distribution.

4. In determining whether and to what extent a power of appointment has been exercised by will, the trustee may rely on any instrument admitted to probate in any jurisdiction as the will of the holder of the power. The trustee may act as if the holder of the power died intestate if the trustee has no notice of a will offered for probate within six (6) months after the holder's death. This subparagraph shall not affect the rights of any appointee or beneficiary against any distributee.

5. No trustee shall be required to give any bond as trustee.

SECTION SEVEN

TRANSACTIONS WITH THIRD PERSONS

No person or corporation dealing with trustee shall be required to investigate trustee's authority for entering into any transaction or to administer the application of the proceeds of any transaction.

SECTION EIGHT

COMPENSATION OF TRUSTEE

The trustee shall be entitled to reasonable compensation for services in administering and distributing the trust property and for reimbursement of expenses.

SECTION NINE

REMOVAL OR RESIGNATION OF TRUSTEE AND APPOINTMENT OF SUCCESSOR

Trustee may be removed at any time by settlor or after settlor's death by Abigail Stewart by written notice to trustee. Trustee may resign by written notice to settlor during settlor's lifetime or after settlor's death to Abigail Stewart. Until the accounts of trustee are settled and trustee is discharged, trustee shall continue to have all the powers and discretions granted to him under this agreement or conferred by law. In the event of the removal or resignation of trustee, settlor or Abigail Stewart may by written instrument appoint a successor trustee. The successor trustee, on executing a written acceptance of the trusteeship and on the settlement of the accounts and discharge of the prior trustee, shall be vested, without further act on the part of anyone, with all the estate, title, powers, duties, immunities, and discretions granted to the original trustee.

SECTION TEN

ACCOUNTING TO INCOME BENEFICIARIES AND REMAINDER BENEFICIARIES

The trustee shall render at least annually to each person who is then an income beneficiary under this trust, and to each person who then holds a remainder interest in the trust principal that can be defeated only by his

---

(continued)

Figure 5-3 (continued)

or her own death, a statement of account showing in detail all receipts, disbursements, and distribution of both principal and income from the trust since the last such statement. Unless the account is objected to in writing within sixty (60) days from its rendition, the account shall be deemed approved as stated. The trustee shall not be required to file any periodic accounting with any court or judicial office, even though otherwise required by law, but this shall not prevent the trustee from having the trustee's accounts judicially settled at any time if the trustee should deem it advisable to do so.

SECTION ELEVEN

GOVERNING LAW

The validity of this trust and the construction of its beneficial provisions shall be governed by the laws of the State of Wisconsin in force from time to time. This article shall apply regardless of any change of residence of a trustee or any beneficiary or the appointment or substitution of a trustee residing or doing business in another state.

Jonathon K. Stewart
Notary Public, State of Wisconsin
My Commission **is permanent.**

Dated this 14th day of June, 2005.
STATE OF WISCONSIN)
)SS
COUNTY OF DANE   )

    This instrument was acknowledged before me on June 14th, 2005, by Jonathon Stewart, as settlor of the trust created by the foregoing agreement.

4. Section Three: Additions to Trust Estate

This provision allows additional property to be placed into the trust fund. It is especially important if the settlor is coupling this trust with a pour-over will or names the trust as the beneficiary on a life insurance policy.

5. Section Four: Disposition of Income

The clause provides how the trust is to be administered. It could also include a disposition of principal.

6. Section Five: Invasion of Principal for Spouse and Descendants

A provision protecting the settlor's spouse and children upon his or her death may be included. It grants payments to them under circumstances as set forth in this section. The language in this trust imposes limits on the payment of principal and retains the trustee's right to use discretionary powers when administering the trust.

7. Section Six: Powers of Trustee

A section enumerating the trustee's powers is typically included. The powers may vary greatly. They could include a wide range of activities, from selling property to leasing it, to lending money, and so on. The paralegal may wish to consult state law on trustees' powers or form books when drafting this section. Please note that this section provides that no bond be required of the trustee.

8. Section Seven: Transactions with Third Persons

This clause provides that the trustee does not have to prove his or her authority when entering into transactions on behalf of the trust.

9. Section Eight: Compensation of Trustee

This vital section states how the trustee will be paid for administering and managing the trust.

10. Section Nine: Removal or Resignation of Trustee and Appointment of Successor

This section states who may remove the trustee from appointment and the procedure for removal or resignation.

11. Section Ten: Accounting to Income Beneficiaries and Remainder Beneficiaries

This provision requires the trustee to file an accounting with designated interested persons. As you recall, the duty of accounting is one of the fiduciary duties that a trustee owes a beneficiary.

12. Section Eleven: Governing Law

It is common practice in all legal agreements to include which state's law will be used.

13. Signature

The date, signature of the settlor, and a jurat should be included.

pour-over will
A will that leaves any property owned by the decedent to an already existing inter vivos trust.

If a revocable inter vivos trust is executed, the settlor may want any property not placed in the trust to be moved to it upon his or her death. The law firm will want to prepare a **pour-over will** to effectuate this purpose and the settlor's wishes. The remaining property owned by the settlor will be probated and transferred into the trust. The trust then retains the property or distributes it as stated in the trust. For example, Peter places $1,000,000 into a revocable inter vivos trust. His desire is to put all his property, his house, car, and so on, into the trust upon his death. He would execute a pour-over will.

The rules for drafting a pour-over will are similar to those for drafting a simple will, as discussed in Chapter 4. This will contains the same types of clauses as those found in a simple will. The exordium, revocation, testimonium, and attestation clauses are found in a pour-over will. The main difference is that the dispositive section leaves the property to the existing trust rather than designated individuals or corporate beneficiaries. (See the pour-over will in Figure 5-4, which corresponds to the revocable inter vivos trust in Figure 5-3.)

The second trust is the testamentary trust. You should recall that this trust is created upon the death of a person. Trust language is included in a will. See the testamentary trust in Figure 5-5. In particular, you should note the following about this trust. The trust corpus is real estate. All other property is passing by will outside the trust. Although the will creates a trust, it retains the requirements of including clauses, as discussed in Chapter 4. A will containing a testamentary trust must comply with the formalities and legal requirements for creating a valid will. It includes an exordium clause, revocation clause, testimonium clause, and attestation clause. It nominates a personal representative. Because the will is from Wisconsin, it requires two witnesses. In addition to standard will provisions, the will contains language creating a trust. In section Third, B, it states that if the youngest grandson has not reached the age of thirty-five, the real estate goes into one trust. A clear intention to place the property in trust is stated. The will goes on to grant discretionary powers to the trustee to administer the trust. It includes a statement of purposes. The goal of the settlor is to provide for the expenses of raising the grandsons and help them with their education. The will contains language about when the trust terminates. The powers of the trustee are enumerated in section Sixth. These powers are similar to those discussed earlier in this chapter and found in the revocable inter vivos trust. The last main distinction between this will with a testamentary trust and a simple will is that this will nominates a trustee and successor trustee, both to serve without bond. All of this language is standard for creating a testamentary trust.

Figure 5-4   A pour-over will

LAST WILL and TESTAMENT
of
Johnathon K. Stewart

I, Johnathon K. Stewart, of Dane County, Wisconsin, revoke all my former wills and codicils and declare this to be my will.

I. DEBTS, TAXES, AND ADMINISTRATION EXPENSES

I have provided for the payment of all my debts, expenses of administration of property wherever situated passing under this will or otherwise, and estate, inheritance, transfer, and succession taxes other than any tax on a generation-skipping transfer that is not a liability on my estate (including interest and penalties, if any) that become due by reason of my death, under the **Stewart Revocable Trust** dated June 14th, 2005. If the trust assets should be insufficient for these purposes, my personal representative shall pay any unpaid items from the residue of my estate passing under this will, without apportionment or reimbursement. In the alternative, my personal representative may demand in a writing addressed to the trustee of the trust an amount necessary to pay all or part of the items, plus claims, pecuniary legacies, and family allowances by court order.

II. RESIDUE

A. If my children survive me, I give the residue of my estate, including any lapsed legacies within or without this residuary clause, but excluding any property over which I have a power of appointment, to the trustee under the **Stewart Revocable Trust** dated June 14th, 2005. The residue of my estate shall be added to, held, and administered as part of that trust, according to the terms of the trust and any amendment made to it before my death.

(continued)

Figure 5-4 (continued)

B. If a disposition mentioned in Paragraph II(A) is inoperative or invalid for any reason, or if the trust referred to in the paragraph fails or is revoked, I incorporate here by reference the terms of that trust, as executed on June 14th, 2005, without giving effect to any amendments made subsequently, and I give the residue of my estate to the trustee named in that trust as trustee, to be held, administered, and distributed as provided in the trust instrument incorporated in this will.

III. PERSONAL REPRESENTATIVE

I nominate Walter P. Stewart as personal representative of my estate. If he is unable or unwilling to serve, I nominate Virginia B. Stewart as personal representative. I direct that my personal representative shall not be required to furnish bond in that capacity.

IV. GUARDIAN

I nominate Hailey J. Stewart to be guardian of the person and property of each of my minor children who survive me. If she does not so serve, I nominate Virginia B. Stewart to be the guardian, and I direct that no bond securing the performance of their duties be required of any of these persons as to property derived through this will.

V. TESTIMONIUM CLAUSE

I freely and willingly subscribe my name to this will consisting of three (3) pages, including this page, on this _____ day of _____, 20 ____, in the presence of these witnesses: Peter C. Johnstone, and Pamela D. Johnstone, each of whom I have requested to subscribe their names in my presence and in the presence of all others.

Dated this _____ day of _____, 20____.

_____
Johnathon K. Stewart

We certify that in our presence on the date appearing above, Johnathon K. Stewart signed, published, and declared the foregoing instrument, consisting of three (3) printed pages, this included, as his will, that at his request and in his presence and in the presence of each other, we have signed our names below as witnesses, and that at the time we believed him to be of sound mind and memory and not acting under any duress or undue influence.

_____ of _____
Peter C. Johnstone

_____ of _____
Pamela D. Johnstone

Figure 5-5   A testamentary trust

LAST WILL and TESTAMENT
of
Megan Elizabeth Cooper

I, Megan Elizabeth Cooper, a resident of Pewaukee, Waukesha County, Wisconsin, hereby revoke my former Wills and Codicils and declare this to be my last Will.

FIRST: I direct the payment of my funeral expenses, administration expenses and legally enforceable debts as provided by law.

SECOND: All of the property which I own at my death subject to the payments set forth in paragraph FIRST above, I hereby give, devise and bequeath to my beloved husband, CADEN COOPER, if he survives me.

THIRD: If my husband, CADEN COOPER, predeceases me, all of my property with the exception of the real estate located at 1234 Woodlane Drive, Pewaukee, Wisconsin 53702, is hereby given to my daughter, LAUREN JONES. The real estate is hereby given as follows:

A. The real estate located at 1234 Woodlane Drive, Pewaukee, Wisconsin 53702 is given in equal shares to my grandson, ALEXANDER JONES, my grandson, ZACHARY JONES, and my grandson, NICHOLAS JONES.

B. If the youngest grandson has reached the age of thirty-five (35) years at such time, ALEXANDER JONES, ZACHARY JONES, and NICHOLAS JONES shall receive their equal shares outright. If the youngest grandson has not reached the age of thirty-five (35) years at such time, the shares of my grandsons, ALEXANDER JONES, ZACHARY JONES, and NICHOLAS JONES, shall be retained by the trustee, in a single trust. The trustee may make such payment, use, application, expenditure, or accumulation of the income and principal thereof as he shall think proper for any grandson's benefit. When the youngest grandson reaches the age of thirty-five (35) years, the trustee shall pay over to my grandsons the principal then remaining plus any accumulated income as provided in Section THIRD B 3 below. The trust shall be administered as directed in Section THIRD B 1-4 below.

1. STATEMENT OF PURPOSES. The provisions of this trust give the trustee the discretion to distribute income and principal. My objective in granting such discretion is to permit the trustee to administer the trust assets and make distribution substantially as I might have done if living, having in mind circumstances as they change from time to time. My primary purpose in establishing this trust is to provide for the expenses of raising my grandsons, including providing or assisting in providing them with an education appropriate to their abilities and interests. Secondarily, it is my hope that additional funds will be available to make the lives of my grandsons more comfortable and financially secure. The trustee shall have no duty to preserve principal intact to the extent he considers its current use in the best interests of the current beneficiaries. Distributions may be made for a beneficiary's care, comfort, maintenance, education (including graduate or technical education), purchases of homes, or any other worthwhile purpose. The trustee shall have no liability to any person for any good faith exercise of his power to make or withhold distributions of income or principal. The trustee may consider other resources known to him to be available to the beneficiaries.

2. INCOME AND PRINCIPAL UNTIL DIVISION AND DISTRIBUTION. The net income and principal of this trust may be distributed to or applied for the benefit of any one or more of my grandsons in such amounts and at such times as the trustee, in his absolute discretion, may determine. Any undistributed net income shall be added to trust principal.

(continued)

Figure 5-5 (continued)

3. DIVISION AND DISTRIBUTION. When the youngest living grandson reaches age thirty-five (35), the then remaining net trust assets shall be divided into equal shares so that there is one share for each of my then living grandsons.

4. FAILURE OF BENEFICIARIES. If a grandson dies before all trust assets are fully withdrawn or distributed, the then remaining assets shall be divided into equal shares so that there is one for each of my then living grandsons. Each share for a then living grandson shall be added to the assets of, or distributed pursuant to the provisions of, the single trust for my grandsons under Section THIRD B 1-4.

FOURTH: If my daughter, LAUREN JONES, predeceases me, the interest which would have passed to her had she survived me is hereby given with right of representation to the descendants of said deceased child who survive me. If there is no surviving descendant of said deceased child, my property is hereby given in such shares and to such beneficiaries as would have been the distribution under this Will if that child had never lived.

FIFTH: If any beneficiary dies prior to the entry of an order, decree, or judgment in my estate, distributing the property in question, or within six months after the date of my death, whichever is earlier, any interest which would have passed to said beneficiary under other provisions of the Will are to be disposed of according to the plan of distribution which would have been effective under this Will if such beneficiary had predeceased me. It is my intention that any property or interest which is distributed from my estate as a result of Court order, decree, or judgment will not be revoked or otherwise affected by the subsequent death of the distributee.

SIXTH: A. The personal representative, trustee, and any successors shall have the following powers, exercisable without obtaining prior authority from any court:

1. To retain, invest, and reinvest in any property without regard to whether the same may be authorized by law and regardless of any risk, lack of diversification, or unproductivity involved.
2. To lend.
3. To borrow.
4. To pay, collect, enforce, and compromise claims.
5. To allot, assign, convey, convert, divide, exchange, hold, improve, insure, lease, maintain, mortgage, operate, repair, grant and exercise options on, pledge, sell at public or private sale, or exchange all or part of the estate or trust property.
6. To purchase life, liability, and any other type of insurance.
7. To exercise all incidents of ownership of insurance policies.
8. To pay, from the residue of the estate or trust, packing, storage, and shipping expenses for, and related insurance premiums on, any property even though specifically given in this Will.
9. To participate in any way in the continuation, organization, operation, discontinuance, or dissolution of business in corporate, partnership, or other forms.
10. To vote stock and other rights by proxy or otherwise.
11. To hold title to property without disclosing fiduciary capacity.
12. To employ agents, assistants, counsel, and brokers and to delegate powers to them and to pay their reasonable fees and expenses.
13. To demolish or erect structures.
14. To make income and gift tax returns.
15. To establish adequate reserves for appropriate purposes.
16. To continue as personal representative or trustee and to deal with the estate or trust without regard to conflicts of interest.

(continued)

Figure 5-5 (continued)

17. To make divisions and distributions in kind or cash, or partly in each.
18. To distribute property to a custodian for a minor beneficiary under applicable Uniform Transfers to Minors Act or similar law.
19. To allocate property proportionately or disproportionately among beneficiaries or heirs.
20. To allocate in his discretion all receipts and disbursements between principal and income where uncertainty exists about proper allocation under applicable law.
21. To make tax elections, allocations, and decisions (in doing so, he shall seek to minimize the present and future income and transfer tax burden to the estate or trust and beneficiaries, and he shall make no reimbursement or adjustments between any beneficial interest, whether income or principal, present or future).
22. To permit occupancy of real property by beneficiaries on any terms.
23. To accept additions of any kind to the trust.
24. To waive, release, or delegate, temporarily or irrevocably, any power, authority, or discretion.
25. In general, without limitation by reason of the foregoing, to do any and every act and thing that the personal representative or trustee would have the right to do as personal representative or trustee under applicable law or as absolute owner of property.

B. The personal representative or trustee shall not be liable for loss caused to any person by any good faith decision.

SEVENTH: A. I hereby appoint JEFFREY ANDERSON Personal Representative of this Will. If JEFFREY ANDERSON cannot so act, I appoint MICHAEL DAVIDSON as such Personal Representative. If MICHAEL DAVIDSON cannot so act, I appoint LINDSAY ROBINSON, Personal Representative.

B. I appoint MICHAEL DAVIDSON as Trustee of the trust created under this Will. If he does not so act or ceases to act, I appoint LINDSAY ROBINSON as Trustee.

C. No bond shall be required of any Personal Representative, Trustee, or Successor.

I freely and willingly subscribe my name to this will consisting of four pages on this the 30th day of May, 2006, at Pewaukee, County of Waukesha, State of Wisconsin, in the presence of these witnesses: John Doe and Jane Doe, each of whom I have requested to subscribe their names in my presence and in the presence of all the others.

(Seal)

_____

Megan Elizabeth Cooper

The foregoing instrument consisting of four (4) pages was signed and published by said MEGAN ELIZABETH COOPER as her Last Will, that at her request and in her presence and in the presence of each other, we have hereunto subscribed our names as witnesses. We each certify that at the time of the execution of the Will said MEGAN ELIZABETH COOPER was mentally competent and acting voluntarily.

_____ of _____, Wisconsin.

_____ of _____, Wisconsin.

KEY **TERMS**

beneficiary (p. 66)
cestui que trust (p. 66)
constructive trust (p. 73)
cy-pres doctrine (p. 74)
equitable title (p. 66)
express trust (p. 73)
implied trust (p. 73)
inter vivos trust (p. 75)

irrevocable trust (p. 75)
legal title (p. 67)
letters of trust (p. 67)
pour-over will (p. 84)
private trust (p. 73)
public trust (p. 73)
resulting trust (p. 73)

revocable trust (p. 75)
settlor (p. 66)
spendthrift trust (p. 76)
testamentary trust (p. 75)
totten trust (p. 76)
trust (p. 66)
trustee (p. 66)

REVIEW **QUESTIONS**

1. Under what circumstances might a trust be an effective estate planning device for a client?

2. Name the four essential elements of a trust.

3. Explain equitable title. What party to a trust has only equitable title?

4. Name three powers a trustee has.

5. Does a trust that is funded with a parcel of real estate need to be in writing? Explain.

6. Why can't the same person be a trustee and a beneficiary to a trust?

7. Create an example of an express private revocable living trust. Explain how your example meets these qualifications.

8. What is the purpose of creating a spendthrift trust?

9. What is a totten trust? Give an example of how one could be created.

10. List and explain three methods of terminating a trust.

11. Explain a pour-over will. Under what circumstances would this document be used?

ROLE-PLAYING **ACTIVITY**

1. Many other trusts besides those explained in this chapter exist. As a class, create a list of different trusts. Choose two other trusts to research; present information regarding the trusts to the class. Can your classmates determine which type of trust it is?

RESEARCH **ASSIGNMENTS**

1. What is the cy-pres doctrine? Find a cy-pres case in your state.

2. Research your state's law on a trustee's (a) fiduciary duties, (b) powers, and (c) compensation.

3. Research what a sprinkling trust is. What language placed in a trust would make it a sprinkling trust?

4. Research your state's law regarding the validity of and requirements to create a spendthrift trust.

PART II

ESTATE ADMINISTRATION

Chapter **six**

OVERVIEW OF ESTATE ADMINISTRATION AND THE PERSONAL REPRESENTATIVE

Following Through on the Plan: The Administration of the Estate

We have now reached the second phase with regard to the estate. The plan, if there is one, has been created and outlined on written instruments, such as a will or trust. Our testator or settlor has left this world, and now others must put into action the individual's dreams, goals, and plans. The court oversees that the plan is carried out properly. The personal representative, with the help of the law firm, carries out the directions left by the decedent. For the plan to materialize, the law firm must follow a series of steps that make up the estate administration procedure. The decedent's dream should now become a reality, and much work must be done during this process.

Chapter 6 provides a brief overview of the work that must be completed to transfer the decedent's wealth to its new rightful owners, and it introduces you to the steps involved. Chapter 6 also introduces you to the new key player in making the decedent's plan come to life: the personal representative. Finally, it provides additional information about the four case examples in Chapter 1, so you can expand your portfolio.

OBJECTIVES

After studying this chapter, you should be able to:

- Understand that the estate plan is now ready to be administered.
- Identify the different types of probate and recognize when they would be implemented.
- Understand, in general, Step One: The Issuance of Letters of Appointment.
- Explain, in general, Step Two: Inventory and Appraisal.
- Describe, in general, Step Three: Creditors' Claims.
- Explain, in general, Step Four: Tax Documents.
- Understand, in general, Step Five: Final Account.
- Explain, in general, Step Six: Closing the Estate.
- Describe the role of the personal representative.
- Differentiate among the types of personal representatives.

- Name a personal representative's powers and where these powers come from; list a personal representative's duties and understand where these duties originate; and explain the compensation of a personal representative.
- Define bond, explain its purpose, identify under what circumstances bond would be required, and explain how the amount of bond is determined.
- List and explain the circumstances under which a personal representative's duties are terminated.

probate
(a) The process of a court admitting a will as valid or (b) The process of administering a decedent's estate.

estate administration
The process of managing a decedent's property under court supervision; it includes collection of decedent's assets, payment of debts and taxes, and distribution of remaining property.

formal probate
A proceeding before a judge to determine if the decedent left a valid will.

informal probate
A process supervised by a court official to probate a will or appoint a personal representative.

The remaining chapters of the book detail each step: the documents to prepare and file, the fact gathering that must be done, the taxes that may be incurred, and the decisions that must be made. Chapter 7 details documents for issuance of letters of appointment. Chapter 8 discusses the inventory, appraisals, and creditors' claims. Chapter 9 discusses taxes, and Chapter 10 details the process for the final account and closing of the estate. The estate administration process can be a complicated one; however, by approaching it in an organized and systematic manner, you can accomplish it efficiently and effectively. Let us begin our new journey: effectuating the plan, administering the estate.

An Overview of the Six-Step Procedure for Administration of an Estate

Upon commencing the probate or estate administration procedure, the paralegal must be knowledgeable about the state requirements. Multiple variations of estate administration exist. Many choices about how to proceed with the decedent's wishes abound. Often two expressions denote this process. They are *probate* and *estate administration*. The term **probate** is the court procedure to prove a will. This term, through expansion, often refers to the process of working through the estate administration. **Estate administration** references the settlement of an estate. It includes the steps involved to have the decedent's wishes carried out. Probate and estate administration are represented in the six-step procedure outlined here.

Different types of probate may occur. Traditionally, probates can be solemn or regular. A solemn probate is formal and requires court supervision and approval. A regular probate requires filing of documents and less court approval. The Uniform Probate Code (UPC) distinguishes between formal and informal probate. The UPC explains **formal probate** as follows:

> A formal testacy proceeding is litigation to determine whether a decedent left a valid will. UPC § 3-401.

It defines formal proceedings as "proceedings conducted before a judge with notice to interested persons." UPC § 1-201(18). The UPC outlines a formal probate in UPC §§ 3-401 through 3-414. A formal probate requires the court and judge to monitor and rule on the progress being made on an estate. The procedure is more rigid, requires notice to interested persons, and may include more hearings than an informal proceeding.

An **informal probate** is supervised by the registrar or other court officials and does not require hearings or formal judicial approval of the procedure. It may not require notice to be given to interested persons. The Uniform Probate Code defines informal proceedings as "those conducted without notice to interested persons by an officer of the court acting as a registrar for probate of a will or appointment of a personal representative" UPC § 1-201(23). The UPC outlines informal probate in §§ 3-301 through 3-322. Although several states have adopted the UPC, many hybrid approaches to the procedures have been created. The goal of this chapter and the remainder of the book is to provide the paralegal with knowledge of how to proceed with an estate administration. Certain documents are common for both a formal and an informal proceeding. Some may be used in only one or the other. The best approach is to become familiar with those documents used in formal probate and informal probate in your state.

Another category of administration exists. The broad category for this is called administration for small estates. Names such as *summary administration* or *transfer by affidavit* are often given to this type of procedure. This type of administration, along with ancillary administration, is discussed in Chapter 10.

At this time, you may be asking: Which procedure do I use to probate an estate? This is the attorney's decision. If the law firm is debating between formal or informal probate versus summary administration, statutory law sets limits of when the summary administration can be done. These limits are usually based on dollar amounts, types of property held, or who is receiving the property. The decision between choosing formal versus informal probate may depend on whether an heir or beneficiary is contesting the will or is disgruntled with the amount inherited. If beneficiaries are fighting among each other, formal probate may be preferred. If a couple of individuals are desirous of becoming the administrator, formal administration may be required. In some states, it may be possible to move back and forth between a formal and an informal administration. The more an attorney wants court control and supervision, the more a formal probate is desirable. Usually the formal probate is the most expensive and the most time consuming, and requires the most documentation. However, it is the most-reviewed procedure because the judge plays such an active role. The informal probate probably requires less money, time, and paperwork. The summary administration usually requires the least amount of money, time, and documents.

Most law firms have an estate administration checklist that outlines the steps and documents to be completed during the process. This checklist lists the documents in chronological order and is a wonderful organizational tool that demonstrates the progress being made on the estate. It is often kept in a front section of the client's file. Familiarize yourself with your law firm's checklist. If the law firm does not have one, create and use your own checklist. A sample estate administration checklist based on Illinois forms is shown in Figure 6-1.

A valuable paralegal is one who is knowledgeable about the alternatives available in the state and has a sense for the tasks involved and the documents that must be prepared. Let us focus on the six steps required to accomplish a formal and/or informal administration.

Step One: Issuance of Letters of Appointment

During the first step, the law firm is contacted by someone whose relative, friend, or business client has just died. An initial interview is conducted. The law firm must get a personal representative appointed by the court before the wishes of the decedent can materialize. During this stage, there is the initial rush of preparing and filing a variety of court documents. This process normally takes one to four weeks, depending on the jurisdiction. The petition or application begins the estate administration process, and several other documents follow. Upon completion of this step, the court issues the letters of appointment called letters testamentary or letters of administration. This document demonstrates that the court has confirmed the appointment of the personal representative. The personal representative can now move forward with the duties of estate administration. This procedure is discussed at length in Chapter 7.

Figure 6-1 Estate administration checklist

ESTATE ADMINISTRATION CHECKLIST

ESTATE OF _____

Date of Death _____ Probate County _____

Decedent's Last Address _____

Social Security # _____ Will _____ Codicil _____

Personal Representative _____ Relationship _____

Address _____ Phone # _____

Enter date RECEIVED, FILED, MAILED, or PUBLISHED

INTERNAL

_____ Obtain retainer agreement

_____ Obtain names, addresses, and phone numbers of beneficiaries/heirs

EXTERNAL

_____ Petition for probate of will and testamentary letters

_____ Letters to heirs, banks, insurance companies, etc.

_____ SS4 FORM

_____ Oath and bond of representative

_____ Proof of heirship

_____ Order declaring heirship

_____ Order admitting will to probate and appointing executor

_____ Issuance of letters of appointment

_____ Spousal election

_____ Notice to heirs and legatees

_____ Claim notice

_____ Inventory

_____ Decedent's final income tax return

　　　　_____ Federal

　　　　_____ State

_____ Fiduciary income tax return

　　　　_____ Federal

　　　　_____ State

_____ Federal estate tax return

(continued)

Figure 6-1   (continued)

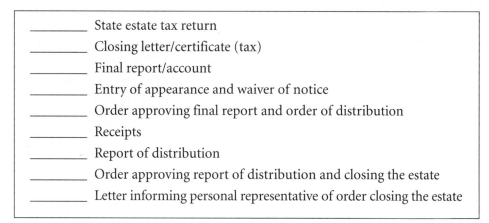

```
_____    State estate tax return
_____    Closing letter/certificate (tax)
_____    Final report/account
_____    Entry of appearance and waiver of notice
_____    Order approving final report and order of distribution
_____    Receipts
_____    Report of distribution
_____    Order approving report of distribution and closing the estate
_____    Letter informing personal representative of order closing the estate
```

Step Two: Inventory and Appraisal

The second step concerns the financial holdings of the decedent. The personal representative and the law firm determine what assets the decedent owned. They determine how the asset was titled and its value. Certain assets may be appraised, though not all assets must have an appraisal. Once the assets and fair market value are determined, a document called the inventory is prepared and filed with the court. Interested persons may receive notice that the inventory has been completed and then have an opportunity to inspect and review it. This process is discussed more thoroughly in Chapter 8.

Step Three: Creditors' Claims

The third step, creditors' claims, requires the personal representative and the law firm to locate, assess, and either allow or disallow payment of the decedent's debts. Where Step Two dealt with the decedent's assets, Step Three encompasses the decedent's liabilities.

Law firms publish notice of the decedent's death in local newspapers so that creditors can present claims. The procedure for notice, how a creditor must present a claim, and the options available to pay the debt are covered in Chapter 8. This step is important because creditors get paid before inheritances may be kept. Sometimes there are not enough assets in the estate to pay all of the creditors; in this case, preferences are given to certain creditors. Chapter 8 includes the order of preference.

Step Four: Tax Documents

Step Four involves the preparation of tax documents. Another one of the personal representative's responsibilities is to make certain the appropriate filing of tax returns and payment of tax liabilities occur. Four types of taxes exist: the final income tax return of the decedent, estate tax, inheritance tax, and fiduciary tax. The evaluation of tax liability encompasses both state and federal government tax consequences. A closing certificate or document confirming payment of taxes may be received by the law firm or personal representative. This document must be filed with the probate court before the estate administration can be closed. Chapter 9 discusses tax documents.

Step Five: Final Account

The fifth step is the final account. This document is a financial report to the court and interested persons, and includes the estate's income and outflow of money and property while the estate is open. It reports the payment of taxes, debts, and distributions, and who received the money. The remaining amount of funds to be distributed to the heirs and beneficiaries awaiting their inheritances is reported as well. The preparation of the final account is discussed further in Chapter 10.

Step Six: Closing the Estate

The sixth and final step is the closing of the estate. It requires receipts to be collected from the interested persons who have received estate money or property. The receipts are then filed with the court. Next, the personal representative signs and files a court document stating that he or she has performed all required estate administration tasks and that the work is done. Upon reviewing the filed documents, the court officially closes the estate. The decedent's plan has been accomplished. This step is more thoroughly discussed in Chapter 10.

The Personal Representative

The above discussion referenced the importance of the personal representative. This individual is in charge of making certain the administration is properly carried out and completed. However, the duties of the personal representative are many and can be complicated; thus, the individual often requires the assistance of a law firm. Before you study in depth the procedure required for estate administration, you should look more closely at types of personal representatives, how they are appointed, their powers and duties, the requirement of bond, and termination of the personal representative's authority.

Types of Personal Representatives

personal representative
Also known as administrator or executor; a legal representative who is appointed by the court to administer the decedent's estate.

The Uniform Probate Code defines **personal representative** to include "executor, administrator, successor personal representative, special administrator, and persons who perform substantially the same function under the law governing their status" UPC § 1-201(36). The term *personal representative* is used broadly to mean the individual or entity who is administering the estate. The personal representative works through the six steps previously outlined. With the assistance of the law firm, the individual or entity prepares and files proper court and tax documents, pays creditors and taxes, and distributes property to those entitled to inherit. Usage of the term *personal representative* is widespread and is the broader, all-encompassing term for *executor* or *administrator*.

executor
A person nominated in the will to carry out the gifts and directions contained in the will.

    Executor references a person or entity nominated in the decedent's will to carry out the gifts and directions of the will once the court confirms the appointment. The term *executor* is the masculine variation, and *executrix* is the feminine. Often the testator nominates a family member, a spouse, parent, or adult child to serve. Sometimes a friend or business associate is selected. A corporate entity may also be chosen.

If the decedent died intestate, the court appoints an **administrator**, man, or *administratrix*, woman, to administer the estate. An administrator's duties are the same as those of an executor. Two other situations where an executor is not appointed is when the will does not nominate someone, or the decedent nominated an individual who predeceased the decedent and is unable to serve. In these cases, a special type of administrator called an administrator cum testamento annexo or administrator with the will annexed is appointed. The initials C.T.A. designate the special type of administrator. The duties of the administrator, C.T.A., are the same as those of the administrator or executor.

If an emergency situation exists, a special administrator may be appointed by the court "to preserve the estate or secure its proper administration including its administration in circumstances where a general personal representative cannot or should not act" UPC § 3-614(2). The other circumstance for appointment of a special administrator would be "to protect the estate of a decedent prior to appointment of a general personal representative or if a prior appointment has been terminated . . ." by death or disability; UPC § 3-614(1). A document granting this authority would be issued by the court. See Wisconsin's letters of special administration in Figure 6-2.

The estate can be administered by co–personal representatives or co-executors if the decedent specified such in a will. For example, George wishes his two adult children, Amy and Jessica, to administer the estate together and the court could appoint them as co-executors.

Finally, it is often recommended in will drafting to nominate a successor executor. This person would act if the previously nominated or appointed person could not. A successor personal representative can also be an administrator appointed by the court. The Uniform Probate Code defines a successor personal representative as "a personal representative, other than a special administrator, who is appointed to succeed a previously appointed personal representative" UPC § 1-201(47).

State statutes may require or limit who may serve as a personal representative. Usually, the individual must be an adult who is mentally competent. Further, the personal representative cannot be convicted of a crime. Often the person must be a U.S. citizen or more specifically a resident of the state where the court has jurisdiction over the probate.

Appointment

The court must appoint the personal representative in order for him or her to conduct business for the estate. A South Dakota statute lists the order of priority of appointment as (1) the person nominated in the will; (2) the decedent's surviving spouse, who is also a beneficiary; (3) decedent's other beneficiaries; (4) the decedent's surviving spouse; (5) other heirs of the decedent; and (6) forty-five (45) days after the decedent's death, any other qualified person; S.D. Codified Laws § 29A-3-203. If an executor is appointed, the document is often called testamentary letters. If an administrator is appointed, the document is called letters of administration. Chapter 7 outlines the process.

Powers and Duties

Once the personal representative is appointed, he or she has certain powers and duties regarding the estate. In general, the duties of the personal representative are to preserve, collect, and manage the estate's assets; to pay expenses, creditors' claims,

administrator
The court-appointed legal representative, not named in the will, who manages the administration of the decedent's estate.

Figure 6-2   Wisconsin's letters of special administration

		For Official Use
STATE OF WISCONSIN, CIRCUIT COURT, _____ **COUNTY**		

IN THE MATTER OF THE ESTATE OF

_____

_____   Case No. _____

Letters of Special Administration

To:

The decedent, whose date of birth was _____ and date of death was _____,

died domiciled in _____ County, State of _____.

You are granted letters of special administration, with the following powers:

☐ all the general powers, duties and liabilities as personal representative
    ☐ except: _____

_____

☐ only these specific powers: _____

_____

BY THE COURT:

(Seal)

_____
Circuit Court Judge/Court Commissioner

_____
Name Printed or Typed

_____
Date

Name of Attorney
Address
Telephone Number

PR-1853, 10/00 Letters of Special Administration   §§867.15, 867.17, 879.57, Wisconsin Statutes
This form shall not be modified. It may be supplemented with additional material.

Source: For the most current version of this form, visit www.wicourts.gov.

and taxes; and to distribute the remaining assets to the beneficiaries and heirs. The powers granted to the personal representative enable him or her to accomplish the estate administration, and the duties explain what work must be undertaken and completed by the personal representative.

The powers and duties may be enumerated in the will. The legal professional should consult the will, if one exists, for those powers and duties that have been granted. Another source of powers and duties is statutory law. The law requires the personal representative to have a fiduciary relationship with the heirs and beneficiaries. Recall that a fiduciary duty requires the person to act on behalf of another with trust and confidence. Remember from Chapter 5 that a trustee owes a fiduciary duty to the beneficiary. Many of the powers and duties given to a trustee of a trust also apply to the personal representative of an estate.

Consulting statutory law sheds light on the more specific powers and duties given to the personal representative. The Uniform Probate Code lists the powers, which include the following:

1. Retain assets owned by the decedent pending distribution or liquidation of the estate.
2. Perform, compromise, or refuse performance of decedent's contracts that continue as obligations of the estate.
3. Invest liquid assets of the estate in prudent investments.
4. Acquire or dispose of an asset, including land.
5. Make repairs or alterations in buildings or other structures.
6. Subdivide or develop land.
7. Enter into a lease.
8. Vote stock in person or by proxy.
9. Insure estate assets against damage or loss.
10. Borrow money.
11. Pay taxes and estate administration costs.
12. Employ attorneys, auditors, investment advisors, or agents.
13. Prosecute or defend claims.
14. Sell, mortgage, or lease any real or personal property.
15. Continue a business.
16. Distribute the estate.

Source: UPC § 3-715.

Texas statutory law lists what powers the personal representative can exercise under court order, such as purchasing or exchanging property, versus powers that may be exercised without a court order, such as voting stocks by limited or general proxy; Tex. Prob. Code Ann. § 234.

Duties of the personal representative are enumerated by the Uniform Probate Code, some of which are:

1. A personal representative has a fiduciary duty to act (UPC § 3-703(a)).
2. A personal representative must give notice of his or her appointment to beneficiaries or heirs (UPC § 3-705).
3. A personal representative must prepare and file an inventory of property owned by the decedent and its date of death value (UPC § 3-706).

4. A personal representative may employ qualified and disinterested appraisers to value the decedent's assets (UPC § 3-707).

5. A personal representative takes possession or control of the decedent's property (UPC § 3-709).

Some states contain a list of the duties of the personal representative on court documents and require the personal representative to acknowledge receipt of the information. See California's form for the duties and liabilities of personal representative in Figure 6-3.

The personal representative is allowed to be paid for his or her services. Often the personal representative is a beneficiary or heir to the estate and refuses payment. Any money received as the personal representative's fee is taxable as ordinary income on the individual's income tax return, but his or her inheritance is not. There is a tax benefit to the personal representative for relinquishing payment. However, if the personal representative is unlikely to inherit anything because of abatement or some other reason, the personal representative usually elects to receive payment for services. The UPC provides that "[a] personal representative is entitled to reasonable compensation for his services. . . A personal representative also may renounce his right to all or any part of the compensation. A written renunciation of fee may be filed with the Court" UPC § 3-719.

The fee must be reasonable. In some jurisdictions, a statute may specify the amount. Consider Wisconsin's statute, which computes the fee based on the inventory value "less any mortgages or liens plus net principal gains in the estate proceedings at a rate of two percent . . ." or at a rate the majority inheritors of the estate and the personal representative agree to in writing. This statute also states that the court may determine a larger fee for the personal representative in cases of "unusual difficulty or extraordinary services" Wis. Stat. § 857.05 (2). California law provides a percentage value of the estate to be the personal representative's fee. The percentage amount decreases as the value of the estate increases; Cal. Prob. Code § 10800.

Bond

The personal representative has been entrusted to manage and care for property and money belonging to others. He or she promises to act appropriately and exercise a fiduciary duty. However, it is possible through mismanagement, negligence, embezzlement, or other criminal activity that creditors are not paid, taxes are not paid, and/or beneficiaries or heirs do not receive their inheritance. **Bond** is a protection to these parties. It is a dollar amount that is posted to ensure the estate assets are delivered to the appropriate parties on time and in the correct amount. A California statute states the purpose of bond as follows: "The bond shall be for the benefit of interested persons and shall be conditioned on the personal representative's faithful execution of the duties of the office according to law" Cal. Prob. Code § 8480(b). State statutes dictate the requirements of bond and when it does not have to be posted. The options available are primarily that a state may require bond, bond is waived by the testator or testatrix in the will, bond is not required unless it is requested by an interested person, the will requires it, and/or the court deems it necessary; or bond is required because the decedent died intestate. Let's look more closely at these various rules.

1. Bond is required. In this instance, arrangements must be made to post the amount or obtain a surety. A **surety** charges a fee and agrees to pay the full

bond
Promise of a guarantor to pay the estate if the personal representative fails to properly administer the decedent's estate.

surety
One who promises to pay money if the personal representative fails to properly administer the decedent's estate.

Figure 6-3 California's duties and liabilities of personal representative (Courtesy of California Judicial Branch)

	DE-147
ATTORNEY OR PARTY WITHOUT ATTORNEY (*Name, state bar number, and address*):	*FOR COURT USE ONLY*

TELEPHONE NO.:   FAX NO. *(Optional)*:

E–MAIL ADDRESS *(Optional)*:

ATTORNEY FOR *(Name)*:

SUPERIOR COURT OF CALIFORNIA, COUNTY OF

STREET ADDRESS:

MAILING ADDRESS:

CITY AND ZIP CODE:

BRANCH NAME:

ESTATE OF *(Name)*:

                                                     DECEDENT

DUTIES AND LIABILITIES OF PERSONAL REPRESENTATIVE and Acknowledgment of Receipt	CASE NUMBER:

DUTIES AND LIABILITIES OF PERSONAL REPRESENTATIVE

When the court appoints you as personal representative of an estate, you become an officer of the court and assume certain duties and obligations. An attorney is best qualified to advise you about these matters. You should understand the following:

1. MANAGING THE ESTATE'S ASSETS

a. Prudent investments

You must manage the estate assets with the care of a prudent person dealing with someone else's property. This means that you must be cautious and may not make any speculative investments.

b. Keep estate assets separate

You must keep the money and property in this estate separate from anyone else's, including your own. When you open a bank account for the estate, the account name must indicate that it is an estate account and not your personal account. Never deposit estate funds in your personal account or otherwise mix them with your or anyone else's property. Securities in the estate must also be held in a name that shows they are estate property and not your personal property.

c. Interest-bearing accounts and other investments

Except for checking accounts intended for ordinary administration expenses, estate accounts must earn interest. You may deposit estate funds in insured accounts in financial institutions, but you should consult with an attorney before making other kinds of investments.

d. Other restrictions

There are many other restrictions on your authority to deal with estate property. You should not spend any of the estate's money unless you have received permission from the court or have been advised to do so by an attorney. You may reimburse yourself for official court costs paid by you to the county clerk and for the premium on your bond. Without prior order of the court, you may not pay fees to yourself or to your attorney, if you have one. If you do not obtain the court's permission when it is required, you may be removed as personal representative or you may be required to reimburse the estate from your own personal funds, or both. You should consult with an attorney concerning the legal requirements affecting sales, leases, mortgages, and investments of estate property.

2. INVENTORY OF ESTATE PROPERTY

a. Locate the estate's property

You must attempt to locate and take possession of all the decedent's property to be administered in the estate.

b. Determine the value of the property

You must arrange to have a court-appointed referee determine the value of the property unless the appointment is waived by the court. You, rather than the referee, must determine the value of certain "cash items." An attorney can advise you about how to do this.

c. File an inventory and appraisal

Within four months after Letters are first issued to you as personal representative, you must file with the court an inventory and appraisal of all the assets in the estate.

Page 1 of 2

Form Adopted for Mandatory Use Judicial Council of California DE-147 [Rev. January 1, 2002]	**DUTIES AND LIABILITIES OF PERSONAL REPRESENTATIVE** (Probate)	Probate Code, § 8404

(continued)

Figure 6-3 (continued)

ESTATE OF *(Name):*	CASE NUMBER:
⌐ DECEDENT	

d. File a change of ownership
At the time you file the inventory and appraisal, you must also file a change of ownership statement with the county recorder or assessor in each county where the decedent owned real property at the time of death, as provided in section 480 of the California Revenue and Taxation Code.

3. NOTICE TO CREDITORS

You must mail a notice of administration to each known creditor of the decedent within four months after your appointment as personal representative. If the decedent received Medi-Cal assistance, you must notify the State Director of Health Services within 90 days after appointment.

4. INSURANCE

You should determine that there is appropriate and adequate insurance covering the assets and risks of the estate. Maintain the insurance in force during the entire period of the administration.

5. RECORD KEEPING

a. Keep accounts
You must keep complete and accurate records of each financial transaction affecting the estate. You will have to prepare an account of all money and property you have received, what you have spent, and the date of each transaction. You must describe in detail what you have left after the payment of expenses.

b. Court review
Your account will be reviewed by the court. Save your receipts because the court may ask to review them. If you do not file your accounts as required, the court will order you to do so. You may be removed as personal representative if you fail to comply.

6. CONSULTING AN ATTORNEY

If you have an attorney, you should cooperate with the attorney at all times. You and your attorney are responsible for completing the estate administration as promptly as possible. **When in doubt, contact your attorney.**

NOTICE: **1. This statement of duties and liabilities is a summary and is not a complete statement of the law. Your conduct as a personal representative is governed by the law itself and not by this summary.**
2. If you fail to perform your duties or to meet the deadlines, the court may reduce your compensation, remove you from office, and impose other sanctions.

ACKNOWLEDGMENT OF RECEIPT

1. I have petitioned the court to be appointed as a personal representative.

2. My address and telephone number are *(specify):*

3. I acknowledge that I have received a copy of this statement of the duties and liabilities of the office of personal representative.

Date:

_____   ▶   _____
(TYPE OR PRINT NAME)   (SIGNATURE OF PETITIONER)

Date:

_____   ▶   _____
(TYPE OR PRINT NAME)   (SIGNATURE OF PETITIONER)

CONFIDENTIAL INFORMATION: If required to do so by local court rule, you must provide your date of birth and driver's license number on supplemental Form DE-147S. (Prob. Code, § 8404(b)).

DE-147 [Rev. January 1, 2002]   **DUTIES AND LIABILITIES OF PERSONAL REPRESENTATIVE**   Page 2 of 2
(Probate)

amount if the personal representative does something wrong. A surety is usually an insurance company. The surety then goes after the personal representative for payment if any loss is covered.

2. Bond is not required because the testator or testatrix waives it in the will. Recall from Chapter 4 that a clause may be included in the will that waives bond. The testator nominates an individual he trusts, so the requirement of bond is just an added expense to the estate. Most attorneys recommend that this language be incorporated in the will. A court may order bond regardless of such language if it deems it necessary and the state statute so allows. California statutory law allows the bond to be waived by will; Cal. Prob. Code § 8481.

3. Bond is not required by statute but an interested person requests it, the will requires it, and/or the court deems it necessary. Some states may not require bond to be posted; however, an interested person can petition the court, asking for bond to be required. If the written demand is filed, it is possible that bond will automatically be required. It is also possible that the testator expressly states in the will that the personal representative is to serve with bond. If this is the case, the court orders bond to be posted. This is the method stated in the Uniform Probate Code; UPC §§ 3-603, 3-605.

4. Bond is required because the decedent died intestate. The decedent has not left a will waiving bond. No planning has been done, and the court needs to protect the heirs. The court will be especially concerned and may require bond if minor children are inheriting.

The value of the bond given is usually determined by the value of the estate, the types of assets contained within the estate, and the personal representative's relationship to heirs and beneficiaries. The Uniform Probate Code determines the amount based on

the best estimate of the value of the personal estate of the decedent and the income expected from the personal and real estate during the next year, [the bond amount should be] . . . in an amount not less than the estimate; UPC § 3-604.

A California statute allows the court, at its discretion, to determine the amount of bond but specifies a ceiling on the amount; Cal. Prob. Code § 8482.

The procedure for providing bond and the preparation of related court documents is discussed in more detail in Chapter 7.

Termination

The duties of the personal representative may be terminated under several circumstances, including:

1. Estate completion.
2. Death or disability.
3. Resignation.
4. Removal.

1. Estate Completion

Once the personal representative has faithfully completed all six steps of the estate administration, he or she is discharged. Chapter 10 outlines the procedure for court discharge of the personal representative when the estate has been completed.

2. Death or Disability

If the personal representative dies or becomes mentally incompetent while the probate is pending, he or she can no longer act. A personal representative must be mentally competent. Under these circumstances, the court appoints a special administrator or a successor personal representative to replace the deceased or disabled personal representative.

3. Resignation

The personal representative may request the court to be discharged of his or her duties prior to the completion of all probate steps. This would amount to a resignation of the personal representative. A new personal representative would need to be appointed.

4. Removal

The court has the authority to remove the personal representative from administering the estate. Some causes for removal include: when it is in the best interest of the estate, the personal representative misrepresented material facts when seeking appointment, the personal representative has disregarded a court order, the personal representative has mismanaged the estate, or the personal representative is incapable of discharging the duties; UPC § 3-611. Grounds for removal in California include the following: the personal representative was wasteful, embezzled, mismanaged, or committed a fraud against the estate; is incapable of properly administering the estate; or has wrongfully neglected the estate; or removal is necessary for the protection of the estate or interested persons; Cal. Prob. Code § 8502. Upon removal, a successor personal representative or special administrator may be put into office. An interested person may petition the court for removal of the personal representative. California so provides in Cal. Prob. Code § 8500. California law further provides, "[O]n removal of a personal representative from office, the court shall revoke any letters issued to the personal representative, and the authority of the personal representative ceases" Cal. Prob. Code § 8501.

Now that you have been introduced to an overview of estate administration and have a solid knowledge of the duties and powers of the personal representative, let us look more closely at how to effectuate the decedent's plan. Our first step is to learn more about the procedure for the issuance of the letters of appointment.

The Estate Planning and Estate Administration Portfolio

Recall from Chapter 1 that this textbook offers you the opportunity to create an estate planning and administration portfolio. This chapter contains the four estate administration case examples that may be used when preparing requested documents. Within each case example are several drafting assignments. They are cross-referenced to the chapter that covers that material. The Build Your Portfolio section found at the end of each chapter also contains assignments requiring you to complete certain documents. You should refer to the case examples contained in Chapter 1 to obtain needed information.

ESTATE ADMINISTRATION CASE **EXAMPLES**

A. The Richardson Estate

1. Edward Allen Richardson recently passed away on August 5, 20___. Review his will and codicil. Surviving Edward are his four children: Elizabeth Richardson, Mary Richardson, Donald Richardson, and Mark Richardson. His brother, Matthew Richardson, also survives him. Claudia Louise Richardson, his wife, has predeceased him. All of his beneficiaries are adults.

   a. Draft a petition or application for estate administration to be signed by Beverly Corey. She has agreed to act as the personal representative.

   b. Draft three (3) other documents required to initiate the estate administration. Of the three, make certain one is an order.

   c. Draft the appropriate letter of appointment declaring Beverly Corey as the executrix (Chapter 7).

2. Edward Richardson had the following assets, titled only in his name, with the following date-of-death values:

   a. His home, located at 777 Pivot Drive: tax bill value of $400,000.00, with a $100,000.00 mortgage.

   b. A checking account at Gold Bank: account number 10108, with a date-of-death value of $3,000.00.

   c. A savings account at Gold Bank: account number 200065, with a balance of $7,893.16 on the date of death and accrued interest of $56.13.

   d. One hundred (100) shares of Rock, Incorporated stock: the stockbroker stated that, on August 5, 20__, the stock had a value of $62.00 per share.

   e. Cash on hand of $1,250.00.

   f. The Corvette: serial number 44556677, valued at $42,000.00, with a $10,000.00 lien on it.

   g. The Harley Davidson motorcycle: serial number 2783645, valued at $23,000.00, with no existing lien on it.

   h. Life insurance payable to the estate: valued at $150,000.00 as of the date of death.

   i. Personal property, furnishings, clothing, and so on, valued at $10,000.00.

   Prepare an inventory (Chapter 8).

3. Prepare a notice to creditors to present claims form (Chapter 8).

4. Prepare an SS4 form (Chapter 9).

5. While the estate was pending, the following financial events occurred:

   a. The house was sold for $500,000.00, and the $100,000.00 mortgage was paid off.

   b. The Gold Bank savings account paid an additional $32.12 in interest.

   c. The 100 shares of Rock, Incorporated stock paid two dividends of $20.00 per share.

d. The Rock, Incorporated stock was sold, and the estate received a capital gain of $1,200.00.

e. The estate paid funeral costs of $15,000.00 for Edward's casket and burial plot. It paid $7,000.00 for the funeral service. The cost of the flowers was $500.00, and the funeral luncheon was $750.00.

f. Claims that were paid consisted of the following:

(1) Credit card: $3,110.00.

(2) Dr. Black: $1,750.00.

(3) Slippery Oil Company: $ 263.10.

g. Taxes:

(1) No federal estate tax was due.

(2) No state estate or inheritance tax was due.

(3) Federal final income tax paid: $2,200.00.

(4) State final income tax paid: $835.00.

(5) Federal fiduciary tax paid: $1,300.00.

(6) State fiduciary tax paid: $712.00.

h. Costs of the estate administration include filing fees of $600.00, mailing and photo-copying fees of $280.00, attorney's fees of $7,280.00, personal representative's fees of $4,300.00, and appraiser's fees of $590.00.

i. The car and motorcycle have been delivered to Matthew Richardson. A sum of $5,000.00 was distributed to Mark Richardson, and $60,000.00 has been given in equal shares to Elizabeth Richardson, Mary Richardson, and Donald Richardson.

Prepare a final account (Chapter 10).

6. Prepare a receipt (Chapter 10).

7. Prepare a document closing the estate and discharging the personal representative (Chapter 10).

B. The Diggle Estate

1. Mae Josephine Diggle died on January 10, 20___. Review her will and codicil. Kelly Foxworth, Robert Diggle, and Carolyn Diggle all survive her.

a. Draft a petition or application for estate administration to be signed by Robert Diggle and Carolyn Diggle as co-executors.

b. Draft three other documents required to initiate the estate administration. Of the three, make certain one is an order.

c. Draft the appropriate letter of appointment declaring Robert Diggle and Carolyn Diggle as co-executors (Chapter 7).

2. Mae Diggle had the following property titled only in her name, with the following date-of-death values:

a. A checking account at East Towne Bank: account number 44332, with a date-of-death value of $5,857.00.

b. A money market account at East Towne Bank: account number 52938, with a date-of-death balance of $12,332.65 and accrued interest of $323.18.

c. Sixty-three (63) shares of Foxtrot, Incorporated stock, with a value on her date of death of $125.00 per share.

d. A corporate bond from Bolero, Incorporated, with a date-of-death value of $6,000.00 and accrued interest of $650.00.

e. Personal property, furnishings, clothing, and so on, valued at $5,000.00.

f. Her bone china tea set is valued at $3,200.00.

g. The cookbook collection has a value of $350.00.

Prepare an inventory (Chapter 8).

3. Prepare a notice to creditors to present claims form (Chapter 8).

4. Prepare an SS4 form (Chapter 9).

5. While the estate was pending, the following financial events occurred:

a. The money market account paid an additional $56.32 of interest.

b. The Foxtrot stocks paid a dividend of $12.00 per share.

c. The Foxtrot stocks had a capital gain of $1,200.00.

d. The Bolero, Incorporated bond paid additional interest of $1,350.00.

e. The estate paid funeral costs of $6,000.00 for Mae's casket and burial plot. It paid $3,000.00 for the funeral service. Flowers cost $650.00, and the funeral luncheon cost $375.00.

f. Mae had medical expenses from her last illness. These were paid as follows:

(1) Dr. Cologne: $3,500.00.

(2) Revere Hospital: $8,000.00.

g. The estate also paid an electric bill of $78.39.

h. Taxes:

(1) No federal estate tax was due.

(2) No state estate or inheritance tax was due.

(3) Federal final income tax paid: $900.00.

(4) State final income tax paid: $250.00.

(5) Federal fiduciary tax paid: $580.00.

(6) State fiduciary tax paid: $150.00.

i. Administration costs of the estate include filing fees of $500.00, attorney's fees of $2,800.00, personal representative's fees were not taken by Robert Diggle or Carolyn Diggle, and appraiser's fees were $100.00.

j. The tea set has already been delivered to Kelly Foxworth, and $5,000.00 for each was given to Robert Diggle and Carolyn Diggle. The cookbooks have already been donated to the library. Prepare a final account (Chapter 10).

6. Prepare a receipt (Chapter 10).

7. Prepare a document closing the estate and discharging the co-executors (Chapter 10).

C. The Weber Estate

1. Jeanne Morgan Weber died on November 9, 20___. Jeanne has drafted a new will leaving all property to her three children in equal shares. She still wants Martha to be her executrix. Jeanne is survived by her three children: Pamela Barker, Martha Weber, and Kyle Weber. Daryl Weber and Julie Williams have predeceased her. All of her children are adults.

   a. Draft a petition or application for estate administration to be signed by Martha Weber, the executrix.

   b. Draft three other documents required to initiate the estate administration. Of the three, make certain one is an order.

   c. Draft the appropriate letter of appointment declaring Martha Weber as the executrix (Chapter 7).

2. Jeanne Weber had the following assets, titled only in her name, with the following date-of-death values:

   a. A ranch located at 125 Cattle Drive: valued at $1,000,000.00, with a $100,000.00 mortgage.

   b. A checking account at Vines Bank: account number 9865402, with a balance of $20,000.00. This was an interest-paying checking account, with accrued interest of $333.00.

   c. An investment portfolio consisting of mutual funds at Gordon's Investments: valued at $250,000.00, with accrued interest of $1,212.00.

   d. Five hundred (500) shares of Jazzerlee stock valued at $12.00 per share.

   e. Personal property, furnishings, clothing, and so on, valued at $30,000.00.

   f. Three horses, at a total value of $9,000.00.

   Prepare an inventory (Chapter 8).

3. Prepare a notice to creditors to present claims form (Chapter 8).

4. Prepare an SS4 form (Chapter 9).

5. While the estate was pending, the following financial events occurred:

   a. The ranch was transferred into the three children's names.

   b. The checking account paid an additional $300.00 interest.

   c. The investment portfolio made an additional $2,000.00 and then was distributed in equal shares to the three children.

   d. The Jazzerlee stock paid dividends of $2.00 per share, three times.

   e. The Jazzerlee stock was sold and realized a capital loss of $2,000.00.

   f. The three horses were distributed, one to each child.

   g. The estate paid funeral expenses of $15,000.00 for the funeral service. A monument was erected for $50,000.00. The casket cost $12,000.00, flowers cost $6,000.00, and the funeral dinner cost $3,500.00.

   h. The estate paid the following creditor's claims:

      (1) Horse trailer lien: $25,000.00.

      (2) Mastercard: $2,000.00.

   i. Taxes:

      (1) No federal estate tax was due.

      (2) No state estate or inheritance tax was due.

      (3) Federal final income tax paid: $7,000.00.

      (4) State final income tax paid: $4,000.00.

      (5) Federal fiduciary tax paid: $6,300.00.

      (6) State fiduciary tax paid: $3,700.00.

   j. Administration costs of the estate include filing fees of $4,250.00, attorney's fees of $12,985.00, personal representative's fees of $1,100.00, photocopying and mailing fees of $800.00, and accountant's fees of $6,000.00.

   k. In addition to the other distributions made, each child has also received $50,000.00 in cash.

Prepare a final account (Chapter 10).

6. Prepare a receipt (Chapter 10).

7. Prepare a document closing the estate and discharging the executrix (Chapter 10).

D. The Ehlers Estate

1. Marvin Cole Ehlers died on December 12, 20____. Please review his will and codicil. Marvin is survived by his two children, Elaine Spears and Luke Ehlers, and his three grandchildren, Amanda Spears, William Spears, and Beth Ehlers. His three grandchildren are still minors. He is also survived by Elaine's husband, Mike Spears.

    a. Draft a petition or application for estate administration to be signed by Elaine Spears and Luke Ehlers as co-executors.

    b. Draft three other documents required to initiate the estate administration. Of the three, make certain one is an order.

    c. Draft the appropriate letter of appointment declaring Elaine Spears and Luke Ehlers co-executors (Chapter 7).

2. Marvin Ehlers had the following assets, titled only in his name, with the following date-of-death values:

    a. Three real estate rental properties. One is a business property located at 926 Profit Drive, and it is worth $600,000.00, with a $150,000.00 mortgage on it. One is a duplex located at 362 Pilgrim Way; it is worth $300,000.00, with no mortgage. The third is a four-family housing complex located at 450 Longest Drive; it is worth $500,000.00, with a $300,000.00 mortgage. They were all owned by him as a sole proprietor.

    b. A checking account at Community Bank: account number 000234, with a balance of $895.00.

    c. A savings account at Community Bank: account number 973218, with a balance of $35,000.00 and accrued interest of $900.00.

    d. Three hundred twenty-five (325) shares of stock in Honling Manufacturing, valued at $110.00 per share.

    e. Personal property and furnishings, including his home office equipment, valued at $15,000.00.

    f. A baseball card collection valued at $7,500.00.

    g. A gold pocket watch valued at $1,635.00.

    h. A diamond tie clip valued at $3,250.00.

    Prepare an inventory (Chapter 8).

3. Prepare a notice to creditors to present claims form (Chapter 8).

4. Prepare an SS4 form (Chapter 9).

5. While the estate was pending, the following financial events occurred:

    a. The business rental property paid $16,650.00 in rent. It was transferred to Elaine Spears and Luke Ehlers.

    b. The duplex paid $3,000.00 worth of rent, and it was also transferred to Elaine Spears and Luke Ehlers.

    c. The four-family apartment complex was sold, with a capital gain of $50,000.00.

    d. The savings account paid an additional $1,500.00 in interest.

    e. The Honling Manufacturing stock paid one dividend of $25.00 per share.

    f. The baseball card collection, gold pocket watch, and diamond tie clip have all been distributed to the legatees.

    g. The estate paid funeral expenses of $12,000.00 for the funeral service. The casket was $1,000.00, and the burial plot had been prepaid by Marvin. The flowers cost $400.00, and the funeral dinner cost $625.00.

    h. The estate paid $17,500.00 in real estate taxes for the rental properties.

    i. The estate also paid:

        (1) Utilities: $3,900.00.

        (2) Community Bank line of credit: $6,350.00.

        (3) Visa: $4,728.36.

    j. Taxes:

        (1) No federal estate tax was due.

        (2) No state estate or inheritance tax was due.

        (3) Federal final income tax paid: $12,000.00.

        (4) State final income tax paid: $8,000.00.

(5) Federal fiduciary tax paid: $5,750.00.

(6) State fiduciary tax paid: $3,900.00.

k. Administration costs of the estate include filing fees of $2,200.00, attorney's fees of $10,980.00, personal representative's fees of $2,300.00, appraisal fees of $1,500.00, and accountant's fees of $5,400.00.

l. No distributions other than those previously mentioned were made.

Prepare a final account (Chapter 10).

6. Prepare a receipt (Chapter 10).

7. Prepare a document closing the estate and discharging the co-executors (Chapter 10).

KEY **TERMS**

administrator (p. 99)
bond (p. 102)
estate administration (p. 94)

executor (p. 98)
formal probate (p. 94)
informal probate (p. 94)

personal representative (p. 98)
probate (p. 94)
surety (p. 102)

REVIEW **QUESTIONS**

1. Compare and contrast probate and estate administration.

2. What is the difference between formal and informal probate?

3. List and briefly explain the six-step procedure for completing an estate administration.

4. Define the following: executrix, administrator cum testamento annexo, special administrator, and successor personal representative.

5. Explain three powers that a personal representative may have. Name two duties of a personal representative.

6. Explain bond and why it may be ordered.

7. Name and briefly explain under what four circumstances a personal representative may be terminated.

ROLE-PLAYING **ACTIVITY**

1. Pair up with a classmate. One student should be an attorney advising the other student, the newly appointed personal representative, of his or her powers and duties for administering the estate.

RESEARCH **ASSIGNMENTS**

1. Research and briefly explain your state's differentiation between formal and informal probate. What statutes outline the procedures?

2. Find your state statute's definition for personal representative. What is it?

3. Research your state law and determine the powers and duties granted to the personal representative of an estate.

4. Research your state law determining how the personal representative's fee is calculated.

5. Research your state law regarding bond. Under what circumstances is it required? How is the amount determined?

6. Research your state's statute regarding grounds for termination of the personal representative.

BUILD YOUR **PORTFOLIO**

1. The case examples in this chapter are continuations of those contained in Chapter 1. Place a copy of the appropriate updated case example from this chapter in your portfolio. (For example, if you chose Case Example A from Chapter 1, continue using Case Example A in Chapter 6.)

2. Draft an estate administration checklist.

Chapter **seven**

STEP ONE— ISSUANCE OF THE LETTERS OF APPOINTMENT

Effectuating the Estate Administration Plan: The Initial Steps

The estate plan has been put into place. A client has executed a will or trust, or perhaps no plan has been made: the person died intestate. Whatever the situation, part two of the estate planning and administration process has begun. The individual has died, and his or her wealth must be distributed. This chapter focuses on the initial steps required to probate a decedent's estate. We will look at the initial client conference to start an estate administration and at some of the initial steps the law firm must take to be able to effectuate the estate administration.

Initial Client Conference

Usually the law firm receives a phone call from a family member, an employee of a bank, or an employee of a trust company (interviewee) inquiring about the necessary procedure to transfer the decedent's wealth. Depending on the protocol at the law firm, a receptionist, legal secretary, or paralegal schedules an appointment for the individual to meet with the attorney. The recipient of the phone call should ask the individual to bring any of the decedent's estate planning documents to the conference. These documents include the last will and testament, codicils, a trust, a death certificate, and any other documents the law firm deems important.

Once the interviewee arrives at the law firm, different interviewing protocols are possible. Most firms ask the individual to complete a general client statistic sheet. Then an attorney may conduct the interview. In some offices, a paralegal may conduct the interview; however, caution

After studying this chapter, you should be able to:

- Outline the initial steps required for the law firm to administer the estate plan.
- Ethically conduct an initial client interview for an estate administration.
- Identify the initial action taken by the law firm once it is hired to administer an estate.
- Understand the importance of compiling financial information and the methods used to verify its accuracy.
- Determine the estate's heirs and/or beneficiaries and accurately compile statistical information about them.
- Explain a petition and its purpose; identify its sections and draft one.
- Recognize and understand the purpose of each additional court document that may be required to initiate the administration and accurately draft them.

- Outline some additional miscellaneous actions to be taken by the law firm; explain an SS4 form and draft one.
- Explain the purpose of letters of appointment and draft this document.

should be taken that the paralegal does not violate the ethical rule of the unauthorized practice of law. Often, both an attorney and a paralegal meet and interview the potential client. The attorney can give legal advice and answer legal questions as well as discuss the fee arrangement. The paralegal can take down statistical information. This way, the interviewee knows the team of legal professionals working on the estate.

The individual who has contacted the law firm may be appointed by the court as the executor, administrator, or personal representative. Although the law firm represents the estate, the firm works closely with the personal representative to conduct the estate administration. An executor or administrator could perform the work by him- or herself; however, the individual is usually not knowledgeable enough in the area of estate administration or taxes and requires the expertise of a law firm. (See Chapter 6 for a full discussion on the role of the personal representative.)

Many law firms use a probate or estate administration interview checklist (see Figure 7-1) when conducting the initial client interview. If your law firm does not

Figure 7-1   Probate checklist for initial client conference

Name of Client: _____

Name of Deceased: _____

Relationship of Client to the Deceased: _____

1. Determine if Valid Will or Died Intestate

   a. Review will, date _____

   b. Review codicil, date _____

   c. No will.

2. Determine Interested Persons

   a. Heirs

   b. Beneficiaries named in will

   c. Person acting as trustee of any trust

   d. Personal representative

   e. Others named by the court

   f. Unknown or unborn beneficiaries

   Obtain for each:

      (1) Name

      (2) Address

      (3) Telephone number

      (4) Social security number

      (5) Minor or incompetent

      (6) May contest will

      (7) Special financial consideration

3. Determine Assets

   a. Real estate (deeds, title policies, mortgages)

   b. Securities (stocks, brokerage statements, bonds)

(continued)

Figure 7-1　(continued)

c. Bank accounts (check book, statements, savings passbooks, CDs)
d. Vehicles (titles)
e. Life insurance (policies, claim forms)
f. Retirement benefits (plan statements, IRAS, beneficiary designation forms)
g. Household/personal property

4. **Discuss Asset Transfer Process**

   a. Autos
   b. Joint property
   c. Personalty
   d. Safe deposit box

5. **Obtain:**

   a. Tax returns for the past three to five years
   b. Premarital agreement or marital property agreement
   c. Gift tax return
   d. Determine business agreements (buy-sell)

6. **Estimate Cash Requirements**

   a. Rough calculations of funeral expenses
   b. Debts, mortgages
   c. Bequests
   d. Administrative transfer costs
   e. Fees
   f. Final income tax
   g. Estate or inheritance tax

7. **Discuss Insurance Needs (Home/Auto/Liability)**

8. **Discuss Creditors' Claims**

9. **Miscellaneous**

   a. Obtain death certificate
   b. Precautions
      (1) Cut up credit cards, close accounts
      (2) Security of home
      (3) Tangible personal effects
      (4) Plants, animals
   c. Outline estate administration process
      (1) Time frame
      (2) How your office processes estates
      (3) Introduce client to key staff members

10. **Consider Formal Versus Informal Administration** (consider other methods such as transfer by affidavit or summary settlement)

11. **Discuss Fees**

12. **Discuss Next Step** (such as initial hearing or preparation of the petition/ application)

have one, it might be wise to create one. The checklist reminds the attorney or paralegal what information to cover during the initial meeting.

Throughout the interview, good interviewing techniques, which were discussed in Chapter 4, should be employed. During the interview, several areas are generally covered. First, statistical information is gathered. This information includes the interviewee's name, address, telephone number, social security number, employment, and relationship to the decedent. Second, information regarding the decedent is gathered. This information includes the decedent's name, address, and date of birth. A list of the decedent's surviving relatives and their addresses, telephone numbers, ages, social security numbers, and relationships is created. The legal professional may ask for a copy of the death certificate if one was acquired. Third, the attorney reads the will if one has been provided by the interviewee. The attorney looks for beneficiaries' names and who is nominated to serve as the personal representative. If the interviewee cannot produce a will, then the firm needs to determine if one exists and where it may be located. The law firm must obtain the will. If it is determined that the decedent died intestate or the will does not nominate an executor, the attorney discusses with the interviewee who would be a good person to serve as an administrator. Often this person is the closest family member: a spouse, adult child, or parent of the decedent.

Fourth, depending upon how knowledgeable the interviewee is, the paralegal obtains information on the decedent's wealth. Financial questions are posed; for example, how much property was owned by the decedent and what is its value? This includes real estate, bank accounts, investments, cars, collections, and so on. In addition, questions regarding how the ownership was held should be asked. For example, was the property owned severally or concurrently with someone who had survivorship rights? Another good question is, were there were any liens or mortgages on the property? Questions about liabilities are asked. Creditors' names, addresses, amounts owed, and the basis of the claims are discussed. If the individual present does not possess the information, the law firm must obtain it through other family members and friends of the decedent, or by other means.

Fifth, a variety of other miscellaneous issues are covered. Does the client anticipate a will contest from a disgruntled heir? Are any inter vivos trusts in existence? Did the decedent have life insurance, pension plans, or a 401(k) retirement fund? If the decedent lived alone, is the house secure? Does a minor child or unemployed spouse need financial assistance while the estate is being administered?

During the initial conference, one additional consideration should be kept in mind. The individual may be grieving the loss of a loved one. The paralegal should be prepared for the possibility of tears. Remember to remain professional, supportive, and sympathetic to the person's concerns and fears.

The interviewee is encouraged to ask questions throughout the interview. In the estate administration interview, the law firm can typically anticipate three questions that the interviewee will ask:

1. How much will the estate administration cost?
2. How long will the estate administration take?
3. I am supposed to inherit. When will I get my money or property?

A paralegal cannot ethically answer the first question. To answer it, the paralegal would be setting fees, which only an attorney is allowed to do. The answer depends on so many variables that it usually cannot be answered here. The variables includehow complicated the estate administration will be, the amount that is charged in the jurisdiction, and the amount the particular attorney who is working on the case earns. Estate administration is typically billed on a per-hour basis. The attorney quotes his or her hourly rate. However long it takes to finish the estate administration is then factored into the hourly rate and the final bill is calculated. Some law firms might charge a flat fee to complete the estate administration, for example, $5,000.00. In some states, statutory law sets the fee that an attorney may charge. Typically, the fee is set at a percentage value of the gross estate or must be at a reasonable rate. Your state law should be consulted. An estate administration is not done on a contingent-fee arrangement because there is no money to win from an opponent.

A paralegal should defer the second question and its answer to the attorney. The answer about the time it takes to administer the estate depends on many factors. Is the estate administration procedure going to be done by a summary settlement, informal probate procedure, or formal probate procedure? Does real estate need to be sold? Is a will contest or fighting among heirs or beneficiaries anticipated? Are there complicated tax matters involved? If closing tax certificates are required from the state or federal government, the probate will probably take at least six months. States often have laws requiring deadlines for certain documents. Knowledge of these deadlines is helpful in determining an estimated completion time. After working in this area for awhile, the legal professional gets a sense for how long an estate administration takes.

Once the interviewee hears the estate may take one year or more to finish, he or she is fearful that the receipt of the inheritance, the subject of the third question, may also take a year or more. Again a "depends" answer is most appropriate. Creditors and taxes must be paid before anyone inherits anything. Different styles may be used by different attorneys with regard to inheritance. Consult with your employer/attorney regarding the law firm's preference. The attorney should answer this question. If it is a small article of personal property and the property does not need to be sold to pay creditors or taxes, the item can be delivered to the heir or beneficiary relatively early in the estate administration process.

Let's say the individual is to receive a sum of money in the amount of $50,000.00. The timing for the beneficiary to receive the money depends on many factors. Is this sum of money already in a bank account or in investments that can be easily sold, or is it tied up in a parcel of real estate to be sold? If it is relatively liquid, no problems exist with creditors or taxes, and no fights among heirs or beneficiaries are anticipated, the attorney might authorize a disbursement before the closing of the estate. Partial distribution of assets may be allowed. Of course, if your state places restrictions on this, you must abide by the law. If the law does not restrict a partial distribution, the attorney would advise the recipient that the money might need to be paid back to the estate if an unsuspected creditor's claim or tax problem arises. Therefore, the individual may not have to wait to receive the property until the estate administration procedure is completed. An heir or beneficiary must sign a receipt or similar document indicating the acceptance of the distribution. Again the practice varies among attorneys. The law firm's rules and any state laws in connection with partial distribution must be followed.

Initial Action of the Law Firm

Provided the interview goes well and the person decides to hire the law firm to represent the estate, the law firm then begins preparation of the initial documents and other tasks required to commence the estate administration. The law firm creates a client file, and an agreement setting forth the fee and services to be provided by the law firm is signed by both the client and attorney. The estate administration procedure is now underway.

Compile Financial Information

The individual who initially meets with the law firm may provide some financial information regarding the decedent, and this person is certainly the first place to start to acquire financial information. Depending on the interviewee's relationship to the decedent or the decedent's preparation of documents listing assets and liabilities, the law firm may gain a great deal of knowledge or very little from the initial client conference. How the law firm receives financial information and records can vary from case to case. Sometimes the firm receives precise accountings; other times, a lot of paperwork must be sorted through to determine the decedent's financial holdings. The law firm may receive all paperwork found in the decedent's desk or fireproof safe, in which case, the paralegal must sort out the important documents from the extraneous ones. The law firm may receive computer printouts of business records, tax returns, bank statements, and so on. This information must be validated, compiled, and analyzed. The compilation of financial information can be relatively easy or daunting. A paralegal who is organized and familiar with the estate administration procedure is a great asset to the law firm at this time.

After a new client has delivered to the law firm all the relevant documents, the law firm must check into all the financial information provided. Telephone calls and written correspondence are used to locate financial information. Letters are sent to banks, insurance companies, stockbrokers, and others who have knowledge of the decedent's assets. For example, a letter sent to a bank inquires about the decedent's accounts that the law firm is aware of, the balance in the accounts as of the date of death, the account numbers, who had title to the accounts, and if the decedent had any other accounts at the bank that the law firm should know about. (See Figure 7-2.)

Why is collecting financial information an initial step? It takes time to gather all the financial information. The financial information is required to prepare the inventory for the estate, which is discussed in Chapter 8. The inventory must contain a list of the decedent's assets and the date-of-death values of these assets.

Determine Heirs and/or Beneficiaries

The law firm must determine the heirs and/or beneficiaries of the estate. Through the interview process, a good understanding can be acquired. If a will exists, the attorney reads it and determines the beneficiaries. The attorney or paralegal should also ask the interviewee about the decedent's heirs. This information is vital if the decedent died intestate. Not all heirs must be determined; however, those first and second in line to inherit should be discovered and named. A paralegal who is knowledgeable about the state statutes of descent and distribution can successfully determine the identity of those individuals.

Figure 7-2   Correspondence inquiring about a decedent's bank accounts

---

Ramthun and Pratt
219 Courthouse Road
Waukesha, WI 53186
(262) 999-8305

July 20, 2006

ABC Bank
123 Financial Lane
Waukesha, WI 53186

Re: Timothy Benson, deceased
       Date of Death: July 3, 2006
       Checking Account Number: 003421

Dear Sir or Madam:

Please be informed that our law firm has been retained to represent the Estate of Timothy Benson. Mr. Benson died on July 3, 2006. According to our records, he possessed a non-interest-bearing checking account at your bank, account number 003421. Please provide us with the checking account's balance on July 3, 2006.

According to our information, Mr. Benson did not possess any other accounts at your bank. We would greatly appreciate if you would verify this information as accurate. In the event that Mr. Benson had other accounts at your financial institution, please provide us with the following information: type of account, account number, how the account was titled, and the account balance with any accrued interest as of the date of death.

Thank you in advance for your cooperation. If you have any questions, please feel free to contact me.

Sincerely,

Attorney Frank Pratt

Along with the beneficiaries' and heirs' names, additional information must be learned. A beneficiary's or heir's address, telephone number, social security number, and relationship to the decedent should all be gathered. If an heir was disinherited or is disgruntled with the amount given to him or her, the law firm needs to be aware of the possibility or likelihood of a will contest. Information regarding beneficiaries and heirs is required to complete the initial court document to begin the estate administration: the petition. Most states require all interested persons to be named in the petition. These people are entitled to information regarding the progress of the estate. The interested persons are advised of court hearings and receive copies of a variety of the documents filed with the probate court.

Prepare Petition

petition
A document that initiates a legal proceeding.

As with many legal cases, a **petition** begins the legal process in the court. A petition or application for estate administration initiates the probate. Different types of petitions are used, depending on whether formal or informal administration has been selected or whether it is a testate versus intestate case. The petitions have several names, including petition for formal administration; application for probate and letters; petition for probate of a will; and petition for adjudication of intestacy, determination of heirs, and formal appointment of personal representative. Each state prescribes its own procedure. You must research and be knowledgeable about the correct documents. Some states have standard fill-in-the-blank forms to be completed, while others require the law firm to prepare a computer-generated petition. Many states have their own websites listing all of the estate administration forms. For example, Wisconsin forms are found at www.courts.state.wi.us. Another great website is findlaw.com. A visit to your local probate register or clerk of courts probate division is another way to acquire the appropriate forms for each estate administration case.

The petition is usually very straightforward and not difficult to draft or complete. The information can be gathered from the family or future personal representative with ease. Certain information is needed in the petition, which is discussed in the following subsections.

1. A Caption

caption
The top section of a court document.

The **caption** contains the jurisdiction and venue of the appropriate court. It requires the decedent's name and may require the date of death. The name of the document is also included in this section. The court's file number or case number is included. Some states' captions require more information, such as the applicant's name and address, and the attorney's name, address, and bar number. This information may not be required in the caption in some states' petitions, but it could be included in other sections of the petition for those states.

2. The Body

The body of the petition can vary widely in its organization, but most states require similar information. The petition includes the decedent's name, date of death, age, and address. It includes information regarding the named executor or person proposed to be the administrator, such as name, address, and relationship to the decedent. Bond information may be included. The value of the estate is listed. Some petitions require a lot of detail about the decedent's property, and others just want an estimated dollar figure. The interested persons, beneficiaries, or heirs are named, and their addresses and relationships are included. Some petitions require the date of birth if the interested person is a minor. Many require information about a surviving spouse. Finally, a discussion about the will and/or codicil and its date is stated, or an indication that the person did not have a will is mentioned. These items are most often found in the body of a petition.

3. The Closing

The closing of the petition also varies from jurisdiction to jurisdiction. It demands the precise relief sought. It asks for the will to be admitted to probate or for the court to grant intestate administration of the estate. It also requests the court appointment of the personal representative and the issuance of letters of appointment.

The closing contains a signature line for the petitioner or applicant, a space for the individual's address, and a date line. The end of the document may ask for information regarding the estate's attorney, address, and bar number. Finally a jurat may be included. In this situation, the petitioner's signature must be notarized. A sample standardized form from Colorado is included in Figure 7-3. Compare this form to the computer-generated petition from Illinois in Figure 7-4.

Prepare Other Court Documentation

The petition or application is the initial document prepared by the law firm to begin the estate administration. If the decedent died leaving a valid will, the will is filed with the petition in the appropriate court office. Some other initial court documents are prepared to effectuate the court appointment of the personal representative. Each state varies concerning the documents that must be prepared and filed with the court. Knowledge of your state's procedure is a must.

The following discussion includes some of the main documents that may be required. It is possible your state could require others as well. Some of the documents are:

1. Proof of heirship.
2. Notice for hearing.
3. Oath.
4. Bond.
5. Orders: order admitting will or order for administration, order of heirship, and order issuing letters of appointment.

1. Proof of Heirship

Because it is a court document, the **proof of heirship** contains a caption. Some states have preprinted forms, and other states require the law firm to generate the document. The proof of heirship outlines the decedent's family tree, and it names the closest relatives. The proof of heirship includes each relative's name, address, and relationship to the decedent. It should indicate if the relative is living or deceased and adult or minor. The form is completed whether the decedent died testate or intestate. The court wants to be informed about the natural objects of the decedent's bounty and to track those individuals who would by statute have rights to the decedent's estate. It informs the court of the overall picture of the decedent's family. Remember, the decedent may have altered the statutory preference of inheritance by executing a will or trust. This document alerts the court to any potential problems that may arise from a disinherited or disgruntled heir. See Wisconsin's standard fill-in-the-blank proof of heirship in Figure 7-5 and Illinois's computer-generated proof of heirship in Figure 7-6.

proof of heirship
A court document that lists the decedent's heirs.

Figure 7-3   Colorado's petition

☐ District Court ☐ Denver Probate Court _____ County, Colorado Court Address: **IN THE MATTER OF THE ESTATE OF:** **Deceased**	
Attorney or Party Without Attorney (Name and Address):	▲ **COURT USE ONLY** ▲ Case Number:
Phone Number: E-mail: FAX Number: Atty. Reg. #:	Division Courtroom

**PETITION FOR FORMAL PROBATE OF WILL
AND FORMAL APPOINTMENT OF PERSONAL REPRESENTATIVE**

1. Petitioner, (Name) _____
   as _____, is an interested person. (§15-10-201, C.R.S.)

2. The decedent died on the date of _____, at the age of _____ years,
   domiciled in the City of _____, County of _____, State of _____.

3. Venue for this proceeding is proper in this county because the decedent:

   ☐ was a domiciliary of this county on the date of death.
   ☐ was not a domiciliary of Colorado, but property of the decedent was located in this county on the date of death.

4. ☐ No personal representative has been appointed by a Court in this state or elsewhere.
   ☐ A personal representative of the decedent has been appointed by a Court in this state or elsewhere as shown on the
      attached explanation. (§15-12-301, C.R.S.)

5. Petitioner:

   ☐ has not received a demand for notice and is unaware of any demand for notice of any probate or appointment
      proceeding concerning the decedent that may have been filed in this state or elsewhere.
   ☐ has received, or is aware of, a demand for notice. See attached demand or explanation.

6. The date of decedent's last will is _____. The dates of all codicils are _____
   _____.

   The will and any codicils are referred to as the will. The will:

   ☐ was deposited with this Court before the decedent's death. (§15-11-515, C.R.S.)
   ☐ has been lodged with this Court since the decedent's death. (§15-11-516, C.R.S.)
   ☐ is filed with this petition.
   ☐ has been probated in the State of _____. Authenticated copies of the will and of the
      statement probating it are filed with this petition. (§15-12-402, C.R.S.)
   ☐ is lost, destroyed, or otherwise unavailable. See attached explanation. (§15-12-402, C.R.S.)

7. Except as may be disclosed on an attached explanation and after the exercise of reasonable diligence, petitioner is
   unaware of any instrument revoking the will, is unaware of any prior wills which have not been expressly revoked by a later
   instrument, and believes that the will is the decedent's last will and was validly executed.

8. ☐ No statutory time limitation applies to the commencement of these proceedings. (§15-12-108, C.R.S.)
   ☐ More than 3 years have passed since decedent's death. A statutory time limitation would apply to the commencement
      of these proceedings except for the circumstances described in an attachment to this petition.

9. _____
   Name, address, and telephone number of the nominee for Personal Representative

   is 21 years of age or older, and has priority for appointment because of:

CPC 9   R7/04   PETITION FOR FORMAL PROBATE OF WILL AND   Page 1 of 2
               FORMAL APPOINTMENT OF PERSONAL REPRESENTATIVE
This form conforms in substance to CPC 9.

(continued)

Figure 7-3   (continued)

☐ nomination by the will.
☐ statutory priority. (§15-12-203, C.R.S.)
☐ reasons stated in the attached explanation.

10. The nominee is to serve:

☐ without bond   ☐ in unsupervised administration
☐ with bond (§15-12-604, C.R.S.)   ☐ in supervised administration

11. The decedent ☐ was ☐ was not   married at time of death.

12. Listed below are the names and addresses of decedent's spouse, children, heirs and devisees, and the names and addresses of guardians or conservators of incapacitated or protected persons. (See instructions below.)

NAME (Include spouse, if any)	ADDRESS (or date of death)	AGE AND DATE OF BIRTH OF MINORS (or nature of disability)	INTEREST AND RELATIONSHIP (See instructions)

PETITIONER REQUESTS that the Court set a time and place of hearing; that notice be given to all interested persons as provided by law; that after notice and hearing, the Court determine the heirs of the decedent and formally admit the decedent's will to probate; that the nominee:

☐ be formally appointed as personal representative   ☐ be formally confirmed as personal representative
☐ without bond   ☐ with bond
☐ in unsupervised administration   ☐ in supervised administration (additional fee required)

and that Letters Testamentary be issued to the personal representative or confirmed. Petitioner also requests:

☐ a setting aside of prior informal findings as to testacy,
☐ a setting aside of prior informal appointment of personal representative,
☐ _____

_____   _____   _____   _____
Signature of Attorney for Petitioner   Date   Signature of Petitioner   Date
(Type or Print name below)   (Type or Print name, address and telephone # below)

_____   _____

                                                            _____

                                                            _____

                                                            _____

INSTRUCTIONS FOR PARAGRAPH 12:

Include any statements of legal disability or other incapacity required by Rule 10, C.R.P.P.

List the names and dates of death of any deceased devisees. (See applicable antilapse statute, §§15-11-601 and 603, C.R.S.)

Where a listed person is an heir, detail the relationship to the decedent which creates heirship. Examples: son, daughter of pre-deceased son. (§§15-11-101 to 114, C.R.S.)

Attach additional sheets if necessary.

CPC 9 R7/04   PETITION FOR FORMAL PROBATE OF WILL AND   Page 2 of 2
               FORMAL APPOINTMENT OF PERSONAL REPRESENTATIVE
This form conforms in substance to CPC 9.

Source: Used by permission of the Supreme Court State of Colorado.

Figure 7-4   Illinois's petition

STATE OF ILLINOIS
IN THE CIRCUIT COURT
OF THE SEVENTEENTH
JUDICIAL CIRCUIT
COUNTY OF WINNEBAGO

IN THE MATTER OF THE ESTATE OF   )
)
Robert A. Benson,   )   No.
)
Deceased.   )
)
)

PETITION FOR PROBATE OF WILL AND FOR TESTAMENTARY LETTERS

Ruth A. Benson, on oath states:

1. Robert A. Benson, whose place of residence at the time of death was: 1234 Bluebird Road, Rockford, Winnebago County, Illinois, died August 12, 2006, in Rockford, Illinois, leaving a Will dated February 5, 1994, which the petitioner believes to be the valid last Will of the testator.
2. Estimated value of the estate in Illinois: Real and Personal $500,000.00; Income from real estate—NONE.
3. The names and post office addresses of the testator's heirs and legatees are:

Ruth A. Benson	Spouse	H/L Adult	1234 Bluebird Road Rockford, IL 61103
Samuel Benson	Son	H/L Adult	564 Robin Lane Rockford, IL 61103
Sarah Hart	Daughter	H/L Adult	798 Blackbird Lane Rockford, IL 61103
Julie Benson	Daughter	H Adult	652 Pierce Drive Dallas, TX 12561
Timothy Benson	Brother	H/L Adult	12 Jameson Lane Rockford, IL 61104

4. The testator nominated as Executrix the following, qualified and willing to act:

Ruth A. Benson   1234 Bluebird Road
                                      Rockford, IL 61103

(continued)

Figure 7-4   (continued)

Petitioner asks that the Will be admitted to probate and testamentary letters issued.

_____
Ruth A. Benson
1234 Bluebird Road
Rockford, Illinois 61103

SUBSCRIBED and SWORN to
Before me this _____ day of
_____, 20 ___.

_____
        Notary Public
        My commission expires: _____

Carrie L. Smith
Attorney for the Estate
Attorney No. 5858
8755 Glacier Drive
Byron, Illinois 61010
(815) 555-1212

---

2. Notice for Hearing

This step varies greatly from jurisdiction to jurisdiction. The laws of the state must be consulted. It may also depend upon whether formal or informal probate is chosen. An initial hearing on the estate administration may be scheduled. If the hearing is required, notice must be sent to the interested persons named in the petition. The document includes a caption and the subject matter of the hearing. See California's notice of petition to administer estate in Figure 7-7 and Wisconsin's order setting time to hear petition for administration and notice to creditors in Figure 7-8.

The hearings themselves also vary. Some may require witnesses to the will to testify to prove it is genuine and the testator had testamentary capacity. Some hearings require proof of heirship information to be entered on the record during the hearing. Some may question the personal representative and make certain the individual is willing and able to serve. In California, the court could require a witness to attend and give testimony on several matters, including:

(1) The time, place, and manner of the decedent's death. (2) The place of the decedent's domicile and residence at the time of death. (3) The character and value of the decedent's property. (4) Whether or not the decedent left a will; Cal. Prob. Code § 8005.

Figure 7-5   Wisconsin's proof of heirship

STATE OF WISCONSIN, CIRCUIT COURT, _____ COUNTY	*For Official Use*

IN THE MATTER OF THE ESTATE OF

_____

_____   Case No. _____

Proof of Heirship
☐ **Informal**
☐ **Formal**

Under oath, I answer the following questions:

---

1. What is your name, address and relationship to the decedent?

Name   Address   Relationship

---

2. Was the decedent survived by a spouse?   ☐ Yes ☐ No
    If YES, give name:

3a. Did the decedent have any children?   ☐ Yes ☐ No
    (living or deceased; natural or adopted)
        If YES, list all names: (If deceased, indicate date of death.)
    Name

3b. For each deceased child in 3a, list his or her name and the names of his or her children (living or deceased; natural or adopted). If any of his or her children are deceased, indicate the date of death of that child and his or her descendants (living or deceased; natural or adopted).   ☐ See attached schedules.
    Name

4. If there is a surviving spouse, are all of the decedent's children listed
    in 3a, also the children of the surviving spouse?   ☐ Yes ☐ No
    If NO, give details:

Instructions:
Are there living persons listed in answers to questions 2 through 4?
• If yes, go to question 8.
• If no, go to question 5.

PR-1806, 10/00 Proof of Heirship (Informal and Formal Administration)   §§852.01 and 863.23, Wisconsin Statutes
This form shall not be modified. It may be supplemented with additional material.
Page 1 of 2

(continued)

Figure 7-5   (continued)

| **Proof of Heirship** | Page 2 of 2 | Case No. _____ |

---

5. Did the decedent leave surviving parents?   ☐ Yes ☐ No
     If YES, list names:
   <u>Name</u>

6a. Did the decedent have brothers or sisters?   ☐ Yes ☐ No
    (living or deceased; whole blood, half blood, adopted)
        If YES, list all names: (If deceased, indicate date of death.)
    <u>Name</u>

6b. For each deceased brother or sister in 6a, list his or her name and the names of his or her children (living or
    deceased; natural or adopted). If any of his or her children is deceased, indicate the date of death of that child
    and his or her descendants (living or deceased; natural or adopted).   ☐ See attached schedules.
    <u>Name</u>

7. If there are no living persons listed in questions 2 through 6, list names and trace the relationship of any other
    persons related to the decedent on the decedent's paternal (father) side and the decedent's maternal (mother)
    side: ☐ See attached schedules.
    <u>Name</u>   <u>Explain Relationship</u>

8. Did any of the persons named in questions 2 through 7
    die within 120 hours after the death of the decedent?   ☐ Yes ☐ No
        If YES, list names:
    <u>Name</u>

Subscribed and sworn to before me
on _____

_____
Formal: Court Official
Informal: Notary Public/Court Official

My commission expires: _____

_____
Signature

_____
Name Printed or Typed

_____
Date

Name of Attorney	Telephone Number
Address	

PR-1806, 10/00 Proof of Heirship (Informal and Formal Administration)   §§852.01 and 863.23, Wisconsin Statutes
This form shall not be modified. It may be supplemented with additional material.
Page 2 of 2

Source: For the most current version of this form, visit www.wicourts.gov.

Figure 7-6   Illinois's computer-generated proof of heirship

STATE OF ILLINOIS
IN THE CIRCUIT COURT OF THE SEVENTEENTH JUDICIAL CIRCUIT
COUNTY OF WINNEBAGO

IN THE MATTER OF THE ESTATE OF	)	
	)	
Robert A. Benson,	)	
	)	Case No.
Deceased.	)	
STATE OF ILLINOIS	)	
	) SS	**PROOF OF HEIRSHIP**
COUNTY OF WINNEBAGO	)	

Ruth A. Benson, being duly sworn upon oath, deposes and says:

I reside at 1234 Bluebird Road, Rockford, Illinois 61103. I am the spouse of the decedent, Robert A. Benson, who died on August 12, 2006, in Rockford, Illinois.

The decedent was married once in his lifetime. Three children were born as a result of this marriage, namely:

1. Julie Benson who is a living adult;
2. Samuel Benson who is a living adult;
3. Sarah Benson a/k/a (also known as) Sarah Hart who is a living adult.

Parents of the decedent were Charles and Agnes Benson, who are both deceased. Two children were born as a result of this marriage, namely:

1. Robert A. Benson, decedent herein;
2. Timothy Benson who is a living adult.

_____
Ruth A. Benson

SUBSCRIBED and SWORN to
Before me this _____ day of
_____, 20____.

_____
     Notary Public
     My commission expires: _____

Carrie L. Smith
Attorney for the Estate
Attorney No. 5858
8755 Glacier Drive
Byron, Illinois 61010
(815) 555-1212

Figure 7-7   California's notice of petition to administer estate (Courtesy of California Judicial Branch.)

DE-121

ATTORNEY OR PARTY WITHOUT ATTORNEY *(Name, State Bar number, and address)*:

FOR COURT USE ONLY

TELEPHONE NO.: FAX NO. *(Optional)*:
E-MAIL ADDRESS *(Optional)*:
ATTORNEY FOR *(Name)*:

SUPERIOR COURT OF CALIFORNIA, COUNTY OF
STREET ADDRESS:
MAILING ADDRESS:
CITY AND ZIP CODE:
BRANCH NAME:

ESTATE OF *(Name)*:

DECEDENT

NOTICE OF PETITION TO ADMINISTER ESTATE OF
(Name):

CASE NUMBER:

1. To all heirs, beneficiaries, creditors, contingent creditors, and persons who may otherwise be interested in the will or estate, or both, of *(specify all names by which the decedent was known)*:

2. A **Petition for Probate** has been filed by *(name of petitioner)*: in the Superior Court of California, County of *(specify)*:

3. The Petition for Probate requests that *(name)*: be appointed as personal representative to administer the estate of the decedent.

4. ☐ The petition requests the decedent's will and codicils, if any, admitted to probate. The will and any codicils are available for examination in the file kept by the court.

5. ☐ The petition requests authority to administer the estate under the Independent Administration of Estates Act. (This authority will allow the personal representative to take many actions without obtaining court approval. Before taking certain very important actions, however, the personal representative will be required to give notice to interested persons unless they have waived notice or consented to the proposed action.) The independent administration authority will be granted unless an interested person files an objection to the petition and shows good cause why the court should not grant the authority.

6. **A hearing on the petition will be held in this court as follows:**
   a. Date: Time: Dept.: Room:
   b. Address of court: ☐ same as noted above ☐ other *(specify)*:

7. **If you object** to the granting of the petition, you should appear at the hearing and state your objections or file written objections with the court before the hearing. Your appearance may be in person or by your attorney.

8. **If you are a creditor or a contingent creditor of the decedent**, you must file your claim with the court and mail a copy to the personal representative appointed by the court within four months from the date of first issuance of letters as provided in Probate Code section 9100. The time for filing claims will not expire before four months from the hearing date noticed above.

9. **You may examine the file kept by the court.** If you are a person interested in the estate, you may file with the court a *Request for Special Notice* (form DE-154) of the filing of an inventory and appraisal of estate assets or of any petition or account as provided in Probate Code section 1250. A *Request for Special Notice* form is available from the court clerk.

10. ☐ Petitioner ☐ Attorney for petitioner *(name)*:

(Address):

(Telephone):

NOTE: If this notice is published, print the caption, beginning with the words NOTICE OF PETITION TO ADMINISTER ESTATE, and do not print the information from the form above the caption. The caption and the decedent's name must be printed in at least 8-point type and the text in at least 7-point type. Print the case number as part of the caption. Print items preceded by a box only if the box is checked. Do not print the italicized instructions in parentheses, the paragraph numbers, the mailing information, or the material on page 2.

Page 1 of 2

Form Adopted for Mandatory Use
Judicial Council of California
DE-121 [Rev. January 1, 2006]

NOTICE OF PETITION TO ADMINISTER ESTATE
(Probate—Decedents' Estates)

Probate Code, § 8100
www.courtinfo.ca.gov

American LegalNet, Inc.
www.USCourtForms.com

(continued)

Figure 7-7   (continued)

DE-121

ESTATE OF *(Name):*	CASE NUMBER:
DECEDENT	

PROOF OF SERVICE BY MAIL

1. I am over the age of 18 and not a party to this cause. I am a resident of or employed in the county where the mailing occurred.
2. My residence or business address is *(specify):*

3. I served the foregoing *Notice of Petition to Administer Estate* on each person named below by enclosing a copy in an envelope addressed as shown below **AND**

   a. ☐ **depositing** the sealed envelope with the United States Postal Service on the date and at the place shown in item 4, with the postage fully prepaid.

   b. ☐ **placing** the envelope for collection and mailing on the date and at the place shown in item 4 following our ordinary business practices. I am readily familiar with this business's practice for collecting and processing correspondence for mailing. On the same day that correspondence is placed for collection and mailing, it is deposited in the ordinary course of business with the United States Postal Service, in a sealed envelope with postage fully prepaid.

4. a. Date mailed: b. Place mailed *(city, state):*

5. ☐ I served, with the *Notice of Petition to Administer Estate*, a copy of the petition or other document referred to in the notice.

I declare under penalty of perjury under the laws of the State of California that the foregoing is true and correct.

Date:

▶

_____   _____
(TYPE OR PRINT NAME OF PERSON COMPLETING THIS FORM)   (SIGNATURE OF PERSON COMPLETING THIS FORM)

NAME AND ADDRESS OF EACH PERSON TO WHOM NOTICE WAS MAILED

	Name of person served	Address *(number, street, city, state, and zip code)*
1.		
2.		
3.		
4.		
5.		
6.		

☐ Continued on an attachment. *(You may use form DE-121(MA) to show additional persons served.)*

Assistive listening systems, computer-assisted real-time captioning, or sign language interpreter services are available upon request if at least 5 days notice is provided. Contact the clerk's office for *Request for Accommodations by Persons With Disabilities and Order* (form MC-410). (Civil Code section 54.8.)

DE-121 [Rev. January 1, 2006]   **NOTICE OF PETITION TO ADMINISTER ESTATE**   Page 2 of 2
(Probate—Decedents' Estates)

Figure 7-8   Wisconsin's order setting time to hear petition for administration and notice to creditors

STATE OF WISCONSIN, CIRCUIT COURT, _____ COUNTY		*For Official Use*
IN THE MATTER OF THE ESTATE OF _____ _____ Case No. _____	**Order Setting Time to Hear Petition for Administration and Heirship and Notice to Creditors**	

A petition has been filed for administration of the estate and determination of heirship of the decedent, whose date of birth was _____ and date of death was _____. The decedent died domiciled in _____ County, State of _____, with a post office address of :

_____

IT IS ORDERED THAT:

1. The petition be heard at the _____ County Courthouse, _____, Wisconsin, Room _____, before _____ Court Official, on _____ at _____ or when scheduled thereafter.
   Date   Time

2. Heirship will be determined on the date set for hearing on the final account.

   You need not appear unless you object. The petition may be granted if no objection is made.

3. Creditor's claims must be filed with the court on or before _____.
   Date

4. Publication of this notice shall constitute notice to any persons whose names or addresses are unknown.
   **The names or post office addresses of the following persons interested (if any) are not known or reasonably ascertainable: _____

*Notice shall be given by publication of this notice once a week for three consecutive weeks in the following newspaper: _____.
The first publication date shall be within 15 days from the date of this notice; AND

1. By mailing, at least 20 days before the hearing, a copy of this notice and a copy of the will to every person entitled to notice; OR
2. By personal service, at least 10 days before the hearing.

* The personal representative is responsible for mailing this notice to all known or reasonably ascertainable creditors.

If you need help in this matter because of a disability, please call: ☐ **Please check with attorney/petitioner below for exact time and date.**	**BY THE COURT:** _____ Circuit Court Judge/Court Commissioner
Name of Attorney	_____ Name Printed or Typed
Address	_____ Date
Telephone Number	Bar Number

*Notice to Printers - DO NOT PRINT this text when publishing notice. **DO NOT PRINT this text if left blank.
PR-1903, 12/01 Order Setting Time to Hear Petition for Administration and Heirship and Notice to Creditors   §§856.11, 859.07, 879.03, and 879.05, Wisconsin Statutes
This form shall not be modified. It may be supplemented with additional material.

Source: For the most current version of this form, visit www.wicourts.gov.

3. Oath

Another initial court document may be an oath, consent to serve, or acceptance of appointment document signed by the executor or administrator. Many states require the personal representative to take an oath prior to issuance of the letters of appointment. A Washington statute states:

> Before letters testamentary or of administration are issued, each personal representative or an officer of a bank or trust company qualified to act as a personal representative, must take and subscribe an oath, before some person authorized to administer oaths, that the duties of the trust as personal representative will be performed according to law, which oath must be filed in the cause. Wash. Rev. Code Ann. § 11.28.170.

A Washington case held that the alleged personal representative could not accept service of process on behalf of the estate. She had petitioned the probate court for appointment but had not yet complied with a court order to file a bond and her oath. The court had concluded that because not all requirements were fulfilled, and the letters of administration had not been issued, she was not the personal representative for the estate and had no authority to accept the service of process. See *Williams-Moore v. Estate of Shaw*, 122 Wash. App. 871, 96 P. 3d 433 (2004).

The document, containing a caption, indicates that the person is willing to serve and includes a promise to act in a trustworthy, fiduciary capacity. See North Carolina's oath in Figure 7-9. Some states may combine this document with the bond. See Illinois's oath and bond form in Figure 7-10.

4. Bond

bond
Required by the court to be filed by the personal representative to ensure proper performance of duties.

States usually require **bond** of the personal representative. Consider Wis. Stat. § 856.25 (1):

> A person shall not act as personal representative, nor shall letters be issued to the person until the person has given a bond . . . with one or more sureties, conditioned on the faithful performance of the person's duties, to the judge of the court, or until the court has ordered that the person be appointed without being required to give bond.

Chapter 6 includes a lengthy discussion regarding bond.

The bond document contains a caption and indicates the amount of the bond, the name and address of the surety, and often a jurat. See Colorado's bond of personal representative in Figure 7-11.

You may recall from Chapter 4 that one advantage to executing a will is that the testator may waive bond. Different states may apply this law differently. Consider Wis. Stat. § 856.25 (4):

> A direction or request in a will that the personal representative serve without bond is not binding on the court.

If bond is waived, another type of form may be required to be filed with the court. See North Carolina's waiver of personal representative bond in Figure 7-12.

5. Orders

order
A court ruling on an issue raised during a proceeding.

After the initial papers have been filed, the court may issue a variety of orders. The orders are prepared by the law firm for the judge's signature. A petition is the law firm's application to the court for some type of action; the **order** is the court's determination regarding the action requested. The court grants or denies the request. In this step of estate administration, three main types of orders may be issued: orders admitting the

Figure 7-9   North Carolina's oath

STATE OF NORTH CAROLINA

_____ County

File No.

In The General Court Of Justice
Superior Court Division
Before The Clerk

IN THE MATTER OF THE ESTATE OF:
Name Of Decedent/Minor/Incompetent/Trust

OATH/AFFIRMATION

N.C. Constitution, Art. VI., Sec. 7; G.S.11-7, 11-11; 28A-7-1

I, the undersigned, do solemnly ☐ swear ☐ affirm that I will support and maintain the Constitution and laws of the United States, and the Constitution and laws of North Carolina not inconsistent therewith; that I will be faithful and bear true allegiance to the State of North Carolina, and to the constitutional powers and authorities which are or may be established for the government thereof; and that I will endeavor to support, maintain and defend the Constitution of said State, not inconsistent with the Constitution of the United States, to the best of my knowledge and ability; and that I will faithfully discharge the duties of my office as indicated below;
☐ so help me, God. ☐ and this is my solemn affirmation.

(check office below)

☐ **OATH OF ADMINISTRATOR**

I ☐ swear ☐ affirm that I believe that the above named decedent died without leaving any Last Will and Testament; that I will well and truly administer all and singular the goods and chattels, rights and credits of the deceased and a true and perfect inventory thereof return according to law; and that all other duties appertaining to the charge reposed in me, I will well and truly perform, according to law and with my best skill and ability;
☐ so help me, God. ☐ and this is my solemn affirmation.

☐ **OATH OF EXECUTOR**

I ☐ swear ☐ affirm that I believe this paper writing to be and contain the Last Will and Testament of the above named decedent; and that I will well and truly execute the same by first paying the decedent's debts and then the decedent's legacies; as far as the said estate shall extend or the law shall charge me; and that I will well and faithfully execute the office of an executor, agreeably to the trust and confidence reposed in me, and according to law; ☐ so help me, God. ☐ and this is my solemn affirmation.

☐ **OATH OF ADMINISTRATOR CTA**

I ☐ swear ☐ affirm that I believe this paper writing to be and contain the Last Will and Testament of the above named decedent; and that I will well and truly execute the same by first paying the decedent's debts and then the decedent's legacies, as far as the said estate shall extend or the law shall charge me; and that I will well and faithfully execute the office of an administrator cta to the best of my skill and ability and according to the law;
☐ so help me, God. ☐ and this is my solemn affirmation.

☐ **OATH OF FIDUCIARY**

I ☐ swear ☐ affirm that I will faithfully and honestly discharge the duties reposed in me according to the best of my skill and ability, and according to law; ☐ so help me, God. ☐ and this is my solemn affirmation.

Name Of Fiduciary 1 | Name Of Fiduciary 2

Signature Of Fiduciary | Signature Of Fiduciary

☐ **SWORN** ☐**AFFIRMED AND SUBSCRIBED TO BEFORE ME** | ☐ **SWORN** ☐**AFFIRMED AND SUBSCRIBED TO BEFORE ME**

Date | Date

Signature Of Person Authorized To Administer Oaths | Signature Of Person Authorized To Administer Oaths

☐ Deputy CSC   ☐ Assistant CSC   ☐ Clerk Of Superior Court | ☐ Deputy CSC   ☐ Assistant CSC   ☐ Clerk Of Superior Court

☐ Notary | Date My Commission Expires | Date My Commission Expires | ☐ Notary

SEAL | County Where Notarized | County Where Notarized | **SEAL**

AOC-E-400, Rev. 3/07
© 2007 Administrative Office of the Courts

Original-File

Source: North Carolina Administrative Office of the Courts.

Figure 7-10 Illinois's oath and bond form

STATE OF ILLINOIS
IN THE CIRCUIT COURT
OF THE SEVENTEENTH
JUDICIAL CIRCUIT
COUNTY OF WINNEBAGO

IN THE MATTER OF THE ESTATE OF   )
)
    Robert A. Benson,   )
)   Case No.
        Deceased.   )
)

OATH AND BOND OF REPRESENTATIVE—NO SURETY

    I, Ruth A. Benson, on oath state that I will faithfully discharge the duties of the office of Representative; and I acknowledge that I am bound to the People of the State of Illinois to the faithful discharge of those duties in the amount equal to double the value from time to time of the personal estate.

_____
Ruth A. Benson
1234 Bluebird Road
Rockford, Illinois 61103

SUBSCRIBED and SWORN to
Before me this _____ day
of _____, 20 _____.

_____
    Notary Public
    My commission expires: _____

APPROVED:

_____
        JUDGE

Carrie L. Smith
Attorney for the Estate
Attorney No. 5858
8755 Glacier Drive
Byron, Illinois 61010
(815) 555-1212

Figure 7-11   Colorado's bond of personal representative

<table>
<tr><td>

☐ District Court   ☐ Denver Probate Court

_____ County, Colorado

Court Address:

_____

IN THE MATTER OF THE ESTATE OF:

☐ Deceased ☐ Protected Person

</td><td>

▲   **COURT USE ONLY**   ▲

</td></tr>
<tr><td>

Attorney or Party Without Attorney (Name and Address):

Phone Number: E-mail:

FAX Number: Atty. Reg.#:

</td><td>

Case Number:

Division   Courtroom

</td></tr>
</table>

BOND OF   ☐ PERSONAL REPRESENTATIVE   ☐ CONSERVATOR

TO WHOM IT MAY CONCERN: We, _____

(Name)

as principal, and _____ of _____

(Name)   (address)

and _____ of _____

(Name)   (address)

as surety, are held and firmly bound unto the People of the State of Colorado for the benefit of persons interested in this estate

in the penal sum of _____ Dollars,

lawful money of the United States of America, for which payment we, and each of us, do hereby bind ourselves, our heirs,

personal representatives, successors and assigns, jointly and severally.

The condition of this obligation is that if the principal, as ☐ personal representative ☐ conservator of this estate, shall

faithfully discharge the duties of such office as provided by law and orders of Court, then this obligation shall be void,

otherwise it shall be and remain in full force and effect.

Executed on _____, at _____, Colorado.

(Date)

Approved on _____

(Date)   _____

                                          Signature of Principal

_____   _____

Judge/Registrar   Signature of Principal

                                          _____

                                          Signature of Surety

                                          _____

                                          Signature of Surety

The undersigned, being sworn, states: That the ☐ value of the personal estate of the deceased ☐ aggregate capital value

of the property of the estate of the protected person in the undersigned's control, less the value of such property deposited

with the Clerk of this Court or held subject to Court order, is estimated to be $_____, and that the income

expected from the personal and real property of this estate during the next year is estimated to be $_____.

STATE OF _____   _____

                                            Signature of Principal

_____COUNTY OF _____

Subscribed and sworn to before my by _____, as Principal on _____.

My commission expires _____.

                                            _____

                                            Notary Public/(Deputy) Clerk of Court

CPC 19   R7/00   BOND OF ☐ Personal representative ☐ Conservator   1

(continued)

Figure 7-11 (continued)

JUSTIFICATION OF SURETIES

STATE OF _____

_____ COUNTY OF _____

I, (Name) _____ being sworn, state: That I reside at

_____
and am seized and possessed in my own right, over and above all my just debts, liabilities and liens, of property within the State of Colorado of a value at least equal to the penal sum of this Bond; that such property is not exempt by law from levy and sale under execution; that I have made and assigned such property to the People of the State of Colorado, as obligee, for the use and benefit of all persons interested in this estate; and that such property is described as follows:

_____   _____
Signature of Surety   Date

Subscribed and sworn to before me on _____.

My commission expires _____.

_____
Notary Public/(Deputy) Clerk of Court

CPC 19   R7/00   BOND OF ❑ Personal representative   ❑ Conservator   2

Source: Used by permission of the Supreme Court state of Colorado.

Figure 7-12   North Carolina's waiver of personal representative bond

STATE OF NORTH CAROLINA	File No. ▶
_____ County	In The General Court Of Justice Superior Court Division Before The Clerk

IN THE MATTER OF THE ESTATE OF: _Name Of Decedent_	**WAIVER OF PERSONAL REPRESENTATIVE'S BOND** G.S. 28A-8-1(b)(6)

I certify that I am an heir of the above named decedent, and I am over eighteen (18) years of age.

I waive the requirement for bond for the personal representative of this estate, who resides in the State of North Carolina, and agree to relieve him/her from the necessity of giving the statutory bond.

I understand that this means that there will be no bond to go against if the personal representative does not properly administer the estate and distribute the assets to the heirs.

I have read this Waiver, and I fully understand its meaning and effect.

Date	Signature Of Witness	Signature Of Heir
Date	Signature Of Witness	Signature Of Heir
Date	Signature Of Witness	Signature Of Heir
Date	Signature Of Witness	Signature Of Heir
Date	Signature Of Witness	Signature Of Heir
Date	Signature Of Witness	Signature Of Heir
Date	Signature Of Witness	Signature Of Heir
Date	Signature Of Witness	Signature Of Heir
Date	Signature Of Witness	Signature Of Heir
Date	Signature Of Witness	Signature Of Heir
Date	Signature Of Witness	Signature Of Heir
Date	Signature Of Witness	Signature Of Heir
Date	Signature Of Witness	Signature Of Heir
Date	Signature Of Witness	Signature Of Heir
Date	Signature Of Witness	Signature Of Heir
Date	Signature Of Witness	Signature Of Heir
Date	Signature Of Witness	Signature Of Heir
Date	Signature Of Witness	Signature Of Heir
Date	Signature Of Witness	Signature Of Heir

AOC-E-404, Rev. 4/97
© 1997 Administrative Office of the Courts   Original - File

Source: North Carolina Administrative Office of the Courts.

will or commencing intestate administration, orders of heirship, and orders issuing the letters of appointment. A state may combine the orders into one document or have separate documents for each order. A wide variety of other orders may be issued by the court at this time. Let's take a closer look at these three types of orders.

a. Orders Admitting Will or Commencing Intestate Administration

These orders contain a caption. They state that the court has agreed that the will is valid and the probate may commence, or that the decedent died intestate and the estate may be administered. In some jurisdictions, the law firm files a computer-generated document. See Illinois's order admitting will to probate and appointing executor in Figure 7-13. Other jurisdictions have standard fill-in-the-blank forms.

Figure 7-13   Illinois's order admitting will to probate and appointing executor

---

STATE OF ILLINOIS
IN THE CIRCUIT COURT
OF THE SEVENTEENTH
JUDICIAL CIRCUIT
COUNTY OF WINNEBAGO

IN THE MATTER OF THE ESTATE OF   )
)
        Robert A. Benson,   )
)   Case No. 06 P 420
            Deceased.   )
)

ORDER ADMITTING WILL TO PROBATE AND APPOINTING EXECUTOR

On the verified petition of Ruth A. Benson for admission to probate of the Will of Robert A. Benson, who died August 12, 2006.

IT IS ORDERED that the Will of Robert A. Benson dated February 5, 1994, is admitted to probate;

IT IS FURTHER ORDERED that testamentary letters be issued to Ruth A. Benson as Executrix of the ESTATE OF ROBERT A. BENSON, deceased.

_____
                                              JUDGE

ENTERED:

_____

PREPARED BY:

Carrie L. Smith
Attorney for the Estate
Attorney No. 5858
8755 Glacier Drive
Byron, Illinois 61010
(815) 555-1212

See California's order for probate in Figure 7-14. These orders must be signed and dated by the judge. Please note that the two examples in Figures 7-13 and 7-14 combine orders to admit the will and to appoint the executor.

b. Orders for Heirship   A jurisdiction may require the judge to approve the proof of heirship form and sign a document declaring heirship. This document contains a caption, states the decedent's heirs, and is signed by the judge. See Illinois's order of heirship in Figure 7-15.

c. Orders Issuing Letters of Appointment   A jurisdiction may have a separate order appointing the personal representative and stating that the letters of appointment should be issued. Containing a caption; language stating the appointment, name, and address of the personal representative; and signature of the judge, these orders are the precursors to the letters of appointment. This document can stand on its own or, as mentioned earlier, can be combined with an order approving the will. See North Carolina's order authorizing issuance of letters in Figure 7-16.

Miscellaneous Actions

As the law firm gears up to commence work on a new estate administration case, certain other miscellaneous actions must be taken. These may be done by the soon-to-be personal representative or members of the law firm, or a combination of both.

The law firm starts on a fact-finding mission to determine financial holdings and values immediately. This step was discussed earlier in this chapter. It may include letters sent to banks, stockbrokers, accountants, and so on, to address the worth of the decedent's estate. It might include correspondence to insurance companies inquiring about life insurance. The personal representative may desire the law firm to obtain receipt of any life insurance benefits. Recall from Chapter 1 that life insurance made payable to a designated beneficiary is a nonprobate asset. Working with the life insurance company, the law firm prepares the required forms, and the insurance is paid relatively quickly to the designated beneficiary. If the estate is named as the beneficiary, the funds become part of the probate estate and must go through the entire estate administration process.

Another initial step that may be taken is to locate the original will. Usually the states require it to be filed with the court within a required period of time.

If a will is not brought to the law firm by the family and the family is convinced one exists, locating the will may be a difficult task. Recall from Chapter 4 that the will is typically stored in one of four places: a safety deposit box, a lawyer's office, the courthouse, or a safe place in the decedent's home. If the will is stored in a safety deposit box, access to it may be denied until the letters of appointment are issued. After all, the decedent's valuables are located in the box, and the financial institution cannot allow another person access. However, most states allow an initial access to locate the will. State law must be researched to determine the appropriate procedure. The law firm and the petitioner must request the court to open the box for such a search. See Michigan's petition and order to open safe deposit box to locate will or burial deed in Figure 7-17. Once the order is signed by the judge and presented to the financial institution, the safety deposit box may be opened and the will may be removed. Note that access to the box is allowed in the presence of an officer of the financial institution.

Figure 7-14 California's order for probate (Courtesy of California Judicial Branch.)

DE-140

ATTORNEY OR PARTY WITHOUT ATTORNEY *(Name, state bar number, and address)*:	TELEPHONE AND FAX NOS.:	*FOR COURT USE ONLY*

ATTORNEY FOR *(Name)*:

SUPERIOR COURT OF CALIFORNIA, COUNTY OF

STREET ADDRESS:

MAILING ADDRESS:

CITY AND ZIP CODE:

BRANCH NAME:

ESTATE OF *(Name)*:

DECEDENT

ORDER FOR PROBATE	CASE NUMBER:

ORDER APPOINTING
- ☐ Executor
- ☐ Administrator with Will Annexed
- ☐ Administrator   ☐ Special Administrator

☐ Order Authorizing Independent Administration of Estate
  - ☐ with full authority   ☐ with limited authority

WARNING: THIS APPOINTMENT IS NOT EFFECTIVE UNTIL LETTERS HAVE ISSUED.

1. Date of hearing: Time: Dept./Room: Judge:

THE COURT FINDS

2. a. All notices required by law have been given.
   b. Decedent died on *(date)*:
      (1) ☐ a resident of the California county named above.
      (2) ☐ a nonresident of California and left an estate in the county named above.
   c. Decedent died
      (1) ☐ intestate
      (2) ☐ testate
      and decedent's will dated: and each codicil dated:
      was admitted to probate by Minute Order on *(date)*:

THE COURT ORDERS

3. *(Name)*:
   is appointed **personal representative**:
   a. ☐ executor of the decedent's will   d. ☐ special administrator
   b. ☐ administrator with will annexed   (1) ☐ with general powers
   c. ☐ administrator   (2) ☐ with special powers as specified in Attachment 3d(2)
                                                 (3) ☐ without notice of hearing
                                                 (4) ☐ letters will expire on *(date)*:
   and letters shall issue on qualification.

4. a. ☐ **Full authority** is granted to administer the estate under the Independent Administration of Estates Act.
   b. ☐ **Limited authority** is granted to administer the estate under the Independent Administration of Estates Act (there is no authority, without court supervision, to (1) sell or exchange real property or (2) grant an option to purchase real property or (3) borrow money with the loan secured by an encumbrance upon real property).

5. a. ☐ Bond is not required.
   b. ☐ Bond is fixed at: $ to be furnished by an authorized surety company or as otherwise provided by law.
   c. ☐ Deposits of: $ are ordered to be placed in a blocked account at *(specify institution and location)*:
      and receipts shall be filed. No withdrawals shall be made without a court order. ☐ Additional orders in Attachment 5c.
   d. ☐ The personal representative is not authorized to take possession of money or any other property without a specific court order.

6. ☐ *(Name)*:   is appointed probate referee.

Date:

_____
JUDGE OF THE SUPERIOR COURT

7. Number of pages attached: _____   ☐ SIGNATURE FOLLOWS LAST ATTACHMENT

Form Approved by the Judicial Council of California DE-140 [Rev. January 1, 1998]	**ORDER FOR PROBATE**	Probate Code, §§ 8006, 8400
		American LegalNet, Inc. www.USCourtForms.com

Figure 7-15 Illinois's order of heirship

**STATE OF ILLINOIS
IN THE CIRCUIT COURT
OF THE SEVENTEENTH
JUDICIAL CIRCUIT
COUNTY OF WINNEBAGO**

IN THE MATTER OF THE ESTATE OF)
)
Robert A. Benson,   )
) Case No.
Deceased.   )
)

ORDER OF HEIRSHIP

THIS MATTER OF HEIRSHIP coming on to be heard and the Court being fully advised in the premises, finds:

That Robert A. Benson departed this life on the 12th day of August, 2006, leaving as his heirs-at-law:

Ruth A. Benson,	Adult—Spouse
Samuel Benson,	Adult—Son
Julie Benson,	Adult—Daughter
Sarah Hart,	Adult—Daughter
Timothy Benson,	Adult—Brother

ENTERED:

_____

                                        _____

                                              JUDGE

PREPARED BY:

Carrie L. Smith
Attorney for the Estate
Attorney No. 5858
8755 Glacier Drive
Byron, Illinois 61010
(815) 555-1212

Figure 7-16 North Carolina's order authorizing issuance of letters.

STATE OF NORTH CAROLINA	*File No.*
_____ County	In The General Court Of Justice Superior Court Division Before The Clerk

IN THE MATTER OF THE ESTATE OF:	
Name Of Decedent/Minor/Incompetent/Trust	**ORDER AUTHORIZING ISSUANCE OF LETTERS** G.S. 28A-6-1; 35A-1215, -1226; 36A-107

The Court finds from the Application for Letters in the matter named above that the Fiduciary is entitled and is not disqualified to administer the estate, trust or guardianship.

Based on these findings the Court orders that Letters be issued to the Fiduciary in this matter.

Name And Address Of Fiduciary 1	*Date*
	Clerk Of Superior Court
Title Of Fiduciary 1	**EX OFFICIO JUDGE OF PROBATE**
Name And Address Of Fiduciary 2	*Date Of Issuance*
	Signature
Title Of Fiduciary 2	☐ *Assistant CSC* ☐ *Clerk Of Superior Court*

AOC-E-402, Rev. 6/04
© 2004 Administrative Office of the Courts

Source: North Carolina Administrative Office of the Courts.

Figure 7-17   Michigan's petition and order to open safe deposit box to locate will or burial deed (Courtesy of Michigan Courts.)

Approved, SCAO

OSM CODE: DBP, DBO

STATE OF MICHIGAN PROBATE COURT COUNTY OF	PETITION AND ORDER TO OPEN SAFE DEPOSIT BOX TO LOCATE WILL OR BURIAL DEED	FILE NO.

Estate of _____

PETITION

1. I am an interested person as _____ of decedent, who died _____.
   Heir, devisee, etc.   Date

2. _____ , as lessor, leased to decedent, alone or jointly, safe
   Name of bank, trust company, or safe deposit company

   deposit box number _____ , located at _____ in _____ in this
   Branch   City or township

   county, and the safe deposit box may contain decedent's will or a deed to a burial plot in which the decedent is to be interred.

3. **I REQUEST** that this court issue an order directing the lessor to permit _____
   Name

   to examine the contents of the safe deposit box in the presence of an officer or other authorized employee of lessor for the purpose of locating and removing a will and deed to a burial plot only.

I declare under the penalties of perjury that this petition has been examined by me and that its contents are true to the best of my information, knowledge, and belief.

_____
Date

_____   _____
Attorney signature   Petitioner signature

_____   _____
Name (type or print)   Bar no.   Name (type or print)

_____   _____
Address   Address

_____   _____
City, state, zip   Telephone no.   City, state, zip   Telephone no.

ORDER

IT IS ORDERED:

4. The above petition is granted and the lessor is ordered to permit _____
   to examine the above described safe deposit box in the presence of an officer or other authorized employee of the lessor. Only a will of the decedent and a deed to a burial plot shall be removed from the box and shall be delivered by the above named person to the probate register or deputy register of this court.

5. At the time of the opening of the safe deposit box, all persons in attendance shall execute a written statement certifying whether a will or deed to a burial plot was found and that no other items were removed from the safe deposit box. The person named above shall file that written statement with the probate register or deputy register of this court within 7 days of opening the box.

_____   _____
Date   Judge   Bar no.

Do not write below this line - For court use only

MCL 700.2517; MSA 27.12517

PC 551 (6/00) **PETITION AND ORDER TO OPEN SAFE DEPOSIT BOX TO LOCATE WILL OR BURIAL DEED**

(continued)

Figure 7-17 (continued)

Approved, SCAO

JIS CODE: DBC, DBR

STATE OF MICHIGAN PROBATE COURT COUNTY OF	SAFE DEPOSIT BOX CERTIFICATE AND RECEIPT	FILE NO.

Estate of _____

CERTIFICATE

1. The undersigned certify that they were present on this date at the opening of the safe deposit box number _____

   located in _____,
   Name of bank, trust or safe deposit company

   a. they ☐ did / ☐ did not   find a will of the decedent;

   b. they ☐ did / ☐ did not   find a deed to a burial plot in which decedent is to be buried;

   c. no item or items, other than such deed or will, were removed from the safe deposit box.

Signatures of others present, if any:

_____
Date

_____   _____
Signature of person named in order to examine contents of box   Signature

_____   _____
Signature of bank officer or authorized employee   Signature

REGISTER'S RECEIPT

2. I acknowledge receipt from _____
   Name of person given authority by court order to examine contents of box

   of the following items:

   a. ☐ Will of the decedent

   b. ☐ Burial plot deed

_____
Date

Deputy Probate Register

_____
Do not write below this line - For court use only

PC 552 (9/06) **SAFE DEPOSIT BOX CERTIFICATE AND RECEIPT**

MCL 700.2517

If the will is stored at a lawyer's office, a telephone call and visit to the law firm produces the will. A problem exists if the family is not certain which law firm houses the original document. In this case, several inquiries must be made. It is possible that the will may not be located under these circumstances. The law of lost wills must then be consulted. Review Chapter 3, which discusses revoked and lost wills.

The courthouse may house the original will in the Register of Probates' Office or the Clerk of Courts—Probate Division. An inquiry to the appropriate office would obtain the needed answer. Different states may handle the procedure differently. Consider Wisconsin's approach as found in Wis. Stat. § 856.03:

> If a will has been filed with a court for safekeeping during the testator's lifetime, the court on learning of the death of the testator shall open the will and give notice of the court's possession to the person named in the will to act as personal representative, otherwise to some person interested in the provisions of the will. If probate jurisdiction belongs to any other court, the will shall be delivered to that court.

Finally, the will may be at the decedent's home. In this case, the law firm convinces the family to make a thorough search of the decedent's desk, safe, fireproof box, and other areas where wills are generally stored.

Another initial action taken in the estate administration procedure is to apply for the federal **employer identification number (EIN)**. A tax document step, the application for an EIN is typically done at the same time the proof of heirship and other initial court documents are prepared. Chapter 9 contains more information regarding taxes and estate administration. The federal government requests the completion of an **SS4** application for an employer identification number. Like our social security number that is used to pay taxes, the Internal Revenue Service (IRS) assigns a number, the EIN, to estates to use to pay taxes. The SS4 form is also used to obtain identification numbers for corporations, trusts, and so on. Not all of the form applies for an estate. For example, in the estate of Shirley Mahoney, Shirley is from Milwaukee, Wisconsin, and the executor is Garret Mahoney. The document would be completed as follows: on line one (1) the legal name is Estate of Shirley Mahoney. Line three (3) would include Garret Mahoney's name with the term *executor* following. Line four (4) would contain Garret Mahoney's address. Line six (6) would indicate the county and state where the estate is being administered: Milwaukee County, Wisconsin. In number eight (8a), the box in front of "estate" would be checked and Shirley Mahoney's social security number would be inserted. For question nine (9), the box in front of "Other" would be checked and after "specify," we would write estate. Number ten (10) includes the date of death of the decedent and is so indicated by DOD. Number eleven (11) is typically December, the closing month of accounting for most individuals. Then most questions are skipped until the section marked "Third Party Designee." The law firm may insert its information here. The executor, Garret Mahoney, signs and dates the application. See a sample SS4 form application for federal employer identification number.

There are several ways to submit your application to the IRS. One way is to mail your completed SS4 form. This method may take four to five weeks before you receive your EIN. If you prefer, a completed application may be faxed to your state's service center. The response time is approximately one week if you provide a return fax number. Another option available is to call in the information included on the SS4 form to the toll-free phone number (800) 829-4933. Finally, you may choose to have the

employer identification number (EIN)
The number assigned by the Internal Revenue Service to an estate, to be used by the estate when preparing tax returns and paying taxes.

SS4
The Internal Revenue Service's application used to acquire an employer identification number.

Figure 7-18 SS4 form for application for employer identification number based on the Shirley Mahoney estate

Form **SS-4**	**Application for Employer Identification Number**	OMB No. 1545-0003

Form **SS-4**
(Rev. February 2006)
Department of the Treasury
Internal Revenue Service

Application for Employer Identification Number
(For use by employers, corporations, partnerships, trusts, estates, churches, government agencies, Indian tribal entities, certain individuals, and others.)
▶ See separate instructions for each line.   ▶ Keep a copy for your records.

OMB No. 1545-0003
EIN

Type or print clearly.

1 Legal name of entity (or individual) for whom the EIN is being requested

2 Trade name of business (if different from name on line 1)   **3** Executor, administrator, trustee, "care of" name

4a Mailing address (room, apt., suite no. and street, or P.O. box)   **5a** Street address (if different) (Do not enter a P.O. box.)

4b City, state, and ZIP code   **5b** City, state, and ZIP code

6 County and state where principal business is located

7a Name of principal officer, general partner, grantor, owner, or trustor   **7b** SSN, ITIN, or EIN

8a **Type of entity** (check only one box)
☐ Sole proprietor (SSN) _____
☐ Partnership
☐ Corporation (enter form number to be filed) ▶ _____
☐ Personal service corporation
☐ Church or church-controlled organization
☐ Other nonprofit organization (specify) ▶ _____
☐ Other (specify) ▶

☐ Estate (SSN of decedent) _____
☐ Plan administrator (SSN) _____
☐ Trust (SSN of grantor) _____
☐ National Guard   ☐ State/local government
☐ Farmers' cooperative   ☐ Federal government/military
☐ REMIC   ☐ Indian tribal governments/enterprises
Group Exemption Number (GEN) ▶ _____

8b If a corporation, name the state or foreign country (if applicable) where incorporated   State   Foreign country

9 **Reason for applying** (check only one box)
☐ Started new business (specify type) ▶ _____
☐ Hired employees (Check the box and see line 12.)
☐ Compliance with IRS withholding regulations
☐ Other (specify) ▶

☐ Banking purpose (specify purpose) ▶ _____
☐ Changed type of organization (specify new type) ▶ _____
☐ Purchased going business
☐ Created a trust (specify type) ▶ _____
☐ Created a pension plan (specify type) ▶ _____

10 Date business started or acquired (month, day, year). See instructions.   **11** Closing month of accounting year

12 First date wages or annuities were paid (month, day, year). **Note.** If applicant is a withholding agent, enter date income will first be paid to nonresident alien. (month, day, year) . . . . ▶

13 Highest number of employees expected in the next 12 months (enter -0- if none).
Do you expect to have $1,000 or less in employment tax liability for the calendar year? ☐ **Yes** ☐ **No.** (If you expect to pay $4,000 or less in wages, you can mark yes.)
Agricultural | Household | Other

14 Check **one** box that best describes the principal activity of your business.
☐ Construction ☐ Rental & leasing ☐ Transportation & warehousing
☐ Real estate ☐ Manufacturing ☐ Finance & insurance
☐ Health care & social assistance   ☐ Wholesale–agent/broker
☐ Accommodation & food service   ☐ Wholesale–other   ☐ Retail
☐ Other (specify)

15 Indicate principal line of merchandise sold, specific construction work done, products produced, or services provided.

16a Has the applicant ever applied for an employer identification number for this or any other business? . . . . . ☐ **Yes** ☐ **No**
Note. If "Yes," please complete lines 16b and 16c.

16b If you checked "Yes" on line 16a, give applicant's legal name and trade name shown on prior application if different from line 1 or 2 above.
Legal name ▶   Trade name ▶

16c Approximate date when, and city and state where, the application was filed. Enter previous employer identification number if known.
Approximate date when filed (mo., day, year) | City and state where filed | Previous EIN

Third Party Designee
Complete this section **only** if you want to authorize the named individual to receive the entity's EIN and answer questions about the completion of this form.
Designee's name   Designee's telephone number (include area code) ( )
Address and ZIP code   Designee's fax number (include area code) ( )

Under penalties of perjury, I declare that I have examined this application, and to the best of my knowledge and belief, it is true, correct, and complete.   Applicant's telephone number (include area code) ( )
Name and title (type or print clearly) ▶
Applicant's fax number (include area code) ( )
Signature ▶   Date ▶

For Privacy Act and Paperwork Reduction Act Notice, see separate instructions.   Cat. No. 16055N   Form **SS-4** (Rev. 2-2006)

(continued)

Figure 7-18   (continued)

Form SS-4 (Rev. 2-2006)   Page **2**

Do I Need an EIN?

File Form SS-4 if the applicant entity does not already have an EIN but is required to show an EIN on any return, statement, or other document.[1] See also the separate instructions for each line on Form SS-4.

IF the applicant...	AND...	THEN...
Started a new business	Does not currently have (nor expect to have) employees	Complete lines 1, 2, 4a–8a, 8b (if applicable), and 9–16c.
Hired (or will hire) employees, including household employees	Does not already have an EIN	Complete lines 1, 2, 4a–6, 7a–b (if applicable), 8a, 8b (if applicable), and 9–16c.
Opened a bank account	Needs an EIN for banking purposes only	Complete lines 1–5b, 7a–b (if applicable), 8a, 9, and 16a–c.
Changed type of organization	Either the legal character of the organization or its ownership changed (for example, you incorporate a sole proprietorship or form a partnership)[2]	Complete lines 1–16c (as applicable).
Purchased a going business[3]	Does not already have an EIN	Complete lines 1–16c (as applicable).
Created a trust	The trust is other than a grantor trust or an IRA trust[4]	Complete lines 1–16c (as applicable).
Created a pension plan as a plan administrator[5]	Needs an EIN for reporting purposes	Complete lines 1, 3, 4a–b, 8a, 9, and 16a–c.
Is a foreign person needing an EIN to comply with IRS withholding regulations	Needs an EIN to complete a Form W-8 (other than Form W-8ECI), avoid withholding on portfolio assets, or claim tax treaty benefits[6]	Complete lines 1–5b, 7a–b (SSN or ITIN optional), 8a–9, and 16a–c.
Is administering an estate	Needs an EIN to report estate income on Form 1041	Complete lines 1, 2, 3, 4a–6, 8a, 9-11, 12-15 (if applicable), and 16a–c.
Is a withholding agent for taxes on non-wage income paid to an alien (i.e., individual, corporation, or partnership, etc.)	Is an agent, broker, fiduciary, manager, tenant, or spouse who is required to file Form 1042, Annual Withholding Tax Return for U.S. Source Income of Foreign Persons	Complete lines 1, 2, 3 (if applicable), 4a–5b, 7a–b (if applicable), 8a, 9, and 16a–c.
Is a state or local agency	Serves as a tax reporting agent for public assistance recipients under Rev. Proc. 80-4, 1980-1 C.B. 581[7]	Complete lines 1, 2, 4a–5b, 8a, 9, and 16a–c.
Is a single-member LLC	Needs an EIN to file Form 8832, Entity Classification Election, for filing employment tax returns, **or** for state reporting purposes[8]	Complete lines 1–16c (as applicable).
Is an S corporation	Needs an EIN to file Form 2553, Election by a Small Business Corporation[9]	Complete lines 1–16c (as applicable).

[1] For example, a sole proprietorship or self-employed farmer who establishes a qualified retirement plan, or is required to file excise, employment, alcohol, tobacco, or firearms returns, must have an EIN. A partnership, corporation, REMIC (real estate mortgage investment conduit), nonprofit organization (church, club, etc.), or farmers' cooperative must use an EIN for any tax-related purpose even if the entity does not have employees.

[2] However, do not apply for a new EIN if the existing entity only (a) changed its business name, (b) elected on Form 8832 to change the way it is taxed (or is covered by the default rules), or (c) terminated its partnership status because at least 50% of the total interests in partnership capital and profits were sold or exchanged within a 12-month period. The EIN of the terminated partnership should continue to be used. See Regulations section 301.6109-1(d)(2)(iii).

[3] Do not use the EIN of the prior business unless you became the "owner" of a corporation by acquiring its stock.

[4] However, grantor trusts that do not file using Optional Method 1 and IRA trusts that are required to file Form 990-T, Exempt Organization Business Income Tax Return, must have an EIN. For more information on grantor trusts, see the Instructions for Form 1041.

[5] A plan administrator is the person or group of persons specified as the administrator by the instrument under which the plan is operated.

[6] Entities applying to be a Qualified Intermediary (QI) need a QI-EIN even if they already have an EIN. See Rev. Proc. 2000-12.

[7] See also *Household employer* on page 3. **Note.** State or local agencies may need an EIN for other reasons, for example, hired employees.

[8] Most LLCs do not need to file Form 8832. See *Limited liability company (LLC)* on page 4 for details on completing Form SS-4 for an LLC.

[9] An existing corporation that is electing or revoking S corporation status should use its previously-assigned EIN.

Printed on recycled paper

Figure 7-19 Michigan's letters of authority for personal representative

Approved, SCAO   JIS CODE: LET

STATE OF MICHIGAN PROBATE COURT COUNTY OF	LETTERS OF AUTHORITY FOR PERSONAL REPRESENTATIVE	FILE NO.

Estate of _____

TO: Name and address   Telephone no.

You have been appointed and qualified as personal representative of the estate on _____ You are authorized
to do and perform all acts authorized by law unless exceptions are specified below. Date
☐ Your authority is limited in the following way:
    ☐ You have no authority over the estate's real estate or ownership interests in a business entity that you identified on your acceptance of appointment.
    ☐ Other restrictions or limitations are:

☐ These letters expire: _____
                    Date

_____   _____
Date   Judge (formal proceedings)/Register (informal proceedings)   Bar no.

SEE NOTICE OF DUTIES ON SECOND PAGE

_____
Attorney name (type or print)   Bar no.

Address

_____
City, state, zip   Telephone no.

I certify that I have compared this copy with the original on file and that it is a correct copy of the original, and on this date, these letters are in full force and effect.

_____   _____
Date   Deputy register

Do not write below this line - For court use only

PC 572 (3/07) **LETTERS OF AUTHORITY FOR PERSONAL REPRESENTATIVE**   MCL 700.3103, MCL 700.3307, MCL 700.3414, MCL 700.3504, MCL 700.3601, MCR 5.202, MCR 5.206, MCR 5.307, MCR 5.310

(continued)

Figure 7-19   (continued)

The following provisions are mandatory reporting duties specified in Michigan law and Michigan court rules and are not the only duties required of you. See MCL 700.3701 through MCL 700.3722 for other duties. Your failure to comply may result in the court suspending your powers and appointing a special fiduciary in your place. It may also result in your removal as fiduciary.

CONTINUED ADMINISTRATION: If the estate is not settled within 1 year after the first personal representative's appointment, you must file with the court and send to each interested person a notice that the estate remains under administration, specifying the reasons for the continued administration. You must give this notice within 28 days of the first anniversary of the first personal representative's appointment and all subsequent anniversaries during which the administration remains uncompleted. If such a notice is not received, an interested person may petition the court for a hearing on the necessity for continued administration or for closure of the estate. [MCL 700.3703(4), MCL 700.3951(3), MCR 5.144, MCR 5.307, MCR 5.310]

DUTY TO COMPLETE ADMINISTRATION OF ESTATE: You must complete the administration of the estate and file appropriate closing papers with the court. Failure to do so may result in personal assessment of costs. [MCR 5.310]

CHANGE OF ADDRESS: You are required to inform the court and all interested persons of any change in your address within 7 days of the change.

Additional Duties for Supervised Administration

If this is a supervised administration, in addition to the above reporting duties, you are also required to prepare and file with this court the following written reports or information.

INVENTORY: You are required to file with the probate court an inventory of the assets of the estate within 91 days of the date your letters of authority are issued or as ordered by the court. You must send a copy of the inventory to all presumptive distributees and all other interested persons who request it. The inventory must list in reasonable detail all the property owned by the decedent at the time of death. Each listed item must indicate the fair market value at the time of the decedent's death and the type and amount of any encumbrance. If the value of any item has been obtained through an appraiser, the inventory should include the appraiser's name and address with the item or items appraised by that appraiser. [MCL 700.3706, MCR 5.310(E)]

ACCOUNTS: You are required to file with this court once a year, either on the anniversary date your letters of authority were issued or on another date you choose (you must notify the court of this date) or more often if the court directs, a complete itemized accounting of your administration of the estate. This itemized accounting must show in detail all income and disbursements and the remaining property, together with the form of the property. Subsequent annual and final accountings must be filed within 56 days following the close of the accounting period. When the estate is ready for closing, you are also required to file a final account with a description of property remaining in the estate. All accounts must be served on the required persons at the same time they are filed with the court, along with proof of service.

ESTATE (OR INHERITANCE) TAX INFORMATION: You are required to submit to the court proof that no estate (or inheritance) taxes are due or that the estate (or inheritance) taxes have been paid. **Note:** The estate may be subject to inheritance tax.

Additional Duties for Unsupervised Administration

If this is an unsupervised administration, in addition to the above reporting duties, you are also required to prepare and provide to all interested persons the following written reports or information.

INVENTORY: You are required to prepare an inventory of the assets of the estate within 91 days from the date your letters of authority are issued and to send a copy of the inventory to all presumptive distributees and all other interested persons who request it. You are also required within 91 days from the date your letters of authority are issued, to submit to the court the information necessary to calculate the probate inventory fee that you must pay to the probate court. You may use the original inventory for this purpose. [MCL 700.3706, MCR 5.307]

ESTATE (OR INHERITANCE) TAX INFORMATION: You may be required to submit to the court proof that no estate (or inheritance) taxes are due or that the estate (or inheritance) taxes have been paid. **Note:** The estate may be subject to inheritance tax.

application processed directly through the Internal Revenue Service official website located at www.irs.gov. Click on the businesses tab and follow the prompts. The EIN, once received, allows the personal representative to open the estate bank account. The acquisition of the federal employer identification number is easy.

Obtain Letters of Appointment

letters of appointment:
The appointment of the personal representative is confirmed by court decree and evidenced by this document.

Typically, within two weeks to one month of the petition and the will being filed with the court, the **letters of appointment** are issued. Several names for this document exist: letters of administration, letters of authority, testamentary letters, and domiciliary letters. The letters grant authority to the personal representative to act. The document serves as evidence that the court has appointed a personal representative. Used by the personal representative to conduct business on behalf of the estate, this document allows the personal representative to take action.

The personal representative opens an estate bank account to pay bills and deposit received money. The personal representative may also transfer motor vehicles from the decedent to the beneficiaries, close out bank accounts, and transfer funds to creditors or beneficiaries. Certified copies of the letters may be required by holders of property, and/or the personal representative may be required to appear in person with the letters to transact business. See Michigan's letters of authority for personal representative in Figure 7-19.

The initial step to the estate administration process has been completed. Chapter 8 discusses the next two steps of the procedure: the inventory and appraisal (Step Two) and creditors' claims (Step Three).

KEY **TERMS**

bond (p. 132)
caption (p. 120)
employer identification number (EIN) (p. 145)

letters of appointment (p. 150)
order (p. 132)
petition (p. 120)

proof of heirship (p. 121)
SS4 (p. 145)

REVIEW **QUESTIONS**

1. Generally, what type of information is the law firm trying to obtain during the initial client conference?

2. What is the disadvantage of underestimating the length of time it would take to complete the estate administration? What is the disadvantage of overestimating the time frame?

3. You are in charge of compiling financial information for a new estate. What steps should you take? What types of information should be gathered?

4. Why is it important to determine the heirs and/or beneficiaries of an estate?

5. What is a caption? What information does it contain? Name three estate administration documents that would contain a caption.

6. Distinguish between a petition and an order.

7. Explain the proof of heirship document. What is its purpose?

8. What is the SS4 form? Why complete and submit one?

9. What are letters of appointment? What do they allow the personal representative to do?

ROLE-PLAYING **ACTIVITY**

1. Conduct an interview of a fellow student regarding opening an estate on behalf of a real or hypothetically deceased relative.

RESEARCH **ASSIGNMENTS**

1. Interview a local attorney. What is the common method used to charge for an estate administration case? What is the going fee locally?

2. Research your state's law with regard to a petition or application for estate administration. If standard fill-in-the-blank forms are used, acquire all relevant petitions for formal and informal probate and for testate or intestate administration. If you must prepare an original computer-generated petition, research the specific requirements and information to include in it. What is the document called?

3. Research the additional court documents that must be filed to start an estate administration and acquire letters of appointment in your state.

4. Research your state's law regarding how the court treats a decedent's wishes to waive bond.

5. Contact the time period required by your state to present a will to the court for estate administration.

6. Contact the local courthouse office that contains wills. How is the will transferred to the court upon the death of the testator or testatrix?

7. What is the name of the document in your state that appoints the personal representative? What does it contain? Is it a standard fill-in-the-blank form or must it be computer-generated?

BUILD YOUR **PORTFOLIO**

1. Create an estate administration initial client interview checklist for your portfolio.

2. Using the estate administration case example you chose in Chapter 6, draft a petition or application for estate administration.

3. Using the estate administration case example you chose in Chapter 6, draft three other documents required to initiate the estate administration. Of the three, make certain one is an order.

4. Using the estate administration case example you chose in Chapter 6, draft a letter of appointment or similar document appointing the personal representative.

Chapter **eight**

STEP TWO— INVENTORY AND APPRAISAL AND STEP THREE— CREDITORS' CLAIMS

OBJECTIVES

After studying this chapter, you should be able to:

- Understand and see the estate plan progress.
- Define inventory, explain its purpose, describe the inventory's contents, and prepare one.
- Define appraisal and explain under what circumstances an appraisal would occur.
- Summarize and implement the notification of estate creditors procedure.
- Explain the creditors' options once they learn of the estate, and name the information contained in the creditor's claim document.
- Understand and explain the options available to the estate in responding to known claims.
- List the preference given to creditors in payment of presented claims.

See the Plan Take Form

The initial steps have been taken to effectuate the decedent's plan. The will, if there is one, has been delivered to the court and accepted by it. The personal representative has been appointed by the court and is authorized to conduct business on behalf of the estate. Action can now be taken on behalf of the decedent's plan. The next two steps are major ones with regard to estate administration. The paralegal and the law firm are on a fact-finding mission and must analyze, compile, and present to the court and interested persons an accurate depiction of the estate. This is done in Step Two—the inventory and appraisal. In Step Three—creditors' claims, the personal representative must inform creditors of the decedent's death, learn the decedent's liabilities, and pay each claim or reject it. The creditors must be paid before any beneficiary or heir inherits. For these steps to run smoothly, the paralegal must be aware of deadlines and be organized.

This is an exciting time for the estate. The law firm is beginning the actualization of the decedent's plan. The decedent's wealth is on the verge of being transferred to its next owner and continuing the decedent's legacy.

Inventory

The second step in the estate administration procedure consists of preparing an inventory and acquiring appraisals. The **inventory** is a list of the decedent's assets and their date-of-death values. It lists only the decedent's assets; no liabilities are contained in the inventory. The inventory can be explained as a snapshot picture of the decedent's worth taken on the date of his or her death. The value assigned is a fair-market value of the asset.

inventory
A court document that lists all of the decedent's probatable assets and their date-of-death values.

The inventory is signed by the personal representative, acting as a fiduciary, who swears the information is complete and accurate. Often the personal representative's signature is notarized and a jurat appears on the document. Some state forms also require the attorney for the estate to sign the document. See Colorado's inventory in Figure 8-1.

Most inventories contain the same information. Looking at Colorado's inventory as an illustration, you will find the following:

1. Caption: The caption contains the name of the estate, the proper jurisdiction and venue, the case number, the name of the document, and the attorney's name and address.

2. Signature of personal representative: The inventory includes the signature of the personal representative and a jurat.

3. Asset information: The inventory contains a summary of schedules that have been prepared. It requires the law firm and the personal representative to disclose information regarding the decedent's assets, how the assets are titled, and their value. This information includes real estate, stocks, bonds, cash, insurance, and so on. The assets must be thoroughly described, including the legal description for real estate; account numbers and the names of financial institutions for bank accounts; and other detailed information such as serial numbers, policy numbers, or identification numbers. Schedules detailing the information are attached to the front page of the inventory. The front page contains a summary of the values assigned for each category. The inventory further requires any mortgage or liens on the listed property to be reflected in the "Encumbrances on Inventoried Assets" section. A completed inventory informs the court and interested persons of the value of the estate. Compare Colorado's inventory to Virginia's inventory for decedent's estate in Figure 8-2.

State law prescribes the time limit for filing the inventory. The time frame usually is within a certain time from the date the personal representative was appointed. It ranges from thirty days to six months. The Uniform Probate Code requires the inventory to be filed within three (3) months of the issuance of the letters of appointment. (See UPC § 3-706.) A Delaware case illustrates the importance of filing the inventory as required by statutory law:

In *Adams v. Jankouskas*, 452 A. 2d 148 (Del. Super. Ct. 1982), the executrix argued that a legal defense of laches should be used to prevent the decedent's widower from bringing an action against the estate. (The widower waited too long.) The appellate court stated that the executrix failed to file the estate inventory within three (3) months of her being appointed executrix as required by statutory law. The court stated, "This is no mere ministerial chore to be taken lightly.

Figure 8-1 Colorado's inventory

❏ District Court   ❏ Denver Probate Court

_____ County, Colorado
Court Address:

_____

IN THE MATTER OF THE ESTATE OF:
❏ Deceased ❏ Protected Person

▲ **COURT USE ONLY** ▲

Attorney or Party Without Attorney (Name and Address):

Case Number:

Phone Number: E-mail:
FAX Number: Atty. Reg.#:   Division   Courtroom

INVENTORY

Being sworn, I verify that the attached schedules contain a complete and accurate inventory of the real and personal property of this estate to the best of my knowledge, information and belief.

_____
Signature of ❏ Personal Representative   ❏ Conservator

Subscribed and sworn to before me on _____.

My commission expires _____.

_____
Notary public/(Deputy) Clerk of Court

INSTRUCTIONS

Both decedent's estates and conservatorship:
Within three months after appointment, a personal representative or conservator shall list and value the estate's assets and liabilities, clearly identifying each item and the decedent's or protected person's interest in the item. If additional space is needed, separate sheets may be used. If additional items are discovered after the initial inventory has been completed, a supplemental inventory listing those additional item(s) shall be completed.

Decedent's estates:
Assets shall be listed and the fair market value given as of the date of the decedent's death. The inventory shall be sent to interested persons who request it or the original inventory may be filed with the Court. (Sections 15-12-706, 15-12-707 & 15-12-708, C.R.S., and Rules 28 & 30, C.R.P.P.)

Conservatorship:
Assets shall be listed and the fair market value given as of the date of the conservator's appointment. The inventory must be filed with the Court. A copy must also be provided to the protected person, if 14 years of age or older, and to any parent or guardian with whom the protected person resides. (Section 15-14-418, C.R.S. and Rule 28, C.R.P.P.)

SUMMARY

Schedule A   Real Estate...$_____

Schedule B   Stocks and Bonds.._____

Schedule C   Mortgages and Notes............................._____

              Cash..._____

              Total Mortgages, Notes and Cash.._____

Schedule D   Insurance, Annuities, Pension & Profit Sharing Plans..........................._____

Schedule E   (Conservatorship only) Property Held In Joint Tenancy........................._____

Schedule F   Miscellaneous Property.._____

Total Gross Value...$_____

    Encumbrances on Inventoried Assets...(_____)

Total Net Value..$_____

CPC 20   R7/00   INVENTORY   Page 1 of 4
This form conforms in substance to CPC 20.

(continued)

Figure 8-1 (continued)

Schedule A	Real Estate (State Name in which Title is Held)	Value
	Total Schedule A	$

Schedule B	Stocks and Bonds (State Name in which Title is Held)	Value
	Total Schedule B	$

Schedule C	Mortgages, Notes and Cash (State Name in which Title is Held)	Value
Mortgages and Notes		
	Mortgages and Notes	$

CPC 20   R7/00   INVENTORY
This form conforms in substance to CPC 20.

Page 2 of 4

(continued)

Figure 8-1 (continued)

Cash

Cash	$_____
Total Schedule C	$_____

Schedule D   Insurance, Annuities, Pension and Profit Sharing Plans   Value
(Decedent's estate should include only those items payable to the estate. Conservatorship should include all items in which the protected person has an ownership or beneficial interest.)

Total Schedule D	$_____

Schedule E   (Conservatorship only) Property Held in Joint Tenancy   Value

Total Schedule E	$_____

CPC 20   R7/00   INVENTORY
This form conforms in substance to CPC 20.

Page 3 of 4

(continued)

Figure 8-1 (continued)

Schedule F	Miscellaneous Property (If Titled, State Name in which Title is Held)	Value

Total Schedule F $_____

Encumbrances on Inventoried Assets

Schedule and Item Number	Description	Amount

Total Encumbrances $_____

CPC 20   R7/00   INVENTORY
This form conforms in substance to CPC 20.

Page 4 of 4

Source: Used by permission of the Supreme Court State of Colorado.

Figure 8-2 Virginia's inventory for decedent's estate (Virginia Circuit Court form CC–1670)

INVENTORY FOR DECEDENT'S ESTATE   Court File No.
COMMONWEALTH OF VIRGINIA

Circuit Court of

Decedent's name

Fiduciary(ies) name(s)

Date of fiduciary(s) qualification   Date of decedent's death

This is ☐ the first inventory   ☐ an inventory showing after discovered assets   ☐ an amended inventory restating all assets.

The fiduciary filing this inventory is ☐ an administrator   ☐ an executor   ☐ a curator.

Total value of assets listed in Parts 1 and 3 (estate for bond) . . . . $ _____ 0.00

Total value of assets listed in Parts 1, 3, and 4 (estate for probate tax) . . . . $ _____ 0.00

ATTACH ADDITIONAL SHEETS IF NEEDED

Part 1. The decedent's personal estate under your supervision and control.

DESCRIPTION OF PROPERTY	VALUE
TOTAL VALUE OF PART 1:	0.00

Page 1 of 4

FORM CC-1670 7/02 PDF
VA. CODE §§ 26-12, -12.1

Source: Courtesy of Virginia's Judicial System.   (continued)

Figure 8-2   (continued)

Part 2. The decedent's interest in multiple party accounts and certificates of deposit in banks and credit unions.

DESCRIPTION OF PROPERTY	VALUE
TOTAL VALUE OF PART 2:	0.00

Part 3. The decedent's real estate in Virginia over which you have a power of sale.

DESCRIPTION OF PROPERTY	VALUE
TOTAL VALUE OF PART 3:	0.00

Part 4. The decedent's other real estate in Virginia.

DESCRIPTION OF PROPERTY	VALUE
TOTAL VALUE OF PART 4:	0.00

Page 2 of 4

FORM CC-1670 7/02 PDF
VA. CODE §§ 26-12,12.1

(continued)

Figure 8-2   (continued)

Part 5. The decedent's non-Virginia real estate.

DESCRIPTION OF PROPERTY	VALUE
TOTAL VALUE OF PART 5:	0.00

CERTIFICATE OF ACCURACY, COMPLETENESS, AND MAILING
[Must be signed by each fiduciary.]

1. I (we) hereby certify and affirm under penalty of law, that to the best of my (our) knowledge and belief this is an accurate and complete inventory of this estate made in accordance with my (our) responsibilities under Virginia law.

2. I (we) hereby also certify and affirm that (**choose one**):

   A. [ ] On or before the date of filing this Inventory with the Commissioner of Accounts, I (we) sent a copy of it by first class mail to every person entitled to a copy, pursuant to Virginia Code Section 26-12.4, who made a written request therefor. The names and addresses of the persons to whom copies were sent and the dates they were mailed are shown on Page 4.

   or

   B. [ ] No person entitled to a copy of this Inventory pursuant to Virginia Code Section 26-12.4 made a written request therefor.

Date _____   Fiduciary _____
                                   Address _____
                                   Telephone No.: _____

Date _____   Fiduciary _____
                                   Address _____
                                   Telephone No.: _____

Date _____   Fiduciary _____
                                   Address _____
                                   Telephone No.: _____

CERTIFICATE OF COMMISSIONER

The Commissioner of Accounts has not independently verified the value of the items on the inventory, or the fact that they are the only assets of the estate.

Inspected, found to be in proper form, and approved on _____

_____
Commissioner of Accounts

Received in the Clerk's Office and admitted to record on _____

_____
Clerk

Page 3 of 4

FORM CC-1670 7/02 PDF
VA. CODE §§ 26-12,12.1

(continued)

Figure 8-2   (continued)

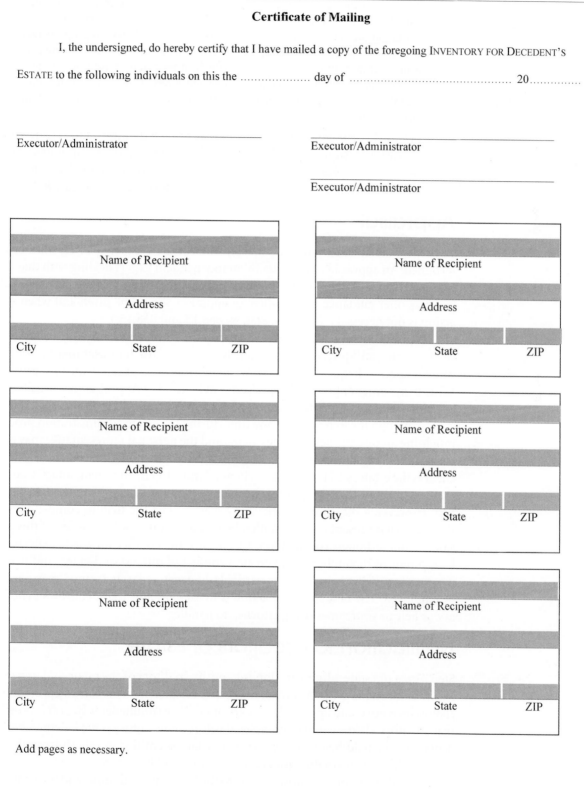

Certificate of Mailing

I, the undersigned, do hereby certify that I have mailed a copy of the foregoing INVENTORY FOR DECEDENT'S ESTATE to the following individuals on this the .... day of .... 20...............

_____   _____
Executor/Administrator   Executor/Administrator

                                          _____
                                          Executor/Administrator

Name of Recipient	Name of Recipient
Address	Address
City State ZIP	City State ZIP

Name of Recipient	Name of Recipient
Address	Address
City State ZIP	City State ZIP

Name of Recipient	Name of Recipient
Address	Address
City State ZIP	City State ZIP

Add pages as necessary.

Page 4 of 4

FORM CC-1670 (MASTER) 6/06
VA. CODE §§ 26-12, -12.1

The purpose and intent of our law is to provide for the expeditious settlement of estates for the benefit of all concerned." *Id*. at 157. The court continued that if she had filed the inventory when required perhaps the executrix could successfully argue the widower had public notice as to the value of his property that was being included in the estate. "However, when a person fails to timely perform a statutory duty, the purpose of which, at least in part, is to put another on notice that his or her vital interests are being affected, then such misfeasance cannot be converted into a shield by the former against the latter." *Id*. at 157–158. The court ultimately denied the executrix's legal defense of laches.

If the personal representative or law firm fails to include information or learns of additional assets, a supplemental inventory may be prepared and submitted. Some states also require notice to be given to interested persons that the inventory has been filed with the court. See Wisconsin's notice of inventory on file in Figure 8-3.

Appraisal

To prepare the inventory, the fair-market value of the decedent's assets must be determined. An appraisal of the asset by an independent expert dealing with that type of property may be required by the court or requested by an interested person. State law may offer guidance about when an appraiser should be hired and when such action is not necessary. (See Wis. Stat. §§ 858.13 and 858.15.)

A professional may be hired to ascertain the value of real estate, a business, artwork, jewelry, antiques, or other expensive property. An appraiser may be asked to value a specific bequest, or the court may order an appraisal on property. See Wisconsin's order appointing appraiser(s) in Figure 8-4. Appraisers are usually paid a fee for their work. This fee is a part of the administration expense of the estate.

Although it can happen at any time during the estate administration process, infighting among the beneficiaries, heirs, and the personal representative may arise at this time. The law firm must be aware of the potential for conflicts. The law firm's client is the estate, and the attorney-client relationship must remain intact. Caution is required about sharing appropriate information with the unhappy beneficiary or heir. However, a disgruntled beneficiary may contact the firm to complain about the personal representative or another beneficiary. You should be aware of this possibility, and although you may want to resolve the conflict for the beneficiary or heir, you must remember not to create a conflict of interest or divulge confidential information. If the beneficiary is particularly upset, separate counsel may need to be employed. The best course of action is to forward any arguments by a beneficiary or heir to your supervising attorney to handle.

Notification to Creditors of Estate

Step Three of estate administration is to notify creditors of the estate and to pay all legally enforceable debts. Although this step is designated as the third step, creditors' claims, inventory, and appraisal work are often done simultaneously, or it is possible that creditors' claims could be completed before an inventory is filed. Remember, all debts must be paid before an heir or beneficiary is entitled to inherit from the estate. See the UPC procedure for creditors' claims in Figure 8-5.

Usually three options are available to the law firm at this time, and the Uniform Probate Code prescribes the options. The law firm may do nothing. If the law firm chooses not to act, the statute of limitations for presenting claims is longest for the

Figure 8-3   Wisconsin's notice of inventory on file

STATE OF WISCONSIN, CIRCUIT COURT, _____ **COUNTY**	*For Official Use*

IN THE MATTER OF THE ESTATE OF

_____

Notice of Inventory on File
(Formal Administration)

_____

Case No. _____

You are notified that an inventory in this estate was filed with the Court on _____ .
                                                                                                    Date

You may obtain a copy or summary of the inventory by making a written request to the personal representative.

Upon receipt of the written request, the copy or summary will be provided to you within five days.

_____
Personal Representative

_____
Address

_____
Date

Name of Attorney
Address
Telephone Number

PR-1908, 10/00 Notice of Inventory on File (Formal Administration)   §858.03, Wisconsin Statutes
This form shall not be modified. It may be supplemented with additional material.

Source: For the most current version of this form, visit www.wicourts.org.

Figure 8-4   Wisconsin's order appointing appraiser(s)

	For Official Use
STATE OF WISCONSIN, CIRCUIT COURT, _____ **COUNTY**	

IN THE MATTER OF

**Order Appointing
Appraiser(s)**
(Probate/Guardianship)

_____

_____   Case No. _____

IT IS ORDERED THAT:

_____
Name(s) & Address(es)

_____

_____

_____

is/are appointed appraiser(s) of this estate and directed to appraise the property and certify its value.

BY THE COURT:

Name of Attorney	
Address	_____
	Circuit Court Judge/Court Commissioner
	_____
	Name Printed or Typed
	_____
Telephone Number	Date

PR-1907, GN-2035, 10/00 Order Appointing Appraiser(s) (Probate/Guardianship)   Chapter 786, and §858.13, Wisconsin Statutes
This form shall not be modified. It may be supplemented with additional material.

Source: For the most current version of this form, visit www.wicourts.org.

Figure 8-5   UPC procedure for creditors' claims

1. Estate notifies creditors.
   a. No notification: claims barred one year after date of death.
   b. Publish notice: claims barred four months after date of first publication.*
   c. Delivery of notice directly to creditor: claims barred sixty days after mailing.*
   * Whichever date is later

2. Creditor's response options.
   a. Do nothing.
   b. Creditor delivers or mails claim to personal representative including basis of claim, claimant's name and address, amount of claim.
   c. Creditor files claim document with clerk of courts.

3. Estate's response to known claims.
   a. Estate pays debt.
   b. Estate disallows debt—mails notice of disallowance.
   c. Estate disallows a portion of the debt—mails notice of partial disallowance.

4. Creditor's response to disallowance.
   a. Creditor petitions court for allowance.

creditor. If no notice is given, all claims that arose before the death of the decedent are barred after one year of the decedent's death (UPC § 3-803). Of course, this is not the recommended course of action for a law firm.

A better option is to publish notice of the claim to creditors. According to UPC § 3-801:

> [A] personal representative upon appointment [may] [shall] publish a notice to creditors once a week for three successive weeks in a newspaper of general circulation in the [county] announcing the appointment . . . and notifying creditors to present their claims within four months after the date of the first publication of the notice or be forever barred.

As you can see, this action shortens the limitations on presentation of claims from one year to four months. Most law firms prepare the required form and request publication. This is standard practice. Many states have a preprinted form that is used to require publication. See Colorado's notice to creditors by publication in Figure 8-6.

Under the Uniform Probate Code, the final option available to the law firm is to give written notice to the creditor. It requires a creditor to present its claim

> [W]ithin four months after the published notice . . . or within sixty (60) days after the mailing or other delivery of the notice, whichever is later, or be forever barred; UPC § 3-801.

See Colorado's notice to creditors by mail or delivery in Figure 8-7.

Certainly each state varies on its creditors' claims procedures and notice requirements. Texas law requires that, within one month of the personal representative receiving his or her letters, notice must be published in a newspaper in the county where the

Figure 8-6 Colorador's notice to creditors by publication

☐ District Court ☐ Denver Probate Court _____ County, Colorado Court Address:	
IN THE MATTER OF THE ESTATE OF	
Deceased	▲ COURT USE ONLY ▲
Attorney or Party Without Attorney (Name and Address):	Case Number:
Phone Number: E-mail: FAX Number: Atty. Reg. #:	Division Courtroom

NOTICE TO CREDITORS BY PUBLICATION

NOTICE TO CREDITORS*

Estate of _____ , Deceased

Case Number _____

All persons having claims against the above-named estate are required to present them to the personal representative or to

☐ District Court of _____ , County, Colorado,

☐ Probate Court of the City and County of Denver, Colorado**-

on or before (date) _____***, or the claims may be forever barred.

_____

_____

_____

Type or Print name and address of Personal Representative

* Publish only this portion of the form.

INSTRUCTIONS TO THE NEWSPAPER:

_____   _____
Name of Newspaper   Signature of Attorney for/or Personal Representative   Date

Publish the above Notice to Creditors once   _____
a week for three consecutive calendar weeks   Type or Print name of Attorney for Personal Representative

**Check whichever Court applies.

***Insert date not earlier than four months from the date of first publication or the date one year from date of decedent's death, whichever occurs first

NOTE: Unless one year or more has elapsed since the death of the decedent, a personal representative shall cause a notice to creditors to be published in some daily or weekly newspaper published in the county in which the estate is being administered, or if there is no such newspaper, then in some newspaper of general circulation in an adjoining county. (§15-12-801, C.R.S.) A copy of this form and the Proof of Publication should be filed with the Clerk of the Court.

CPC 21-A   R7/00   NOTICE TO CREDITORS BY PUBLICATION

Source: Used by permission of the Supreme Court State of Colorado.

Figure 8-7   Colorado's notice to creditors by mail or delivery

☐ District Court   ☐ Denver Probate Court

_____ County, Colorado

Court Address:

IN THE MATTER OF THE ESTATE OF

Deceased:

▲   **COURT USE ONLY**   ▲

Attorney or Party Without Attorney (Name and Address):

Case Number:

Phone Number: E-mail:
FAX Number: Atty. Reg.#:   Division   Courtroom

NOTICE TO CREDITORS BY MAIL OR DELIVERY

NOTICE TO CREDITORS

All persons having claims against the above-named estate are required to present them to the personal representative or the

above-named court on or before _____*, or be forever barred.

(date)

_____
Signature of Attorney for/or Personal Representative   Date

_____

Type or Print name, of Attorney

_____

_____

_____

Type or Print name and address of Personal Representative

* Insert the later of the following two dates:
- The date set in the published Notice to Creditors by Publication (Form CPC 21-A).
- The date sixty days from the mailing or other delivery of this notice, but not later than the date one year following the decedent's death (Section 15-12-801, C.R.S.).

CPC 21-B   R7/00   NOTICE TO CREDITORS BY MAIL OR DELIVERY   1

(continued)

Figure 8-7 (continued)

CERTIFICATE OF SERVICE

I certify that on (date) _____, a copy of this Notice to Creditors by Mail or Delivery was served
on each of the following at the indicated address by:

☐ hand delivery   ☐ certified U.S. mail, postage pre-paid
☐ first class U.S. mail, postage pre-paid   ☐ registered U.S. mail, postage pre-paid

   Name and Address

_____
Signature of Person Certifying Service

NOTE: This certificate of service cannot be used in cases where personal service is required or used. Use CPC7-P (*Personal Service Affidavit*) or CPC8-A (*Waiver of Service*) for each person required to be served personally.

CPC 21-B   R7/00   NOTICE TO CREDITORS BY MAIL OR DELIVERY   2

---

letters were issued. This publication requires anyone with a claim against the estate to present the claim. The notice includes the date of issuance of the letters, the address to which claims may be presented, and an instruction regarding to whom the personal representative wants the claims addressed. The addressee options are:

> [I]n care of representative, in care of representative's attorney, or in care of "Representative, Estate of _____," (naming the estate) (Tex. Prob. Code Ann. § 294(a)).

The representative must prove publication by filing with the court a copy of the printed notice along with the publisher's affidavit swearing it was properly published (Tex. Prob. Code Ann. § 294(b)).

If notice is published,

> [T]he claim may be presented to the personal representative at any time before the estate is closed if suit on the claim has not been barred by the general statutes of limitation (Tex. Prob. Code Ann. § 298(a)).

According to the Texas statutes, if a personal representative fails to give proper notice, the personal representative and sureties on the bond are liable for any damage a person suffers because of neglect, unless the person had notice through some other method (Tex. Prob. Code Ann. § 297).

Texas law provides for another method of giving notice. This method is permissive. The personal representative

> may give notice by certified or registered mail, with return receipt requested, to an unsecured creditor having a claim for money against the estate expressly stating that the creditor must present a claim within four months after the date of the receipt of the notice or the claim is barred, if the claim is not barred by the general statutes of limitation (Tex. Prob. Code Ann. § 294(d)).

The notice must state the date of issuance of letters, address to which claims may be presented, and an instruction of the "in care of" name chosen by the representative. This name would be the attorney, the personal representative, or "Representative, Estate of" listing the estate (Tex. Prob. Code Ann. § 294(d)). If this direct notice is given, it shortens the time for presentation of claims. The Texas statute reads:

> If a claim of an unsecured creditor for money is not presented within four months after the date of receipt of the notice permitted by Section 294(d), the claim is barred (Tex. Prob. Code Ann. § 298(a)).

Creditors' Options

Upon learning of the estate, creditors have two options. The first is to ignore the claim and do nothing. In this case, after the time limitation for presentation of a claim has run out, the creditor is no longer entitled to payment on the debt. The creditor must write off the amount owed as a bad debt.

The second option is to present the claim as required by law. The Uniform Probate Code describes the procedure as follows: the claimant may deliver or mail the claim to the personal representative. The document must include the following: the claim's basis, the claimant's name and address, and the amount claimed. Another option available to the claimant is to file the claim document containing that information with the clerk of court (UPC §3-804(1)).

Each state varies on its requirements. Some states may have required forms that need to be completed, and others may just specify what types of information must be included in the claim. Usually three types of information are included:

1. Name and address of the creditor.
2. Amount claimed.
3. Nature or description of the claim.

See Wisconsin's claim against estate in Figure 8-8.
Texas law requires the claim

to be supported by an affidavit that the claim is just, and that all legal offsets, payments, and credits known to the affiant have been allowed. If the claim is not founded on a written instrument or account, the affidavit shall also state the facts upon which the claim is founded (Tex. Prob. Code Ann. § 301).

In Texas, the notice tells the creditor where the claim should be presented. Another option available to the creditor is to deposit the claim with the clerk of courts. The clerk must then notify the representative or attorney for the estate of the receipt of the claim (Tex. Prob. Code Ann. § 308). In California, the creditor must file a proof of mailing or delivery of claim to the personal representative with the court (Cal. Prob. Code § 9153).

Even if a paralegal does not work in the wills, trusts, and estate administration area, he or she may prepare and submit creditors' claims on behalf of a client for a contract law case.

Estate's Response to Known Claims

Once the creditors' claims have been presented to the personal representative or the attorney for the estate, decisions regarding their payment must be made. The personal representative can choose to pay the debts just as the decedent would have if he or she were still living. All of the debt may be paid or allowed, all may be rejected or disallowed, or a portion of the debt may be allowed and a portion disallowed. Knowledge of contract law and creditor–debtor law is beneficial at this point. If the creditor did inferior performance and breached the contract, the personal representative need not pay. If the decedent has already paid the debt, disallowance is justified. If a contract is unenforceable because of legal defenses against it, the claim would not have to be paid. Examples of legal defenses are statute of frauds, statute of limitations, or duress.

To gain a general knowledge of the procedures available to the personal representative when responding to creditors' claims, let's consult the Uniform Probate Code, which states that the personal representative may mail a notice of disallowance. It also says that if the personal representative fails to mail a notice of action on the claim within sixty (60) days after the presentation-of-claim date has expired, a notice of allowance occurs.

If a disallowance is received by the claimant, the claimant may petition the court for allowance within sixty (60) days after the mailing of the notice. The court then decides the matter. If the claimant has a judgment from another court requiring enforcement of the claim, it is treated as an allowance of the claim (UPC § 3-806). A sample notice of disallowance form from Michigan is shown in Figure 8-9. A petition from Colorado demonstrates the form a claimant might complete after receiving notice of disallowance. See Colorado's petition for allowance of claim(s) by claimant in Figure 8-10.

Figure 8-8   Wisconsin's claim against estate

STATE OF WISCONSIN, CIRCUIT COURT, _____ **COUNTY**

For Official Use

IN THE MATTER OF THE ESTATE OF

_____

_____

Claim Against Estate
☐ Informal
☐ Formal

Case No. _____

Name and address of claimant: _____

_____

Describe nature and amount of claim: (***If claim is based on a written document, attach a complete copy.***)
☐ **See attached.**

If the decedent was survived by a spouse, the classification of the obligation under §766.55(2), Wisconsin Statutes is as follows:
☐ Support obligation owed spouse or child.
☐ Obligation incurred in the interest of the marriage.
☐ Obligation incurred prior to marriage or prior to January 1, 1986.
☐ Tort.
☐ Other: _____

Total amount of claim is $ _____.
This amount is ☐ due ☐ not yet due and will or may become due on (date) _____.
No payments have been made on this claim which are not credited, and there are no offsets except:
_____

I swear that this statement is correct.

Subscribed and sworn to before me

on _____

_____
Notary Public/Court Official
My commission expires: _____

_____
Signature of Claimant

_____
Name Printed or Typed

_____
Address

_____

Name of Attorney for Claimant	
Address	
Telephone Number	Bar Number

Note: A statutory filing fee of $3.00 shall accompany each claim filed.

PR-1819, 10/00 Claim Against Estate (Informal and Formal Administration)
Chapter 859, §766.55, Wisconsin Statutes
This form shall not be modified. It may be supplemented with additional material.

Source: For the most current version of this form, visit www.wicourts.gov.

Figure 8-9 Michigan's notice of disallowance of claim

Approved, SCAO	OSM CODE: NDC

STATE OF MICHIGAN PROBATE COURT COUNTY
CIRCUIT COURT - FAMILY DIVISION

NOTICE OF DISALLOWANCE OF CLAIM

FILE NO.

Estate of _____

TO: Claimant name and address

Your written statement of claim dated _____ for $_____ is disallowed

☐ in whole. ☐ in part as to _____

_____

_____ .

The ☐ entire claim ☐ portion of the claim which has been disallowed will be forever barred unless you start a civil action by filing a complaint against the fiduciary. Your complaint must be filed with the appropriate district, circuit, or probate court not later than **63** days after the mailing or delivery of this notice.

Date _____

Signature of attorney _____

Signature of fiduciary _____

Name of attorney (type or print) _____ Bar no. ____

Name of fiduciary (type or print) _____

Address _____

Address _____

City, state, zip _____ Telephone no. ____

City, state, zip _____ Telephone no. ____

PROOF OF SERVICE

I certify that on _____ I served a copy of this notice on the claimant by
Date

☐ ordinary mail at the address stated above.
☐ delivering personally to the claimant.

I declare under the penalties of perjury that this proof of service has been examined by me and that its contents are true to the best of my information, knowledge, and belief.

Date _____

Signature of fiduciary/attorney _____

Do not write below this line - For court use only

MCL 700.3806; MSA 27.13806,
MCL 700.5429; MSA 27.15429, MCL 700.7507; MSA 27.17507

PC 580 (3/00) **NOTICE OF DISALLOWANCE OF CLAIM**

Source: Courtesy of Michigan Courts.

Figure 8-10   Colorador's petition for allowance of claim(s) by claimant

☐ District Court ☐ Denver Probate Court _____ County, Colorado Court Address: **IN THE MATTER OF THE ESTATE OF:** **Deceased:**	 ▲ **COURT USE ONLY** ▲
Attorney or Party Without Attorney (Name and Address): Phone Number: E-mail: FAX Number: Atty. Reg.#:	Case Number: Division Courtroom
PETITION FOR ALLOWANCE OF CLAIM(S) BY CLAIMANT	

Petitioner (name), _____ , claimant against

this estate, petitions the Court to allow his/her/its claim(s) in the amount(s) set forth below:

CLAIM	**AMOUNT**

In support of this Petition, Petitioner states:

1. Each claim is valid, was presented within the time for presenting claims as provided by law, and has not been paid.

2. As to those claims set forth above which were presented to the personal representative and not filed with the Court, a copy of the written statement of each such claim is attached to this Petition and made a part of it.

3. (State other reasons in support, if any)

DATE: _____

_____
Signature of Attorney for Petitioner

_____
Type or print name of Attorney for Petitioner

_____
Signature of Petitioner

_____
Type or print name, address & tele.# of Petitioner

_____

_____

_____

NOTE: See Section 15-12-806(2) of the Colorado Probate Code for Notice requirements.

CPC 39-C   R7/00   PETITION FOR ALLOWANCE OF CLAIM(S) BY CLAIMANT   1

Source: Used by permission of the Supreme Court State of Colorado.

The Texas procedure can be compared to that required under the UPC. The personal representative has thirty (30) days to prepare a memorandum allowing or rejecting a claim (Tex. Prob. Code Ann. § 309). If the representative does not meet the time requirement, the law treats the claim as rejected (Tex. Prob. Code Ann. § 310). In Wisconsin, the personal representative, a guardian ad litem, or interested person may mail an objection to the claim. In this case, the court sets a date for a pretrial conference and directs what pleadings may be exchanged (Wis. Stat. § 859.33). A Texas statute also provides for any interested person to object in writing to a claim. The Texas court makes a ruling as to the objection (Tex. Prob. Code Ann. § 312).

If the personal representative rejects the claim, the claimant may bring suit to collect the debt. This must be done within ninety (90) days after the rejection or the claim is barred (Tex. Prob. Code Ann. § 313). A Texas statute sets forth who pays the costs of the suit:

> All costs incurred in the probate court with respect to claims shall be taxed as follows:
>
> a. If allowed and approved, the estate shall pay the costs.
> b. If allowed, but disapproved, the claimant shall pay the costs.
> c. If rejected, but established by suit, the estate shall pay the costs.
> d. If rejected, but not established by suit, the claimant shall pay the costs . . .
> e. In suits to establish a claim after a rejection in part, if the claimant fails to recover judgment for a greater amount than was allowed or approved the claimant shall pay all costs (Tex. Prob. Code Ann. § 315).

Some states may require the claimant to file a receipt or other form upon receiving payment of the claim. See Colorado's withdrawal or satisfaction of claim and release in Figure 8-11.

Preference of Creditors

At times, an estate may not have enough assets to cover the decedent's liabilities, costs of administering the estate, funeral expenses, and taxes. Most states have a statute describing the preference of creditors: which claimants get paid first. The Uniform Probate Code order of payment is:

1. Costs and expenses of administration.
2. Reasonable funeral expenses.
3. Debts and taxes with preference under federal law.
4. Reasonable and necessary medical and hospital expenses of last illness of the decedent, including compensation of persons attending decedent.
5. Debts and taxes with preference under other laws of this state.
6. All other claims (UPC § 3-805(a)).

The statute further states:

> No preference shall be given in the payment of any claim over any other claim of the same class (UPC § 3-805(b)).

Other states have similar priority statutes. See the chart in Figure 8-12 comparing Texas and Wisconsin statutes.

After comparing the Uniform Probate Code and the Texas and Wisconsin statutes, you can see that the priority of payment of creditors is similar. Usually costs

Figure 8-11 Colorado's withdrawal or satisfaction of claim and release

☐ District Court ☐ Denver Probate Court _____ County, Colorado Court Address: **IN THE MATTER OF THE ESTATE OF:** ☐ Deceased ☐ Protected Person 	 ▲ **COURT USE ONLY** ▲
Attorney or Party Without Attorney (Name and Address): Phone Number: E-mail: FAX Number: Atty. Reg.#:	Case Number: Division Courtroom
WITHDRAWAL OR SATISFACTION OF CLAIM AND RELEASE	

The undersigned, having filed a claim in the above-captioned estate, concerning the following: (describe nature of claim)

hereby grants a full and final release to the estate and to the fiduciary and any successor for any liability in connection with the claim described above and

☐ withdraws the claim.

☐ acknowledges that the claim has been satisfied.

DATE: _____

_____
Signature of Claimant
(Type or Print name, address & tele. # below)

_____

_____

_____

_____

CPC 22-W   R7/00   WITHDRAWAL OR SATISFACTION OF CLAIM AND RELEASE   1

Source: Used by permission of the Supreme Court State of Colorado.

Figure 8-12   Chart comparing Texas and Wisconsin statutes

Texas Priority: Tex. Prob. Code Ann. §322	Wisconsin Priority: Wis. Stat. §859.25
1. Funeral expenses or expenses of last sickness, not to exceed $15,000.00.	1. Costs and expenses of administration.
2. Expenses of administration, preservation, safekeeping, and management of the estate and unpaid expenses of administration awarded in a guardianship of the decedent.	2. Reasonable funeral and burial expenses.
3. Secured claims for money under Section 306(a) (1) including tax liens. . . .	3. Provision for the family of the decedent. . . .
4. Claims for the principal amount of and accrued interest of delinquent child support arrearages. . . .	4. Reasonable and necessary expenses of the last sickness of the decedent, including compensation of persons attending to the decedent.
5. Claims for taxes, penalties and interest due under Texas Tax Code.	5. All debts, charges, or taxes owing to the United States, this state, or a governmental subdivision or municipality of this state.
6. Claims for costs of confinement. . . .	6. Wages including pension, welfare, and vacation benefits due to employees that have been earned within three (3) months before the date of death of the decedent, not to exceed $300.00 in value to each employee.
7. Claims for repayment of medical assistance payments made by the state under Chapter 32, Human Resources Code, to or for the benefit of the decedent.	7. Property assigned to surviving spouse under § 861.41.
8. All other claims.	8. All other claims allowed.

of administering the estate and attorney's fees vie for the top of the list with funeral expenses. Reasonable funeral expenses usually cover tombstones, grave markers, crypts, or burial plots; funeral services; flowers; a funeral luncheon or dinner; and so on. Case law should be consulted to determine "reasonable" funeral expenses. A Delaware court faced the issue of whether to consider a tombstone a reasonable expense for the estate:

> In *Boyer v. Cole*, 16 Del. Ch. 445, 143 A. 489 (1927), the administrator purchased a tombstone for the deceased with estate funds. Apparently, at common law the purchase of a tombstone was not a proper charge against an estate especially if creditors would be adversely affected. However, the court ruled that a reasonable cost for a tombstone depending partially on the decedent's station in life is now allowed as a funeral expense in America and England. "This rule applies even though the estate be insolvent, though the expenditures are more closely scrutinized and should be more moderate where a creditor is affected thereby." *Id.* at 490. The court ruled the administrator was justified in making a reasonable expenditure for the tombstone because no creditor was injured and the amount

spent appears to be reasonable for the decedent's station in life and the size of the estate.

Texas law has an interesting protection to the surviving spouse in connection with the payment of the funeral expenses. Remember from Chapter 1 that Texas is a community property state. Texas law states:

> When personal representatives pay claims for funeral expenses . . . . They shall charge the whole of such claims to the decedent's estate and shall charge no part thereof to the community share of a surviving spouse (Tex. Prob. Code Ann. § 320A).

Texas directly legislates the estate as paying for the funeral expenses rather than the surviving spouse. Often taxes and payment of health care professionals regarding the decedent's last illness have priority over other claims. Delaware also includes preferences for payment of child-support arrearages, rent not to exceed one year, judgments against the decedent, and mortgages. (See Del. Code Ann. tit. 12 § 2105.)

State statutes' preference lists end with "all other claims." However, not all claims are treated alike. There is a distinction between secured claims and unsecured claims. Secured claims are backed by some type of property or collateral. If the debtor does not pay the debt, the creditor may seize the collateral to help satisfy the claim. For example, home mortgage loans are secured by real estate, and car loans are secured by the specified automobile. Any type of property may be used to secure a loan. This offers more protection to the creditor.

Unsecured claims have no property or collateral to back the debt, and the creditor is more at risk. A typical example of an unsecured debt is credit cards. Therefore, although all other claims may be grouped together, a creditor with a secured claim is more protected than one with an unsecured claim.

Once Steps Two and Three are completed, the law firm prepares the estate tax returns and final account. It supervises the personal representative's satisfaction of tax liability, monitors and reports the income and outflow of the estate, and determines the property remaining for distribution to the beneficiaries and heirs. Chapter 9 discusses Step Four—taxes, and Chapter 10 discusses Step Five—the final account.

KEY **TERM**

inventory (p. 153)

REVIEW **QUESTIONS**

1. Explain the inventory. Who signs it? What type of information does it contain?

2. What is an appraisal? Under what circumstances might one be required?

3. List and briefly summarize the three options available to a law firm for giving notice to creditors about a decedent's death.

4. What information is contained in a creditor's claim document?

5. If the estate decides not to pay a claim, what type of notice should it give to the creditor? What option is available to the creditor?

6. What is the UPC's order of preference for the payment of creditors?

ROLE-PLAYING **ACTIVITY**

1. Pair up with a fellow classmate. One of you is the personal representative and the other the attorney. A creditor has submitted a questionable claim. Discuss the options available, and determine what steps the estate should take.

RESEARCH **ASSIGNMENTS**

1. In your state, what is the time limit for filing the inventory?
2. Research your state's legal requirements for the estate assets that must be specifically appraised.
3. Determine an item that should be appraised. Contact an appropriate expert and have the asset appraised.
4. Research your state's procedure with regard to giving notice to creditors. What options are available? Does giving notice shorten the time for presentation of claims?
5. Find a notice to creditors to present claims in your local paper. What information is included in it?
6. Research your state's requirements for claimant's submission of claims. What information must be included in the document?
7. Determine your state's legal procedure regarding the disallowance of a claim by the personal representative and the options available to a creditor who wants to pursue collection.
8. Research your state's order of priority for the payment of creditors.

BUILD YOUR **PORTFOLIO**

1. Using the case example you chose in Chapter 6, prepare an inventory.
2. Using the case example you chose in Chapter 6, prepare a notice to creditors to present claims form.

Chapter **nine**

STEP FOUR—TAX DOCUMENTS

The Plan Works: Less Wealth to the Government

Most people would like their wealth to be placed in the hands of those they love, those they trust, or those who will use it wisely. Most people, when planning the distribution of an estate, do not tell the law firm that they want all their wealth to go to the government or that they want to pay the most taxes they can. Sometimes a reduction in tax liability is the main reason a person develops an estate plan. The person is determined to pass his or her legacy on to family, friends, or organizations with similar goals.

Through the use of a will, trust, life insurance, or joint tenancy, the decedent may plan to reduce tax liability. This may not be the only goal, but it is usually at least one of them. A solid estate plan, where tax liability has been factored in, reduces the amount of wealth that the government receives.

The goal of this chapter is to introduce the paralegal to basic tax law in estate administration. The federal and state taxing authorities can assess tax liability under four areas: the decedent's final income tax, estate tax, inheritance tax, and fiduciary tax. Let us explore each of the four categories of taxes.

Introduction to Tax Law

A good estate planning and administration paralegal possesses some tax law knowledge. Although tax accountants and tax lawyers are experts in the area, the more tax law knowledge a paralegal has, the more valuable the paralegal is to the law firm. The amount of education and experience required of the paralegal varies from law firm to law firm.

- State under what circumstances a fiduciary tax return is prepared, name the tax forms used, and outline how tax is calculated.
- Explain a closing certificate and its purpose.

A probate paralegal may never be assigned the tax portion of the estate administration, he or she may be required to complete simple tax returns, or he or she may be involved in the research and preparation of extensive and complicated tax returns. Some law firms prefer certified public accountants or tax attorneys with a CPA to complete the tax returns because an accountant signing the return adds protection to the estate in case a mistake is made or an audit is required. If a paralegal has prepared the tax return, he or she should always have the supervising attorney review the completed tax return before it is submitted. A more in-depth study of tax law is recommended for the individual wishing to excel as an estate administration legal professional.

The United States Constitution grants the U.S. government the power to tax. In 1913, the Sixteenth Amendment to the Constitution was passed; it states:

> The Congress shall have power to lay and collect taxes on incomes, from whatever source derived, without apportionment among the several states. . .

The Internal Revenue Code (IRC) was passed by Congress in 1939 and was published as Title 26 of the United States Code. It continues today to be found in Title 26. The tax laws are administered by the Internal Revenue Service (IRS), an administrative agency. Tax law is derived primarily from three sources: statutory law, administrative law, and case law. Tax law is a huge specialty area of the law. Our concern is with the tax law as applied to estate administration. Let us turn our attention to that area.

The Employer Identification Number

employer identification number (EIN)
The number assigned by the Internal Revenue Service to an estate to be used by the estate for the preparation of tax returns and the payment of taxes.

When the estate is initially being administered, one of the first steps is to obtain an **employer identification number (EIN)** for the estate. Like our social security number, this number serves as the estate's number for filing taxes. It is acquired by preparing an SS4 form and submitting it to the federal government. The federal government then assigns a number, the EIN, to the estate to use when paying taxes. The preparation of the SS4 form was discussed in Chapter 7. Please refer to that chapter for the procedure and a sample SS4 form.

Decedent's Final Income Tax

No matter when a person dies, he or she has lived part of a year. If Mary dies April 1, 2006, she has lived three months during the year 2006. If Mark dies November 1, 2006, he has lived for ten months of the year 2006. The person may have earned an income for a portion of that year. If Mark or Mary has made enough taxable income, one more federal income tax must be paid on his or her behalf. The federal government is still entitled to taxes on that income, and death does not excuse the payment of taxes.

Similar to when you and I file and pay our individual income taxes, the personal representative must file tax returns on behalf of the decedent, and the estate must pay taxes owed, including both federal and state income taxes. Certain states do not assess income taxes. These states include Alaska, Florida, Nevada, South Dakota, Texas, Washington, and Wyoming. All other states have some type of income tax assessed. You must consult your state's law.

Our focus is on federal income tax and its requirements. While living, a taxpayer prepares and files a Form 1040 or 1040EZ (see Figure 9-1). The same form is

Figure 9-1 Form 1040: U.S. individual income tax return

Form **1040** Department of the Treasury—Internal Revenue Service
U.S. Individual Income Tax Return 20**06** (99) IRS Use Only—Do not write or staple in this space.

For the year Jan. 1–Dec. 31, 2006, or other tax year beginning , 2006, ending , 20

OMB No. 1545-0074

Label (See instructions on page 16.) **Use the IRS label.** Otherwise, please print or type.

LABEL HERE

Your first name and initial | Last name | Your social security number

If a joint return, spouse's first name and initial | Last name | Spouse's social security number

Home address (number and street). If you have a P.O. box, see page 16. | Apt. no.

▲ You **must** enter your SSN(s) above. ▲

City, town or post office, state, and ZIP code. If you have a foreign address, see page 16.

Checking a box below will not change your tax or refund.

Presidential Election Campaign ▶ Check here if you, or your spouse if filing jointly, want $3 to go to this fund (see page 16) ▶ ☐ **You** ☐ **Spouse**

Filing Status
Check only one box.

1 ☐ Single
2 ☐ Married filing jointly (even if only one had income)
3 ☐ Married filing separately. Enter spouse's SSN above and full name here. ▶
4 ☐ Head of household (with qualifying person). (See page 17.) If the qualifying person is a child but not your dependent, enter this child's name here. ▶
5 ☐ Qualifying widow(er) with dependent child (see page 17)

Exemptions

6a ☐ **Yourself.** If someone can claim you as a dependent, **do not** check box 6a
b ☐ **Spouse**

Boxes checked on 6a and 6b
No. of children on 6c who:
• lived with you
• did not live with you due to divorce or separation (see page 20)
Dependents on 6c not entered above
Add numbers on lines above ▶

c **Dependents:**

(1) First name Last name	(2) Dependent's social security number	(3) Dependent's relationship to you	(4) ✔ if qualifying child for child tax credit (see page 19)
			☐
			☐
			☐
			☐

If more than four dependents, see page 19.

d Total number of exemptions claimed

Income

Attach Form(s) W-2 here. Also attach Forms W-2G and 1099-R if tax was withheld.

If you did not get a W-2, see page 23.

Enclose, but do not attach, any payment. Also, please use Form 1040-V.

7	Wages, salaries, tips, etc. Attach Form(s) W-2	7
8a	**Taxable** interest. Attach Schedule B if required	8a
b	Tax-exempt interest. **Do not** include on line 8a [8b]	
9a	Ordinary dividends. Attach Schedule B if required	9a
b	Qualified dividends (see page 23) [9b]	
10	Taxable refunds, credits, or offsets of state and local income taxes (see page 24)	10
11	Alimony received	11
12	Business income or (loss). Attach Schedule C or C-EZ	12
13	Capital gain or (loss). Attach Schedule D if required. If not required, check here ▶ ☐	13
14	Other gains or (losses). Attach Form 4797	14
15a	IRA distributions [15a] b Taxable amount (see page 25)	15b
16a	Pensions and annuities [16a] b Taxable amount (see page 26)	16b
17	Rental real estate, royalties, partnerships, S corporations, trusts, etc. Attach Schedule E	17
18	Farm income or (loss). Attach Schedule F	18
19	Unemployment compensation	19
20a	Social security benefits [20a] b Taxable amount (see page 27)	20b
21	Other income. List type and amount (see page 29)	21
22	Add the amounts in the far right column for lines 7 through 21. This is your **total income** ▶	22

Adjusted Gross Income

23	Archer MSA deduction. Attach Form 8853 [23]	
24	Certain business expenses of reservists, performing artists, and fee-basis government officials. Attach Form 2106 or 2106-EZ [24]	
25	Health savings account deduction. Attach Form 8889 [25]	
26	Moving expenses. Attach Form 3903 [26]	
27	One-half of self-employment tax. Attach Schedule SE [27]	
28	Self-employed SEP, SIMPLE, and qualified plans [28]	
29	Self-employed health insurance deduction (see page 29) [29]	
30	Penalty on early withdrawal of savings [30]	
31a	Alimony paid b Recipient's SSN ▶ [31a]	
32	IRA deduction (see page 31) [32]	
33	Student loan interest deduction (see page 33) [33]	
34	Jury duty pay you gave to your employer [34]	
35	Domestic production activities deduction. Attach Form 8903 [35]	
36	Add lines 23 through 31a and 32 through 35	36
37	Subtract line 36 from line 22. This is your **adjusted gross income** ▶	37

For Disclosure, Privacy Act, and Paperwork Reduction Act Notice, see page 80. Cat. No. 11320B Form **1040** (2006)

(continued)

Figure 9-1 (continued)

Form 1040 (2006)   Page **2**

Tax and Credits	38	Amount from line 37 (adjusted gross income)	38	

39a Check if: □ **You** were born before January 2, 1942, □ Blind. □ **Spouse** was born before January 2, 1942, □ Blind. } **Total boxes checked** ▶ 39a

b If your spouse itemizes on a separate return or you were a dual-status alien, see page 34 and check here ▶39b □

Standard Deduction for—

- People who checked any box on line 39a or 39b **or** who can be claimed as a dependent, see page 34.

- All others:

Single or Married filing separately, $5,150

Married filing jointly or Qualifying widow(er), $10,300

Head of household, $7,550

40	**Itemized deductions** (from Schedule A) **or** your **standard deduction** (see left margin) . .	40	
41	Subtract line 40 from line 38	41	
42	If line 38 is over $112,875, or you provided housing to a person displaced by Hurricane Katrina, see page 36. Otherwise, multiply $3,300 by the total number of exemptions claimed on line 6d	42	
43	**Taxable income.** Subtract line 42 from line 41. If line 42 is more than line 41, enter -0- .	43	
44	**Tax** (see page 36). Check if any tax is from: **a** □ Form(s) 8814 **b** □ Form 4972 . . .	44	
45	**Alternative minimum tax** (see page 39). Attach Form 6251	45	
46	Add lines 44 and 45 . . . . ▶	46	
47	Foreign tax credit. Attach Form 1116 if required . . .	47	
48	Credit for child and dependent care expenses. Attach Form 2441	48	
49	Credit for the elderly or the disabled. Attach Schedule R .	49	
50	Education credits. Attach Form 8863	50	
51	Retirement savings contributions credit. Attach Form 8880 .	51	
52	Residential energy credits. Attach Form 5695	52	
53	Child tax credit (see page 42). Attach Form 8901 if required	53	
54	Credits from: **a** □ Form 8396 **b** □ Form 8839 **c** □ Form 8859	54	
55	Other credits: **a** □ Form 3800 **b** □ Form 8801 **c** □ Form	55	
56	Add lines 47 through 55. These are your **total credits**	56	
57	Subtract line 56 from line 46. If line 56 is more than line 46, enter -0- . . . . . . ▶	57	

Other Taxes

58	Self-employment tax. Attach Schedule SE	58	
59	Social security and Medicare tax on tip income not reported to employer. Attach Form 4137 . .	59	
60	Additional tax on IRAs, other qualified retirement plans, etc. Attach Form 5329 if required .	60	
61	Advance earned income credit payments from Form(s) W-2, box 9	61	
62	Household employment taxes. Attach Schedule H	62	
63	Add lines 57 through 62. This is your **total tax** . . . . ▶	63	

Payments

If you have a qualifying child, attach Schedule EIC.

64	Federal income tax withheld from Forms W-2 and 1099 . .	64	
65	2006 estimated tax payments and amount applied from 2005 return	65	
66a	**Earned income credit (EIC)**	66a	
b	Nontaxable combat pay election ▶	66b	
67	Excess social security and tier 1 RRTA tax withheld (see page 60)	67	
68	Additional child tax credit. Attach Form 8812	68	
69	Amount paid with request for extension to file (see page 60)	69	
70	Payments from: **a** □ Form 2439 **b** □ Form 4136 **c** □ Form 8885 .	70	
71	Credit for federal telephone excise tax paid. Attach Form 8913 if required	71	
72	Add lines 64, 65, 66a, and 67 through 71. These are your **total payments** . . . . ▶	72	

Refund

Direct deposit? See page 61 and fill in 74b, 74c, and 74d, or Form 8888.

73	If line 72 is more than line 63, subtract line 63 from line 72. This is the amount you **overpaid**	73	
74a	Amount of line 73 you want **refunded to you.** If Form 8888 is attached, check here ▶ □	74a	

▶ **b** Routing number [   ] ▶ **c** Type: □ Checking □ Savings
▶ **d** Account number [   ]

75	Amount of line 73 you want **applied to your 2007 estimated tax** ▶	75	

Amount You Owe

76	**Amount you owe.** Subtract line 72 from line 63. For details on how to pay, see page 62 ▶	76	
77	Estimated tax penalty (see page 62)	77	

Third Party Designee

Do you want to allow another person to discuss this return with the IRS (see page 63)? □ **Yes.** Complete the following. □ **No**

Designee's name ▶   Phone no. ▶ (   )   Personal identification number (PIN) ▶ [   ]

Sign Here

Joint return? See page 17.

Keep a copy for your records.

Under penalties of perjury, I declare that I have examined this return and accompanying schedules and statements, and to the best of my knowledge and belief, they are true, correct, and complete. Declaration of preparer (other than taxpayer) is based on all information of which preparer has any knowledge.

Your signature   Date   Your occupation   Daytime phone number ( )

Spouse's signature. If a joint return, **both** must sign.   Date   Spouse's occupation

Paid Preparer's Use Only

Preparer's signature ▶   Date   Check if self-employed □   Preparer's SSN or PTIN

Firm's name (or yours if self-employed), address, and ZIP code ▶   EIN   Phone no. ( )

Form **1040** (2006)

prepared on behalf of the decedent. It is a very good idea for the paralegal to obtain the decedent's income tax returns for the last three years of his or her life to help with the preparation of the decedent's final income tax return.

The first amount that must be determined is the decedent's **gross income**. The Internal Revenue Code (IRC) defines gross income as "all income from whatever source derived" (26 U.S.C. § 61). Gross income includes salary, royalties, interest, rent received, dividends, capital gains, alimony, and so on. Some income is not taxable; this type of nontaxable income includes accident and health insurance benefits, proceeds from a life insurance policy, gifts, veteran's benefits, scholarships for tuition, and so on.

Although gross income is the starting point for the preparation of the decedent's federal income tax return, this amount is not the amount on which the tax is assessed. That amount is called **taxable income**. Gross income less deductions and exemptions equals taxable income, as shown in Equation 9-1:

$$\text{Taxable income} = \text{gross income} - (\text{deductions} + \text{exemptions}) \qquad (9\text{-}1)$$

Once the gross income is calculated, deductions are subtracted from it. A **deduction** is a reduction in the amount of gross income and translates into less tax being owed. The taxpayer, in our case the personal representative, chooses whether to use a standard deduction or an itemized deduction. The **standard deduction** is an amount set by the Internal Revenue Service (IRS) that allows the taxpayer to subtract the set amount from his or her gross income; the taxpayer does not have to justify the amount. The other option available to the taxpayer is the **itemized deduction**. Itemized deductions are reported on Schedule A of Form 1040. The itemized deductions include medical bills, taxes, interest paid, charitable gifts, losses due to theft or casualty, employment expenses, and miscellaneous expenses. Certain rules, restrictions, and limitations apply to the listed deduction categories, and these categories must be learned and applied by the legal professional in preparation of the schedule. The taxpayer typically prefers to use the type of deduction that lessens tax liability the most.

Another method of reducing the amount of tax liability is exemptions. Exemptions are also subtracted from gross income to determine taxable income (see Equation 9-1). Exemptions are reductions in gross income for a taxpayer and his or her dependents. Two types of exemptions exist:

1. Personal: for the taxpayer.
2. Dependents: for the spouse, children, or other relatives living in the taxpayer's household to which the taxpayer contributes more than half of the money used to support the individual.

After the taxable income is calculated, the tax preparer refers to the tax table prepared by the IRS, which shows the amount of taxable income and the corresponding amount of tax owed. The United States uses a progressive income tax rate: as the taxpayer's income increases, so does the percentage rate of taxes that must be paid. Therefore, if Richard earns $100,000.00 of taxable income and Michael earns $50,000.00, Richard's tax rate is greater than is Michael's.

Once the taxable amount has been determined, **credits** may be applied to reduce the amount of tax liability. Credits provide a dollar-for-dollar reduction in the tax amount owed. Examples of tax credits include child and dependent care, education credit, earned income credit, and so on. After any tax credits are

gross income
All income from whatever source derived.

taxable income
The income calculated by subtracting deductions and exemptions from gross income, or adjusted gross income, to which tax rates are applied to compute tax liability.

deduction
An item allowed to reduce the gross income amount.

standard deduction
A percentage amount, set by the Internal Revenue Service, that the taxpayer may use rather than itemized deductions to reduce gross income.

itemized deduction
A taxpayer expense detailed under an appropriate category to reduce the amount of taxable income.

credits
Amounts subtracted from taxable income to reduce tax liability.

subtracted, the tax due must be paid. The tax return and any taxes owed are due the fifteenth day of the fourth month of the close of the taxable year. Most taxpayers and estates use a calendar year; thus, the tax is due April 15. If the decedent died on May 25, 2006, the tax return and payment was due April 15, 2007.

If the decedent died leaving behind a surviving spouse, a joint return may be filed. For example, Carrie and Jeff are married. Jeff dies July 4, 2006. The estate could file the final 2006 return as a joint return with Carrie on April 15, 2007. Analyzing the tax due, the legal professional or accountant determines if a reduction in taxes results from filing a joint return. The surviving spouse must agree to file the joint return and must not be remarried.

Introduction to Estate Tax

estate tax
A one-time tax imposed on an estate because of the decedent's privilege of transferring property upon death.

The **estate tax** is a one-time tax levied on wealth as it passes from the decedent to heirs or beneficiaries. It is the responsibility of the personal representative, with the assistance of the law firm, to prepare and file the required return. The estate is required to pay any tax that is due. Our focus is on the federal estate tax. At the end of this section, a quick discussion about state estate tax is included. It should be noted that most estates are not subject to a federal estate tax because they are not high enough in value.

Internal Revenue Service Form 706, the U.S. estate tax return, is used for this preparation. An EIN number must be acquired and included on the federal estate tax return. The federal estate tax return and payment of taxes is due nine months from the decedent's date of death. If it is anticipated that more time will be required, Form 4768, application for extension of time to file U.S. estate tax return, should be completed as soon as possible. The government automatically grants an extension for six months. The estate is required to file Form 706, the U.S. estate tax return, only if the taxable estate exceeds the unified credit, or the applicable exclusion amount. Otherwise, the decedent's wealth passes to the heirs or beneficiaries without federal estate tax liability.

The Unified Credit or Applicable Exclusion Amount

unified credit
An amount used to reduce tax liability (credit) that replaces the former lifetime gift tax exemption and estate tax exemption.

Not every estate owes an estate tax. The estate tax catches only the largest estates. Smaller estates need not worry about the filing of the return or tax liability because of the **unified credit**, or applicable exclusion amount. The unified credit acts as an exemption and reduces the amount of estate tax due. It applies to transfers of wealth by an inter vivos gift or testamentary transfer. If the decedent exceeds the exemption on taxable gifts while alive, the amount of the unified credit is reduced. In 2008, the amount excluded is two million dollars ($2,000,000.00). The amount is scheduled to increase. Figure 9-2 lists the applicable exclusion amount and unified credit for estates from 2001 to 2010. This figure is based on the Economic Growth and Tax Reconciliation Act of 2001.

Federal Estate Tax: Form 706

Assume the estate owes estate tax. Let us consider the sections to be completed on Form 706. The form consists of five sections: Part 1—Decedent and Executor, Part 2—Tax Computation, Part 3—Elections by the Executor, Part 4—General

Figure 9-2   Unified credit and applicable exclusion amount

Year	Unified Credit	Applicable Exclusion
2001	$ 220,550.00	$ 675,000.00
2002	$ 345,800.00	$ 1,000,000.00
2003	$ 345,800.00	$ 1,000,000.00
2004	$ 555,800.00	$ 1,500,000.00
2005	$ 555,800.00	$ 1,500,000.00
2006	$ 780,800.00	$ 2,000,000.00
2007	$ 780,800.00	$ 2,000,000.00
2008	$ 780,800.00	$ 2,000,000.00
2009	$ 1,455,800.00	$ 3,500,000.00
2010	Estate tax repealed	

Information, and Part 5—Recapitulation. See Figure 9-3 for a summary of the sections.

Form 706 contains many schedules. Because Form 706 is so lengthy, the schedules that are discussed next are not included in this textbook. The first three pages of Form 706 are included for your reference in Figure 9-4.

The first nine schedules of the federal estate tax return refer to the decedent's assets. They include the type of asset, described at length, and the valuation of the asset. These first nine schedules are Schedule A: Real Estate; Schedule B: Stocks and Bonds; Schedule C: Mortgages, Notes, and Cash; Schedule D: Insurance on the Decedent's Life; Schedule E: Jointly Owned Property; Schedule F: Other Miscellaneous Property Not Reportable Under Any Other Schedule; Schedule G: Transfers During Decedent's Life; Schedule H: Powers of Appointment; and Schedule I: Annuities. A more detailed explanation of Schedules A through I is found in Figure 9-5. The final total amount of these schedules is the total gross estate value. Remember that if the amount is less than the applicable exclusion amount, no tax is due. The calculation and preparation of the federal estate tax can be concluded here. No return needs to be filed.

If the value of the total gross estate exceeds the applicable exclusion amount, then the deduction schedules should be completed. Figure 9-6 summarizes these deduction schedules. These deductions reduce the value of the gross estate and are prepared to determine the decedent's net taxable estate. The current five schedules are Schedule J: Funeral Expenses and Expenses Incurred in Administering Property Subject to Claims; Schedule K: Debts of the Decedent, and Mortgages and Liens; Schedule L: Net Losses During Administration and Expenses Incurred in Administering Property Not Subject to Claims; Schedule M: Bequests, etc., to

Figure 9-3 Form 706: summary of sections

Part 1—Decedent and Executor

This section requires information about the decedent and the executor. The decedent's name, social security number, date of birth, date of death, and where he or she was domiciled at the time of death must be included. The executor's name and address are reported.

Part 2—Tax Computation

This section includes the value of the gross estate minus deductions, application of the unified credit, and other credits. It is a summary of the calculation that appears on twenty attached schedules.

Part 3—Elections by the Executor

The personal representative selects the type of asset valuation used by the estate. The IRS permits the decedent's assets to be valued in one of two ways. The assets' value may be the date-of-death value or it may be based on the assets' value six months after the date of death. The personal representative selects whichever value is lower because that translates into less tax liability. This is an important decision for the personal representative. All assets are valued on the date selected. In this section, the personal representative indicates which valuation method was used and whether the taxes due will be paid in installments.

Part 4—General Information

This section contains general information regarding the estate. A copy of the death certificate is attached. The decedent's business or occupation, a surviving spouse's information, and a list of all persons who inherited, their relationship to the decedent, social security number, and the amount inherited is reported.

Part 5—Recapitulation

The totals appearing on each attached schedule are reported.

---

marital deduction
Property passing to a surviving spouse that is not subject to estate tax.

Surviving Spouse (also known as the **marital deduction**); and Schedule O: Charitable, Public, and Similar Gifts and Bequests.

After the deduction schedules are completed, subtract the deduction amount from the gross taxable estate, which yields the net taxable amount. If the net taxable amount is lower than the applicable exclusion amount, no tax is due. The legal professional or accountant has completed working on the federal estate tax. If the number still exceeds the applicable exclusion amount, calculate the estate tax owed. The estate is allowed certain tax credits and other reductions in tax owed. These remaining schedules, which are summarized in Figure 9-7, are attached to the return. These schedules currently include Schedule P: Credit for Foreign Death Taxes; Schedule Q: Credit for Tax on Prior Transfers; Schedule R: Generation-Skipping Transfer Tax; and Schedule U: Qualified Conservation Easement Exclusion. These tax credits reduce the amount of taxes owed to the government.

Figure 9-4 Form 706: United States estate (and generation-skipping transfer) tax return

Form **706** (Rev. October 2006) Department of the Treasury Internal Revenue Service	**United States Estate (and Generation-Skipping Transfer) Tax Return** Estate of a citizen or resident of the United States (see separate instructions). To be filed for decedents dying after December 31, 2005, and before January 1, 2007.	OMB No. 1545-0015

Part 1—Decedent and Executor

1a Decedent's first name and middle initial (and maiden name, if any)	1b Decedent's last name	2 **Decedent's Social Security No.**

3a County, state, and ZIP code, or foreign country, of legal residence (domicile) at time of death	3b Year domicile established	4 Date of birth	5 Date of death

6b Executor's address (number and street including apartment or suite no. or rural route; city, town, or post office; state; and ZIP code) and phone no.

6a Name of executor (see page 4 of the instructions)

6c Executor's social security number (see page 4 of the instructions)

Phone no. (   )

7a Name and location of court where will was probated or estate administered	7b Case number

8 If decedent died testate, check here ▶ ☐ and attach a certified copy of the will. 9 If you extended the time to file this Form 706, check here ▶ ☐

10 If Schedule R-1 is attached, check here ▶ ☐

Part 2—Tax Computation

1	Total gross estate less exclusion (from Part 5—Recapitulation, page 3, item 12)	1
2	Tentative total allowable deductions (from Part 5—Recapitulation, page 3, item 22)	2
3a	Tentative taxable estate (before state death tax deduction) (subtract line 2 from line 1)	3a
b	State death tax deduction	3b
c	Taxable estate (subtract line 3b from line 3a)	3c
4	Adjusted taxable gifts (total taxable gifts (within the meaning of section 2503) made by the decedent after December 31, 1976, other than gifts that are includible in decedent's gross estate (section 2001(b)))	4
5	Add lines 3c and 4	5
6	Tentative tax on the amount on line 5 from Table A on page 4 of the instructions	6
7	Total gift tax paid or payable with respect to gifts made by the decedent after December 31, 1976. Include gift taxes by the decedent's spouse for such spouse's share of split gifts (section 2513) only if the decedent was the donor of these gifts and they are includible in the decedent's gross estate (see instructions)	7
8	Gross estate tax (subtract line 7 from line 6)	8
9	Maximum unified credit (applicable credit amount) against estate tax . [9]	
10	Adjustment to unified credit (applicable credit amount). (This adjustment may not exceed $6,000. See page 6 of the instructions.) . . . . [10]	
11	Allowable unified credit (applicable credit amount) (subtract line 10 from line 9)	11
12	Subtract line 11 from line 8 (but do not enter less than zero)	12
13	Credit for foreign death taxes (from Schedule(s) P). (Attach Form(s) 706-CE.) . . . . . . [13]	
14	Credit for tax on prior transfers (from Schedule Q) . . . . . [14]	
15	Total credits (add lines 13 and 14)	15
16	Net estate tax (subtract line 15 from line 12)	16
17	Generation-skipping transfer (GST) taxes payable (from Schedule R, Part 2, line 10)	17
18	Total transfer taxes (add lines 16 and 17)	18
19	Prior payments. Explain in an attached statement	19
20	Balance due (or overpayment) (subtract line 19 from line 18)	20

Under penalties of perjury, I declare that I have examined this return, including accompanying schedules and statements, and to the best of my knowledge and belief, it is true, correct, and complete. Declaration of preparer other than the executor is based on all information of which preparer has any knowledge.

Signature(s) of executor(s)   Date

Signature of preparer other than executor   Address (and ZIP code)   Date

For Privacy Act and Paperwork Reduction Act Notice, see page 28 of the separate instructions for this form.   Cat. No. 20548R   Form **706** (Rev. 10-2006)

(continued)

Figure 9-4 (continued)

Form 706 (Rev. 10-2006)

Estate of:

Part 3—Elections by the Executor

Please check the "Yes" or "No" box for each question (see instructions beginning on page 6).

Note. Some of these elections require the posting of bonds or liens.

		Yes	No
1 Do you elect alternate valuation? **1**			
2 Do you elect special-use valuation? . . . . If "Yes," you must complete and attach Schedule A–1. **2**			
3 Do you elect to pay the taxes in installments as described in section 6166? . . . . If "Yes," you must attach the additional information described on pages 9 and 10 of the instructions. **Note. By electing section 6166, you agree to provide security for estate tax deferred under section 6166 and interest in the form of a surety bond or a section 6324A special lien.** **3**			
4 Do you elect to postpone the part of the taxes attributable to a reversionary or remainder interest as described in section 6163? **4**			

Part 4—General Information (Note. Please attach the necessary supplemental documents. **You must attach the death certificate.**) (see instructions on page 11)

Authorization to receive confidential tax information under Regs. sec. 601.504(b)(2)(i); to act as the estate's representative before the IRS; and to make written or oral presentations on behalf of the estate if return prepared by an attorney, accountant, or enrolled agent for the executor:

Name of representative (print or type)	State	Address (number, street, and room or suite no., city, state, and ZIP code)

I declare that I am the ☐ attorney/ ☐ certified public accountant/ ☐ enrolled agent (you must check the applicable box) for the executor and prepared this return for the executor. I am not under suspension or disbarment from practice before the Internal Revenue Service and am qualified to practice in the state shown above.

Signature	CAF number	Date	Telephone number

1 Death certificate number and issuing authority (attach a copy of the death certificate to this return).

2 Decedent's business or occupation. If retired, check here ▶ ☐ and state decedent's former business or occupation.

3 Marital status of the decedent at time of death:

☐ Married

☐ Widow or widower—Name, SSN, and date of death of deceased spouse ▶ -

- -

☐ Single

☐ Legally separated

☐ Divorced—Date divorce decree became final ▶

4a Surviving spouse's name	**4b** Social security number	**4c** Amount received (see page 11 of the instructions)

5 Individuals (other than the surviving spouse), trusts, or other estates who receive benefits from the estate (do not include charitable beneficiaries shown in Schedule O) (see instructions).

Name of individual, trust, or estate receiving $5,000 or more	Identifying number	Relationship to decedent	Amount (see instructions)

All unascertainable beneficiaries and those who receive less than $5,000 . . . . ▶	

Total	

Please check the "Yes" or "No" box for each question.

		Yes	No
6 Does the gross estate contain any section 2044 property (qualified terminable interest property (QTIP) from a prior gift or estate) (see page 11 of the instructions)?			
7a Have federal gift tax returns ever been filed? . . . . If "Yes," please attach copies of the returns, if available, and furnish the following information:			
7b Period(s) covered	**7c** Internal Revenue office(s) where filed		

(continued on next page)

Page 2

(continued)

Figure 9-4 (continued)

Form 706 (Rev. 10-2006)

Part 4—General Information (continued)

If you answer "Yes" to any of questions 8–16, you must attach additional information as described in the instructions.	Yes	No
8a Was there any insurance on the decedent's life that is not included on the return as part of the gross estate?		
b Did the decedent own any insurance on the life of another that is not included in the gross estate?		
9 Did the decedent at the time of death own any property as a joint tenant with right of survivorship in which **(a)** one or more of the other joint tenants was someone other than the decedent's spouse, and **(b)** less than the full value of the property is included on the return as part of the gross estate? If "Yes," you must complete and attach Schedule E		
10 Did the decedent, at the time of death, own any interest in a partnership or unincorporated business or any stock in an inactive or closely held corporation?		
11 Did the decedent make any transfer described in section 2035, 2036, 2037, or 2038 (see the instructions for Schedule G beginning on page 13 of the separate instructions)? If "Yes," you must complete and attach Schedule G		
12a Were there in existence at the time of the decedent's death any trusts created by the decedent during his or her lifetime?		
b Were there in existence at the time of the decedent's death any trusts not created by the decedent under which the decedent possessed any power, beneficial interest, or trusteeship?		
c Was the decedent receiving income from a trust created after October 22, 1986 by a parent or grandparent?		
If "Yes," was there a GST taxable termination (under section 2612) upon the death of the decedent?		
d If there was a GST taxable termination (under section 2612), attach a statement to explain. Provide a copy of the trust or will creating the trust, and give the name, address, and phone number of the current trustee(s).		
e Did decedent at any time during his or her lifetime transfer or sell an interest in a partnership, limited liability company, or closely held corporation to a trust described in question 12a or 12b?		
If "Yes," provide the EIN number to this transferred/sold item. ▶		
13 Did the decedent ever possess, exercise, or release any general power of appointment? If "Yes," you must complete and attach Schedule H		
14 Was the marital deduction computed under the transitional rule of Public Law 97-34, section 403(e)(3) (Economic Recovery Tax Act of 1981)?		
If "Yes," attach a separate computation of the marital deduction, enter the amount on item 20 of the Recapitulation, and note on item 20 "computation attached."		
15 Was the decedent, immediately before death, receiving an annuity described in the "General" paragraph of the instructions for Schedule I or a private annuity? If "Yes," you must complete and attach Schedule I		
16 Was the decedent ever the beneficiary of a trust for which a deduction was claimed by the estate of a pre-deceased spouse under section 2056(b)(7) and which is not reported on this return? If "Yes," attach an explanation		

Part 5—Recapitulation

Item number	Gross estate		Alternate value	Value at date of death
1	Schedule A—Real Estate	1		
2	Schedule B—Stocks and Bonds	2		
3	Schedule C—Mortgages, Notes, and Cash	3		
4	Schedule D—Insurance on the Decedent's Life (attach Form(s) 712)	4		
5	Schedule E—Jointly Owned Property (attach Form(s) 712 for life insurance)	5		
6	Schedule F—Other Miscellaneous Property (attach Form(s) 712 for life insurance)	6		
7	Schedule G—Transfers During Decedent's Life (att. Form(s) 712 for life insurance)	7		
8	Schedule H—Powers of Appointment	8		
9	Schedule I—Annuities	9		
10	Total gross estate (add items 1 through 9)	10		
11	Schedule U—Qualified Conservation Easement Exclusion	11		
12	Total gross estate less exclusion (subtract item 11 from item 10). Enter here and on line 1 of Part 2—Tax Computation	12		

Item number	Deductions		Amount
13	Schedule J—Funeral Expenses and Expenses Incurred in Administering Property Subject to Claims	13	
14	Schedule K—Debts of the Decedent	14	
15	Schedule K—Mortgages and Liens	15	
16	Total of items 13 through 15	16	
17	Allowable amount of deductions from item 16 (see the instructions for item 17 of the Recapitulation)	17	
18	Schedule L—Net Losses During Administration	18	
19	Schedule L—Expenses Incurred in Administering Property Not Subject to Claims	19	
20	Schedule M—Bequests, etc., to Surviving Spouse	20	
21	Schedule O—Charitable, Public, and Similar Gifts and Bequests	21	
22	Tentative total allowable deductions (add items 17 through 21). Enter here and on line 2 of the Tax Computation	22	

Page 3

Figure 9-5   Summary of Schedules A Through I

Schedule A: Real Estate

The real estate schedule reports the fair-market value of all the decedent's real property solely owned or owned as a tenant in common with another. The real estate must be described so the IRS can determine where it is located.

Schedule B: Stocks and Bonds

Stocks must be listed by the name of the corporation, number of shares, and par value. If the stock has a Committee on Uniform Security Identification Procedure (CUSIP) number, it must be included. A CUSIP number identifies securities such as stocks traded on the major stock exchanges. It is a nine-digit number assigned to the stock. If the stock is from a closely held corporation, the EIN must be included in the description.

Bonds are named by the entity that is the payor and include the face amount of the bond. They too require a CUSIP number or EIN.

Schedule C: Mortgages, Notes, and Cash

The personal representative lists all mortgages, promissory notes, contracts to sell land, cash, and checking and savings accounts owned by the decedent. Mortgages and notes listed here are payable to the decedent, not owed by the decedent. To adequately describe mortgages or promissory notes, include the maker's name, face value, unpaid principal, property involved, loan date, maturity date, and so on.

Bank accounts include the name and address of the financial institution, amount deposited, account number, type of account, and accrued interest. The location of all cash must be reported.

Schedule D: Insurance on the Decedent's Life

Schedule D requires inclusion of insurance on the decedent's life payable to the estate and, under certain circumstances, insurance on the decedent's life payable to designated beneficiaries where the decedent has retained incidents of ownership. Instructions for Schedule D should be consulted for the circumstances in which the decedent retains incidents of ownership. A description of insurance includes the insurance company's name and policy number.

Schedule E: Jointly Owned Property

Any property held jointly with right of survivorship or tenancy by the entirety is listed here. The property should be described as it would be if it were included in another schedule. For example, real estate is described as Schedule A required. Consult the instructions for Schedule E for the method of valuing the decedent's interest in any jointly owned property.

(continued)

Figure 9-5   (continued)

Schedule F: Other Miscellaneous Property Not Reported Under Any Other Schedule

This is a catchall schedule. Any other property not previously reported may be included here, for example, collections or artwork with certain values, business interests, royalty rights, and so on.

Schedule G: Transfers During Decedent's Life

Any property the decedent transferred in the last three years of his or her life is reported here. This information includes property transferred into an inter vivos trust. It excludes small gifts.

Schedule H: Powers of Appointment

This schedule includes property in which the decedent has a general power of appointment. A power of appointment is given by one person (the donor) to another person (the donee). The donee has the authority to name who receives property upon the donor testator's death.

Schedule I: Annuities

An annuity is the right to receive periodic payment for a set number of years or life. This schedule requires the inclusion of annuities owned by the decedent. The company providing the annuity policy determines the actuarial value of the annuity and prepares documentation to be attached to the tax return.

Figure 9-6   Summary of Schedules J Through O: Deduction schedules

---

Schedule J: Funeral Expenses and Expenses Incurred Administering Property Subject to Claims

Reasonable funeral expenses are listed here, including, but not limited to, costs for the funeral, burial, or cremation. Administration expenses are reported and include executor's fees, attorney's fees, appraiser's fees, accountant's fees, court costs, and costs of storing and/or maintaining assets. Certain deductions are also permitted on the fiduciary tax return. Some of them cannot be taken on both returns.

Schedule K: Debts of the Decedent, and Mortgages and Liens

This schedule contains information regarding both secured and unsecured debts of the decedent.

Schedule L: Net Losses During Administration and Expenses Incurred in Administering Property Not Subject to Claims

The net losses section lists all losses from casualties such as fires, storms, or theft. The losses reported on this schedule have not been reimbursed

---

(continued)

Figure 9-6   (continued)

---

through insurance or another indemnification source. One example of expenses incurred in administering property not subject to claims is the cost of administrating a trust that was created prior to the decedent's death.

Schedule M: Bequests, etc., to Surviving Spouse

This section is also known as the marital deduction. All property passing to the surviving spouse—whether it is by will, intestate succession, or spousal election—is reported here. This property is inheritable by the surviving spouse without any tax liability.

Schedule O: Charitable, Public, and Similar Gifts and Bequests

Reporting of all gifts given to charitable organizations is done on Schedule O. A charitable organization is one that operates to promote a benefit to the public in education, religion, science, and so on.

Figure 9-7   Summary of Schedules P Through U

Schedule P: Credit for Foreign Death Taxes

This credit is allowed if the decedent owned property located in a foreign country and the estate has paid death taxes to the foreign country.

Schedule Q: Credit for Tax on Prior Transfers

If the decedent received property within the last ten years before his or her death as the beneficiary of another's estate, any estate taxes paid on that property create a credit for this decedent's estate. A sliding scale is applied, depending on when the decedent received the property. The credit is highest for property inherited within two (2) years of the decedent's death; it is lowest for property inherited within nine to ten (9 to 10) years of the decedent's death.

Schedule R: Generation-Skipping Transfer Tax

Schedule R reports any transfer tax imposed on a generation-skipping trust. A tax professional knowledgeable about generation-skipping transfer tax should be consulted because this tax area is complex.

Schedule U: Qualified Conservation Easement Exclusion

If property was owned for at least three (3) years by the decedent and is allocated for conservation, Schedule U provides for a possible reduction in estate tax due.

State Estate Tax

States may also impose a tax on the transfer of the decedent's estate to its new owners, the beneficiaries and heirs. These taxes take three forms: an estate tax, a pickup tax, or an inheritance tax. The inheritance tax is discussed in the next section of this chapter.

The state estate tax is imposed on the privilege of transferring property and measured by the value of the property transferred. The estate tax in many states is referred to as a pickup tax and is determined based on information reported in the federal estate tax return. It takes into consideration the credit available on the return for paying the state death taxes and allows the state to collect on it.

Some states have separate estate taxes not based on the pickup tax. State laws must be consulted to determine what forms must be filed and how to calculate state pickup or estate taxes.

Inheritance Tax

The federal government does not impose an **inheritance tax**; however, some state governments may have one. You should research and become familiar with your state's laws for imposing a tax on the passing of a decedent's wealth to others. An inheritance tax is a tax imposed on the privilege of receiving property from the decedent; it is the opposite of the purpose of an estate tax, which is a tax imposed on the privilege of transferring property upon death. An inheritance tax is usually calculated by determining who the recipients of the property are and the amount being given to each recipient. The closer the beneficiary's or heir's relationship to the decedent, the greater the exemption and the lower the tax rate. In other words, a beneficiary who is a spouse receives an amount that is taxed at a lower amount and at a lower rate than that for someone who is a friend of the decedent.

For example, William dies and leaves $100,000.00 each to his spouse, Rebecca; his uncle Ricco; and his best friend Dan. Rebecca has the greatest exemption amount and no tax may be due on her $100,000.00. Ricco has the second highest exemption, and only a portion of the $100,000.00 may be subject to tax liability. Dan has the lowest or perhaps no exemption, and all of his $100,000.00 may be subject to tax. Likewise, Rebecca has the lowest or no tax rate imposed. Ricco has a higher tax rate than Rebecca, but his is lower than Dan's. Dan has the highest tax rate imposed.

inheritance tax
Tax imposed on the privilege of receiving a decedent's property.

Fiduciary Tax

If an estate earns an income while it is open, the personal representative may need to prepare and file a fiduciary tax return. The estate then pays any tax liability that is due and owed. As you recall, a fiduciary is a person who acts on behalf of another with trust and confidence. Fiduciary tax returns are prepared under two circumstances: (1) by executors and administrators of an estate and (2) by trustees of inter vivos or testamentary trusts. Our focus is on preparation of the fiduciary return in connection with the estate.

Not every estate must file a fiduciary tax return. Currently, only those estates that produce at least $600.00 in annual income or have a beneficiary who is an alien must file. The Internal Revenue Service requires Form 1041, the U.S. tax return for estates and trusts (see Figure 9-8), to be prepared and filed under those circumstances. The return must be filed for every year the estate is open. If the estate is

Figure 9-8 Form 1041: U.S. income tax return for estates and trusts

Department of the Treasury—Internal Revenue Service

Form 1041 U.S. Income Tax Return for Estates and Trusts 2006

OMB No. 1545-0092

A Type of entity (see instr.):
- ☐ Decedent's estate
- ☐ Simple trust
- ☐ Complex trust
- ☐ Qualified disability trust
- ☐ ESBT (S portion only)
- ☐ Grantor type trust
- ☐ Bankruptcy estate–Ch. 7
- ☐ Bankruptcy estate–Ch. 11
- ☐ Pooled income fund

For calendar year 2006 or fiscal year beginning _____ , 2006, and ending _____ , 20___

Name of estate or trust (If a grantor type trust, see page 12 of the instructions.)

Name and title of fiduciary

Number, street, and room or suite no. (If a P.O. box, see page 12 of the instructions.)

City or town, state, and ZIP code

C Employer identification number

D Date entity created

E Nonexempt charitable and split-interest trusts, check applicable boxes (see page 13 of the instr.):
- ☐ Described in section 4947(a)(1)
- ☐ Not a private foundation
- ☐ Described in section 4947(a)(2)

B Number of Schedules K-1 attached (see instructions) ▶

F Check applicable boxes:
- ☐ Initial return
- ☐ Final return
- ☐ Amended return
- ☐ Change in fiduciary
- ☐ Change in fiduciary's name
- ☐ Change in trust's name
- ☐ Change in fiduciary's address

G Pooled mortgage account (see page 14 of the instructions): ☐ Bought ☐ Sold Date: _____

Income

1	Interest income	1
2a	Total ordinary dividends	2a
b	Qualified dividends allocable to: **(1)** Beneficiaries _____ **(2)** Estate or trust _____	
3	Business income or (loss). Attach Schedule C or C-EZ (Form 1040)	3
4	Capital gain or (loss). Attach Schedule D (Form 1041)	4
5	Rents, royalties, partnerships, other estates and trusts, etc. Attach Schedule E (Form 1040)	5
6	Farm income or (loss). Attach Schedule F (Form 1040)	6
7	Ordinary gain or (loss). Attach Form 4797	7
8	Other income. List type and amount _____	8
9	**Total income.** Combine lines 1, 2a, and 3 through 8 ▶	9

Deductions

10	Interest. Check if Form 4952 is attached ▶ ☐	10
11	Taxes	11
12	Fiduciary fees	12
13	Charitable deduction (from Schedule A, line 7)	13
14	Attorney, accountant, and return preparer fees	14
15a	Other deductions **not** subject to the 2% floor (attach schedule)	15a
b	Allowable miscellaneous itemized deductions subject to the 2% floor	15b
16	Add lines 10 through 15b ▶	16
17	Adjusted total income or (loss). Subtract line 16 from line 9	17
18	Income distribution deduction (from Schedule B, line 15). Attach Schedules K-1 (Form 1041)	18
19	Estate tax deduction including certain generation-skipping taxes (attach computation)	19
20	Exemption	20
21	Add lines 18 through 20 ▶	21

Tax and Payments

22	Taxable income. Subtract line 21 from line 17. If a loss, see page 20 of the instructions	22
23	**Total tax** (from Schedule G, line 7)	23
24	**Payments: a** 2006 estimated tax payments and amount applied from 2005 return	24a
b	Estimated tax payments allocated to beneficiaries (from Form 1041-T)	24b
c	Subtract line 24b from line 24a	24c
d	Tax paid with Form 7004 (see page 20 of the instructions)	24d
e	Federal income tax withheld. If any is from Form(s) 1099, check ▶ ☐	24e
f	Credit for federal telephone excise tax paid. Attach Form 8913	24f
	Other payments: **g** Form 2439 _____ ; **h** Form 4136 _____ ; Total ▶	24i
25	**Total payments.** Add lines 24c through 24f, and 24i ▶	25
26	Estimated tax penalty (see page 20 of the instructions)	26
27	**Tax due.** If line 25 is smaller than the total of lines 23 and 26, enter amount owed	27
28	**Overpayment.** If line 25 is larger than the total of lines 23 and 26, enter amount overpaid	28
29	Amount of line 28 to be: **a Credited to 2007 estimated tax** ▶ _____ ; **b Refunded** ▶	29

Sign Here ▶

Under penalties of perjury, I declare that I have examined this return, including accompanying schedules and statements, and to the best of my knowledge and belief, it is true, correct, and complete. Declaration of preparer (other than taxpayer) is based on all information of which preparer has any knowledge.

Signature of fiduciary or officer representing fiduciary | Date | ▶ EIN of fiduciary if a financial institution

May the IRS discuss this return with the preparer shown below (see instr.)? ☐ Yes ☐ No

Paid Preparer's Use Only

Preparer's signature | Date | Check if self-employed ☐ | Preparer's SSN or PTIN

Firm's name (or yours if self-employed), address, and ZIP code ▶ | EIN | Phone no. (   )

For Privacy Act and Paperwork Reduction Act Notice, see the separate instructions.

Cat. No. 11370H

Form **1041** (2006)

(continued)

Figure 9-8 (continued)

Schedule A	Charitable Deduction. Do not complete for a simple trust or a pooled income fund.		
1	Amounts paid or permanently set aside for charitable purposes from gross income (see page 21)	1	
2	Tax-exempt income allocable to charitable contributions (see page 21 of the instructions) .	2	
3	Subtract line 2 from line 1 .	3	
4	Capital gains for the tax year allocated to corpus and paid or permanently set aside for charitable purposes	4	
5	Add lines 3 and 4 .	5	
6	Section 1202 exclusion allocable to capital gains paid or permanently set aside for charitable purposes (see page 21 of the instructions) .	6	
7	**Charitable deduction.** Subtract line 6 from line 5. Enter here and on page 1, line 13 .	7	

Schedule B	Income Distribution Deduction		
1	Adjusted total income (see page 22 of the instructions) .	1	
2	Adjusted tax-exempt interest .	2	
3	Total net gain from Schedule D (Form 1041), line 15, column (1) (see page 22 of the instructions)	3	
4	Enter amount from Schedule A, line 4 (minus any allocable section 1202 exclusion) .	4	
5	Capital gains for the tax year included on Schedule A, line 1 (see page 22 of the instructions)	5	
6	Enter any gain from page 1, line 4, as a negative number. If page 1, line 4, is a loss, enter the loss as a positive number .	6	
7	**Distributable net income (DNI).** Combine lines 1 through 6. If zero or less, enter -0- .	7	
8	If a complex trust, enter accounting income for the tax year as determined under the governing instrument and applicable local law [8]		
9	Income required to be distributed currently .	9	
10	Other amounts paid, credited, or otherwise required to be distributed .	10	
11	Total distributions. Add lines 9 and 10. If greater than line 8, see page 22 of the instructions	11	
12	Enter the amount of tax-exempt income included on line 11 .	12	
13	Tentative income distribution deduction. Subtract line 12 from line 11 .	13	
14	Tentative income distribution deduction. Subtract line 2 from line 7. If zero or less, enter -0-	14	
15	**Income distribution deduction.** Enter the smaller of line 13 or line 14 here and on page 1, line 18	15	

Schedule G	Tax Computation (see page 23 of the instructions)		
1 Tax: **a**	Tax on taxable income (see page 23 of the instructions) .	1a	
b	Tax on lump-sum distributions. Attach Form 4972 .	1b	
c	Alternative minimum tax (from Schedule I, line 56) .	1c	
d	**Total.** Add lines 1a through 1c . ▶	1d	
2a	Foreign tax credit. Attach Form 1116 .	2a	
b	Other nonbusiness credits (attach schedule) .	2b	
c	General business credit. Enter here and check which forms are attached: ☐ Form 3800 ☐ Forms (specify) ▶	2c	
d	Credit for prior year minimum tax. Attach Form 8801 .	2d	
3	**Total credits.** Add lines 2a through 2d . ▶	3	
4	Subtract line 3 from line 1d. If zero or less, enter -0-.	4	
5	Recapture taxes. Check if from: ☐ Form 4255 ☐ Form 8611 .	5	
6	Household employment taxes. Attach Schedule H (Form 1040) .	6	
7	**Total tax.** Add lines 4 through 6. Enter here and on page 1, line 23 . ▶	7	

	Other Information	Yes	No
1	Did the estate or trust receive tax-exempt income? If "Yes," attach a computation of the allocation of expenses Enter the amount of tax-exempt interest income and exempt-interest dividends ▶ $		
2	Did the estate or trust receive all or any part of the earnings (salary, wages, and other compensation) of any individual by reason of a contract assignment or similar arrangement? .		
3	At any time during calendar year 2006, did the estate or trust have an interest in or a signature or other authority over a bank, securities, or other financial account in a foreign country? . See page 25 of the instructions for exceptions and filing requirements for Form TD F 90-22.1. If "Yes," enter the name of the foreign country ▶		
4	During the tax year, did the estate or trust receive a distribution from, or was it the grantor of, or transferor to, a foreign trust? If "Yes," the estate or trust may have to file Form 3520. See page 25 of the instructions .		
5	Did the estate or trust receive, or pay, any qualified residence interest on seller-provided financing? If "Yes," see page 25 for required attachment .		
6	If this is an estate or a complex trust making the section 663(b) election, check here (see page 25) . ▶ ☐		
7	To make a section 643(e)(3) election, attach Schedule D (Form 1041), and check here (see page 25) . ▶ ☐		
8	If the decedent's estate has been open for more than 2 years, attach an explanation for the delay in closing the estate, and check here ▶ ☐		
9	Are any present or future trust beneficiaries skip persons? See page 25 of the instructions .		

Form **1041** (2006)

(continued)

Figure 9-8 (continued)

	Schedule I	Alternative Minimum Tax (AMT) (see pages 26 through 32 of the instructions)	

Part I—Estate's or Trust's Share of Alternative Minimum Taxable Income

1	Adjusted total income or (loss) (from page 1, line 17)	**1**	
2	Interest	**2**	
3	Taxes	**3**	
4	Miscellaneous itemized deductions (from page 1, line 15b)	**4**	
5	Refund of taxes	**5** ( )
6	Depletion (difference between regular tax and AMT)	**6**	
7	Net operating loss deduction. Enter as a positive amount	**7**	
8	Interest from specified private activity bonds exempt from the regular tax . . .	**8**	
9	Qualified small business stock (see page 27 of the instructions)	**9**	
10	Exercise of incentive stock options (excess of AMT income over regular tax income) . . .	**10**	
11	Other estates and trusts (amount from Schedule K-1 (Form 1041), box 12, code A) . . .	**11**	
12	Electing large partnerships (amount from Schedule K-1 (Form 1065-B), box 6) . . .	**12**	
13	Disposition of property (difference between AMT and regular tax gain or loss)	**13**	
14	Depreciation on assets placed in service after 1986 (difference between regular tax and AMT)	**14**	
15	Passive activities (difference between AMT and regular tax income or loss)	**15**	
16	Loss limitations (difference between AMT and regular tax income or loss)	**16**	
17	Circulation costs (difference between regular tax and AMT)	**17**	
18	Long-term contracts (difference between AMT and regular tax income)	**18**	
19	Mining costs (difference between regular tax and AMT)	**19**	
20	Research and experimental costs (difference between regular tax and AMT)	**20**	
21	Income from certain installment sales before January 1, 1987	**21** ( )
22	Intangible drilling costs preference	**22**	
23	Other adjustments, including income-based related adjustments	**23**	
24	Alternative tax net operating loss deduction (See the instructions for the limitation that applies.)	**24** ( )
25	Adjusted alternative minimum taxable income. Combine lines 1 through 24	**25**	

Note: *Complete Part II below before going to line 26.*

26	Income distribution deduction from Part II, line 44	**26**	
27	Estate tax deduction (from page 1, line 19)	**27**	
28	Add lines 26 and 27	**28**	
29	Estate's or trust's share of alternative minimum taxable income. Subtract line 28 from line 25	**29**	

If line 29 is:

- $22,500 or less, stop here and enter -0- on Schedule G, line 1c. The estate or trust is not liable for the alternative minimum tax.
- Over $22,500, but less than $165,000, go to line 45.
- $165,000 or more, enter the amount from line 29 on line 51 and go to line 52.

Part II—Income Distribution Deduction on a Minimum Tax Basis

30	Adjusted alternative minimum taxable income (see page 30 of the instructions)	**30**	
31	Adjusted tax-exempt interest (other than amounts included on line 8)	**31**	
32	Total net gain from Schedule D (Form 1041), line 15, column (1). If a loss, enter -0- . . .	**32**	
33	Capital gains for the tax year allocated to corpus and paid or permanently set aside for charitable purposes (from Schedule A, line 4)	**33**	
34	Capital gains paid or permanently set aside for charitable purposes from gross income (see page 30 of the instructions)	**34**	
35	Capital gains computed on a minimum tax basis included on line 25	**35** ( )
36	Capital losses computed on a minimum tax basis included on line 25. Enter as a positive amount	**36**	
37	Distributable net alternative minimum taxable income (DNAMTI). Combine lines 30 through 36. If zero or less, enter -0-.	**37**	
38	Income required to be distributed currently (from Schedule B, line 9)	**38**	
39	Other amounts paid, credited, or otherwise required to be distributed (from Schedule B, line 10)	**39**	
40	Total distributions. Add lines 38 and 39	**40**	
41	Tax-exempt income included on line 40 (other than amounts included on line 8)	**41**	
42	Tentative income distribution deduction on a minimum tax basis. Subtract line 41 from line 40	**42**	
43	Tentative income distribution deduction on a minimum tax basis. Subtract line 31 from line 37. If zero or less, enter -0-	**43**	
44	**Income distribution deduction on a minimum tax basis.** Enter the smaller of line 42 or line 43. Enter here and on line 26	**44**	

(continued)

Figure 9-8 (continued)

Form 1041 (2006)   Page **4**

Part III—Alternative Minimum Tax

45	Exemption amount			**45**	$22,500	00
46	Enter the amount from line 29	**46**				
47	Phase-out of exemption amount	**47**	$75,000	00		
48	Subtract line 47 from line 46. If zero or less, enter -0-	**48**				
49	Multiply line 48 by 25% (.25)				**49**	
50	Subtract line 49 from line 45. If zero or less, enter -0-				**50**	
51	Subtract line 50 from line 46				**51**	
52	Go to Part IV of Schedule I to figure line 52 if the estate or trust has qualified dividends or has a gain on lines 14a and 15 of column (2) of Schedule D (Form 1041) (as refigured for the AMT, if necessary). Otherwise, if line 51 is—					
	• $175,000 or less, multiply line 51 by 26% (.26).					
	• Over $175,000, multiply line 51 by 28% (.28) and subtract $3,500 from the result . . .				**52**	
53	Alternative minimum foreign tax credit (see page 31 of the instructions)				**53**	
54	Tentative minimum tax. Subtract line 53 from line 52				**54**	
55	Enter the tax from Schedule G, line 1a (minus any foreign tax credit from Schedule G, line 2a)				**55**	
56	**Alternative minimum tax.** Subtract line 55 from line 54. If zero or less, enter -0-. Enter here and on Schedule G, line 1c				**56**	

Part IV—Line 52 Computation Using Maximum Capital Gains Rates

Caution: *If you did not complete Part V of Schedule D (Form 1041), the Schedule D Tax Worksheet, or the Qualified Dividends Tax Worksheet, see page 32 of the instructions before completing this part.*

57	Enter the amount from line 51				**57**	
58	Enter the amount from Schedule D (Form 1041), line 22, line 13 of the Schedule D Tax Worksheet, or line 4 of the Qualified Dividends Tax Worksheet, whichever applies (as refigured for the AMT, if necessary)	**58**				
59	Enter the amount from Schedule D (Form 1041), line 14b, column (2) (as refigured for the AMT, if necessary). If you did not complete Schedule D for the regular tax or the AMT, enter -0-	**59**				
60	If you did not complete a Schedule D Tax Worksheet for the regular tax or the AMT, enter the amount from line 58. Otherwise, add lines 58 and 59 and enter the **smaller** of that result or the amount from line 10 of the Schedule D Tax Worksheet (as refigured for the AMT, if necessary)	**60**				
61	Enter the **smaller** of line 57 or line 60				**61**	
62	Subtract line 61 from line 57				**62**	
63	If line 62 is $175,000 or less, multiply line 62 by 26% (.26). Otherwise, multiply line 62 by 28% (.28) and subtract $3,500 from the result . . . . ▶				**63**	
64	Maximum amount subject to the 5% rate	**64**	$2,050	00		
65	Enter the amount from line 23 of Schedule D (Form 1041), line 14 of the Schedule D Tax Worksheet, or line 5 of the Qualified Dividends Tax Worksheet, whichever applies (as figured for the regular tax). If you did not complete Schedule D or either worksheet for the regular tax, enter -0-	**65**				
66	Subtract line 65 from line 64. If zero or less, enter -0-	**66**				
67	Enter the **smaller** of line 57 or line 58	**67**				
68	Enter the **smaller** of line 66 or line 67	**68**				
69	Multiply line 68 by 5% (.05) . . . . ▶				**69**	
70	Subtract line 68 from line 67	**70**				
71	Multiply line 70 by 15% (.15) . . . . ▶				**71**	
	If line 59 is zero or blank, skip lines 72 and 73 and go to line 74. Otherwise, go to line 72.					
72	Subtract line 67 from line 61	**72**				
73	Multiply line 72 by 25% (.25) . . . . ▶				**73**	
74	Add lines 63, 69, 71, and 73				**74**	
75	If line 57 is $175,000 or less, multiply line 57 by 26% (.26). Otherwise, multiply line 57 by 28% (.28) and subtract $3,500 from the result				**75**	
76	Enter the **smaller** of line 74 or line 75 here and on line 52				**76**	

Form **1041** (2006)

Printed on recycled paper

pending for only one year, a first and final fiduciary return is completed. The return is due on the fifteenth day of the fourth month after the end of the tax year. The personal representative of the estate chooses the initial tax year. A qualified tax preparer should be consulted to determine the most advantageous tax-year-end that would result in the least amount of tax liability. The estate fiduciary tax return is signed by the personal representative. Each beneficiary is sent a Schedule K-1. This form is discussed later in this section.

Federal Form 1041 has similarities to income tax Form 1040. First, income is determined, including salaries, wages, business or trust income, dividends, and so on. This income includes amounts that the decedent has a right to receive but has not been included previously in the decedent's final income tax return. Following the determination of gross income, deductions are subtracted from the gross income. Remember that a deduction reduces the amount of taxes owed. Examples of deductions include mortgage interest, interest on unpaid estate taxes, state and local income taxes, charitable deductions, attorney's fees, accountant's fees, and so on. Once the deductions are subtracted from income, the adjusted total income amount is reached.

Exemptions are also used to lessen the amount of tax liability. The current exemption amount is $600.00. You should check yearly on the exemption amount for the federal fiduciary tax return. Refer again to Equation 9-1 on page 181.

Once the taxable income is calculated, the tax must be computed. Tax credits are applied to the taxable income. A tax credit reduces the amount of taxes owed. It is a dollar-for-dollar reduction in tax liability. Tax credits that may be applied include foreign tax credit, general business credit, and other nonbusiness credits. The taxable income less credits leaves the amount subject to tax. This amount is compared to the tax rates, which are adjusted by the IRS, and the final amount of tax due is determined. The preparation of the federal fiduciary tax return allows the tax preparer an option to compute the tax due using an alternative minimum tax method. A tax professional well versed in preparation of the return should be consulted.

During the final year of the estate, the income or deductions may be passed on to the beneficiaries. The beneficiaries receive a **Schedule K-1:** beneficiary's share of income, deductions, credits, etc. (see Figure 9-9). Schedule K-1 is a document that informs each beneficiary of his or her share of the income and deductions. Only beneficiaries receiving a residuary gift get a Schedule K-1. Those beneficiaries who received a specific bequest do not.

States may also require a fiduciary return to be filed. You should become familiar with your state requirements.

Schedule K-1
A tax document informing an estate's beneficiary or heir of the amount of the estate's income and deductions allocated to him or her.

Closing Certificates

The preparation, filing, and paying of taxes is required to close the estate administration file at the courthouse. Once the returns are filed and any taxes owed are paid, the taxing authority may issue closing certificates or closing letters. These letters state that the personal representative has performed his or her duties with regard to the tax requirements of filing and payment. These closing certificates are filed with the probate court as proof that the taxes owed have been paid. Without them, the court may not allow the estate to be closed.

Figure 9-9   Schedule K-1

		661106
☐ Final K-1	☐ Amended K-1	OMB No. 1545-0092

Schedule K-1
(Form 1041)

2006

Department of the Treasury
Internal Revenue Service

For calendar year 2006,
or tax year beginning _____ , 2006
and ending _____ , 20 _____

Beneficiary's Share of Income, Deductions, Credits, etc.
▶ See back of form and instructions.

Part I	Information About the Estate or Trust
A	Estate's or trust's employer identification number
B	Estate's or trust's name
C	Fiduciary's name, address, city, state, and ZIP code
D ☐	Check if Form 1041-T was filed and enter the date it was filed ___ / ___ / _____
E ☐	Check if this is the final Form 1041 for the estate or trust
F ☐	Tax shelter registration number, if any _____
G ☐	Check if Form 8271 is attached

Part II	Information About the Beneficiary
H	Beneficiary's identifying number
I	Beneficiary's name, address, city, state, and ZIP code
J ☐ Domestic beneficiary ☐ Foreign beneficiary	

Part III	Beneficiary's Share of Current Year Income, Deductions, Credits, and Other Items		
1	Interest income	**11**	Final year deductions
2a	Ordinary dividends		
2b	Qualified dividends		
3	Net short-term capital gain		
4a	Net long-term capital gain		
4b	28% rate gain	**12**	Alternative minimum tax adjustment
4c	Unrecaptured section 1250 gain		
5	Other portfolio and nonbusiness income		
6	Ordinary business income		
7	Net rental real estate income	**13**	Credits and credit recapture
8	Other rental income		
9	Directly apportioned deductions		
		14	Other information
10	Estate tax deduction		

*See attached statement for additional information.

Note: A statement must be attached showing the beneficiary's share of income and directly apportioned deductions from each business, rental real estate, and other rental activity.

For IRS Use Only

For Paperwork Reduction Act Notice, see the Instructions for Form 1041.   Cat. No. 11380D   **Schedule K-1 (Form 1041) 2006**

Now that the tax returns have been filed and the taxes paid, the personal representative can turn his or her attention to the final steps of the estate administration process. Chapter 10 includes the last two remaining steps: Step Five—Final Account and Step Six—Closing the Estate.

KEY **TERMS**

credits (p. 183)
deduction (p. 183)
employer identification number
  (E.I.N.) (p. 180)
estate tax (p. 184)

gross income (p. 183)
inheritance tax (p. 193)
itemized deduction (p. 183)
marital deduction (p. 186)
Schedule K-1 (p. 198)

standard deduction (p. 183)
taxable income (p. 183)
unified credit (p. 184)

REVIEW **QUESTIONS**

1. Where does U.S. tax law originate?
2. What is the formula for taxable income?
3. Explain the difference between a standard deduction and an itemized deduction. Which one should be used?
4. Define credit. Name two examples.
5. Define estate tax. When must a federal estate tax return be filed?
6. Explain the unified credit and applicable exclusion amount. What are the current amounts?

7. What are the five sections of the federal estate tax Form 706?
8. Compare and contrast a pickup tax and an inheritance tax.
9. Under what two circumstances are fiduciary taxes prepared?
10. Explain a Schedule K-1. Who receives it?
11. What tax documents does the probate court require to be filed with it and why?

ROLE-PLAYING **ACTIVITY**

1. Pair up with a classmate. Interview each other to obtain information required to prepare a final income tax return of the decedent or federal estate tax return.

RESEARCH **ASSIGNMENTS**

1. Obtain the CUSIP number for a stock.
2. Research and explain how the fair-market value for Schedule A: Real Estate is determined on the federal estate return.
3. Research and explain how the value in the decedent's Schedule E: Jointly Owned Property is determined.

4. Research your state's requirements for a pickup tax, estate tax, or inheritance tax.
5. Research and summarize your state's requirements for a fiduciary tax.
6. Interview a tax professional about preparation of tax returns on behalf of an estate.

BUILD YOUR **PORTFOLIO**

1. Using the case example you chose in Chapter 6, prepare an SS4 Form.

Chapter **ten**

STEP FIVE—FINAL ACCOUNT AND STEP SIX—CLOSING THE ESTATE: ADDITIONAL ESTATE ADMINISTRATION PROCEDURES

The Plan Culminates in the Final Outcome

The end of the estate administration is in sight. The final two steps of the estate administration are all that remain. The decedent's plan is nearing its complete manifestation. What used to be the decedent's wealth and property is under the personal representative's control.

This chapter contains the final two steps of estate administration. Step Five, the final account, includes information regarding the last remaining financial document to be prepared. Step Six, closing the estate, is a discussion about the final estate administration documents to be prepared. Step Six includes the completion of documents reporting remaining amounts to be distributed, receipts demonstrating that the appropriate distributions were made, and petitions and orders discharging the personal representative from his or her duties. The chapter then discusses will contests and when and how an interested person may challenge a will. Finally, the chapter outlines alternatives to formal and informal administration, including the

OBJECTIVES

After studying this chapter, you should be able to:

- Explain the final outcome of the administration of the estate plan.
- Define final account, list the information contained in one, and draft a final account.
- Outline the procedure for closing the estate, name and explain the three common documents used to close the estate, and draft a receipt and a document that closes the estate and discharges the personal representative.
- Define will contest; list and explain the valid grounds for a will contest.
- Understand the availability of small estate administration for clients, and compare and contrast summary administration and transfer by affidavit.
- Compare and contrast ancillary administration and domiciliary administration, and understand why ancillary administration was created.

procedure for small estate administration, often known as summary settlement or transfer by affidavit.

Now it's time to finish our estate administration procedure.

The Final Account

The **final account**, accounting, or final report is a financial report to the court and interested persons detailing the estate's income and outflow of money and property while the estate is open. It is one of the more complicated estate administration documents. Similar to a balance sheet, the final account includes on one side the inventory amount and all income (rent, dividends, capital gains); on the other side, it reports all amounts paid out: funeral expenses, costs of administration, taxes, distributions. It specifies the sources that generate wealth and the recipients of the decedent's wealth. The remaining funds to be distributed to the heirs and beneficiaries awaiting their inheritance are also reported. A Wisconsin statute defines it as follows:

> The account shall first show the total value of the property with which the personal representative is chargeable according to the inventory; . . . it shall show all income or other property received and gains or losses from the sale of any property; and it shall show all payments, charges, and losses. The final account shall itemize all property available for distribution and all property previously distributed. . . (Wis. Stat. § 862.07)

See Wisconsin's final account in Figure 10-1.

California law lists the information contained in its final report. The accounting includes supporting schedules detailing inventory property, receipts, gains on sales, other property acquired, disbursements, losses on sales, other property dispositions, creditors' claims, and property remaining on hand (Cal. Prob. Code § 10900).

The personal representative and the law firm prepare the final account. Often a paralegal organizes the financial data and compiles it into the final account. The paralegal needs to understand the types of information included and must keep the financial data organized as it is delivered to the law firm. A court may require the personal representative to produce for inspection the documents that support the dollar figure assigned to property valuation, payments, or receipts. See Cal. Prob. Code § 10901. Therefore all supporting documentation must be carefully preserved and organized in the law firm's estate file.

The final account information may be included on preprinted forms like the one from Wisconsin in Figure 10-1, or it may be computer-generated like Illinois's final account in Figure 10-2. A final account typically contains a caption, the inventory amount, the received items, and paid-out items. Next, it contains what amount is left to be distributed. The personal representative signs the document. This signature may be in the presence of a notary public, in which case a jurat would be required. Finally, the attorney information is presented.

The estate administration procedure may require a hearing on the final account and a court order requiring the remaining distributions to be paid. If required by state statute, notice may be given to interested persons, so they may object to the final account. See N.H. Rev. Stat. Ann. § 550:11. Wisconsin's petition for approval of final account and final judgment is shown in Figure 10-3.

It is also possible for interested persons to waive notice of the hearing. See Illinois's entry of appearance and waiver of notice in Figure 10-4.

Figure 10-1   Wisconsin's final account

For Official Use

STATE OF WISCONSIN, CIRCUIT COURT, _____ **COUNTY**

IN THE MATTER OF THE ESTATE OF

_____

_____

Final Account
☐ **Informal**
☐ **Formal**

Case No. _____

I, the personal representative of this estate, certify that this Final Account is true and correct. The following is my account of the administration of this estate from _____ to _____.
(Date of Death or Date of Prior Account)   (Date)

List interested persons on page 2.

RECEIPTS	VALUES	DISBURSEMENTS	VALUES
Inventoried Assets	$	Funeral Expenses (Schedule F)	$
Added Property (Schedule A)		Debts of Decedent (G)	
Dividends (B)		Claims(including those by	
Interest (C)		judgment) (H)	
Capital Gains (Losses) (D)		Taxes Paid (I)	
Other Receipts (E)		Interest Paid (J)	
		Administration Expenses (K)	
		Other Payments (L)	
		Distributions Paid to Date (M)	
		TOTAL DISBURSEMENTS	$
		Assets on Hand (N)	$
BALANCING TOTALS	$		$

Assets on Hand (Schedule N) $ _____
Minus Requested Fees:
    Attorney $ _____
    Personal Representative $ _____
    Guardian Ad Litem $ _____   ($ _____)

Balance Available for Distribution.
    Specific assets must be listed in Schedule 0. $ _____
List of proposed distribution (Schedule P)

_____	_____
Signature of Personal Representative	Signature of Co-personal Representative
Subscribed and sworn to before me	Subscribed and sworn to before me
on _____	on _____
_____	_____
Notary Public/Court Official	Notary Public/Court Official
My commission expires: _____	My commission expires: _____

Name of Attorney	Telephone Number	Bar Number
Address		

PR-1814, 12/04 Final Account (Informal and Formal Administration)   Wis. Stats. §§862.01, 862.05, 862.07, 862.11, 865.16(1)(c)
This form shall not be modified. It may be supplemented with additional material.
Page 1 of 3

(continued)

Figure 10-1   (continued)

Final Account Supporting Schedule

List of Interested Persons

The names and addresses of all interested persons are:

(Include any minor(s) with date of birth, incompetent(s), guardian(s) of estate, guardian ad litem or attorney for a person in the military and note if any person is in the military):

Name	**Relationship**	**Address**	**D. O. B. if Minor**

PR-1814, 12/04 Final Account (Informal and Formal Administration)   Wis. Stats. §§862.01, 862.05, 862.07, 862.11, 865.16(1)(c)
This form shall not be modified. It may be supplemented with additional material.
Page 2 of 3

(continued)

Figure 10-1   (continued)

Schedule Alpha (A - P)	Final Account Supporting Schedules (List details of each schedule)	Total Values

PR-1814, 12/04 Final Account (Informal and Formal Administration)   Wis. Stats. §§862.01, 862.05, 862.07, 862.11, 865.16(1)(c)
This form shall not be modified. It may be supplemented with additional material.
Page 3 of 3

Source: For most current version of this form, visit www.wicourts.org.

Figure 10-2   Illinois's final account

STATE OF ILLINOIS
IN THE CIRCUIT COURT OF THE SEVENTEENTH JUDICIAL CIRCUIT
COUNTY OF WINNEBAGO

IN THE MATTER OF THE ESTATE OF	)	
	)	
Robert A. Benson,	)	
	)	Case No. 06 P 420
Deceased.	)	
	)	

FINAL ACCOUNT

The undersigned, Ruth A. Benson, executrix of the ESTATE OF Robert A. Benson, DECEASED, respectfully submits the following report of her acts and doings as such executrix, from August 31, 2006, the date of her appointment, to the date hereof:

		AMOUNT
INVENTORY	$	548,927.23
ITEMS RECEIVED		
Firstar Savings Account - 322213		12.15
Bank One Certificate of Deposit		200.00
AT&T Stock Dividend		4,000.00
Disney Stock Dividend		1,500.00
Johnson Controls Capital Gain		400.00
Walt Disney Capital Gain		2,300.00
Robert A. Benson's Final Paycheck		515.00
TOTAL RECEIVED:	$	8,927.15
TOTAL	$	**557,854.38**
ITEMS PAID OUT		
FUNERAL EXPENSES		
Christenson Funeral Home, Casket, & Burial Plot		10,000.00
Marble Grave Marker		1,100.00
Flowers		500.00
Luncheon		700.00
TOTAL	$	12,300.00
DEBTS OF DECEDENT		
Master Card		6,200.00
Visa		1,500.00
Sears		150.00
Boston Store		210.00
TOTAL	$	8,060.00

(continued)

Figure 10-2 (continued)

CLAIMS MADE AGAINST THE ESTATE			
Mr. Charles Benson			1,500.00
	TOTAL	$	1,500.00
TAXES			
Federal Final Income Tax of Decedent			2,500.00
State Final Income Tax of Decedent			900.00
	TOTAL	$	3,400.00
DISTRIBUTIONS TO DATE			
Primary Residence			100,000.00
Condominium (Vacation Home)			350,000.00
Cash			10,000.00
	TOTAL	$	460,000.00
ESTATE ADMINISTRATION EXPENSES			
Attorney's Fees			7,800.00
Filing Fees			350.00
Appraisers' Fees			580.00
Mailings, Photocopying, Processing Fees			760.00
Personal Representative			4,850.00
Miscellaneous Fees			110.00
	TOTAL	$	14,450.00
	TOTAL PAID OUT	$	**499,710.00**

RECAPITULATION

INVENTORY:	**$548,927.23**
ITEMS RECEIVED:	**$8,927.15**
TOTAL:	**$557,854.38**
ITEMS PAID OUT:	**$499,710.00**
BALANCE:	**$ 58,144.38**

(continued)

Figure 10-2   (continued)

The undersigned further reports that all claims, taxes, costs of administration, and attorney's fees have been paid, and that there remains the above balance to be distributed to the heirs-at-law entitled thereto under the terms of the Last Will and Testament of Robert A. Benson, as follows:

TO:	Timothy Benson	$ 350.00
	Ruth A. Benson	$ 28,897.18
	Samuel Benson	$ 14,448.60
	Sarah Hart	$ 14,448.60
	TOTAL:	$ 58,144.38

The undersigned prays that she may be allowed to make the distribution as above set forth.

_____

                                                                Ruth A. Benson

STATE OF ILLINOIS   )
COUNTY OF WINNEBAGO   )

Ruth A. Benson, being first duly sworn upon oath, deposes and says that the following is a true and correct account of all monies taken in and paid out by her on the estate account from August 31, 2006, the date of her appointment, to the date hereof.

_____

SUBSCRIBED and SWORN to
Before me this _____ day of
_____, 20 ____.

_____
                    Notary Public
                    My commission expires: _____

Carrie L. Smith
Attorney for the Estate
Attorney No. 5858
8755 Glacier Drive
Byron, Illinois 61010
(815) 555-1212

Figure 10-3 Wisconsin's petition for final approval of final account and final judgment

---

STATE OF WISCONSIN, CIRCUIT COURT, _____ COUNTY

IN THE MATTER OF THE ESTATE OF

_____

_____

Petition for Approval of Final Account and Final Judgment
(Formal Administration)

Case No. _____

For Official Use

Under oath, I state that:

1. I am the personal representative of this estate.

2. My final account of the administration of this estate from _____ to _____
   (Date of Death or Date of Prior Account)   (Date)

   is attached and the estate is ready for final judgment.

3. All allowances, debts, taxes, funeral expenses, and expenses of administration as shown in the final account have been paid.

4. Any unfiled claims against the estate which I have paid in good faith were just demands against the estate and were paid on or before the deadline for filing claims or with the consent of the heirs or beneficiaries affected by the payment, as shown in the final account.

I request that:

1. A time and place be set for hearing this petition;
2. Heirship be determined by the court;
3. The account be allowed, and any life estate and joint tenancy of decedent be declared terminated; and
4. The assets of the estate be assigned according to law.

_____
Signature of Personal Representative

Subscribed and sworn to before me

on _____

_____
Notary Public/Court Official

My commission expires: _____

_____
Signature of Co-personal Representative

Subscribed and sworn to before me

on _____

_____
Notary Public/Court Official

My commission expires: _____

Name of Attorney

Address

Telephone Number	Bar Number

PR-1910, 05/02 Petition for Approval of Final Account and Final Judgment (Formal Administration)   §§859.47, 862.09, 862.15, 863.25, Wisconsin Statutes
This form shall not be modified. It may be supplemented with additional material.

Source: For the most current version of this form, visit www.wicourts.org.

Figure 10-4 Illinois's entry of appearance and waiver of notice

STATE OF ILLINOIS
IN THE CIRCUIT COURT OF THE SEVENTEENTH JUDICIAL CIRCUIT
COUNTY OF WINNEBAGO

IN THE MATTER OF THE ESTATE OF ....)
....)
.... Robert A. Benson, ...)
....)   Case No. 06 P 420
.... Deceased. ....)
....)

ENTRY OF APPEARANCE AND WAIVER OF NOTICE

The undersigned hereby enters her appearance in the matter of a hearing on the Final Report filed herein; and consents to the entry of an Order Approving the Final Report and an Order of Distribution, together with an Order Closing the Estate, all without further notice.

_____
Ruth A. Benson

Carrie L. Smith
Attorney for the Estate
Attorney No. 5858
8755 Glacier Drive
Byron, Illinois 61010
(815) 555-1212

Closing the Estate

After the final account has been accepted by the court, a few final court documents must be completed. These documents constitute Step Six, closing the estate. Most state procedures require the following documents: receipts, an order for distribution, and an order discharging the personal representative. It is possible other miscellaneous documents may be required. A paralegal must consult the law in the jurisdiction where he or she is working to determine the exact documents required. Now we turn to the common remaining court documents.

1. Receipts

receipts:
Documents demonstrating that beneficiaries or heirs obtained money or property from the estate.

As their name suggests, **receipts** prove that money or property was received by a beneficiary or heir. Many states have standard fill-in-the blank receipts; in some states, the law firm may use computer-generated receipts. The receipts have a caption, indicate the property and its value or the amount of money received, and report if this is in partial or full satisfaction of the amount to be inherited. The

Figure 10-5   Colorado's receipt and release

☐ District Court ☐ Denver Probate Court	
_____ County, Colorado Court Address: **IN THE MATTER OF THE ESTATE OF:** ☐ Deceased ☐ Protected Person	▲ **COURT USE ONLY** ▲
Attorney or Party Without Attorney (Name and Address): Phone Number: E-mail: FAX Number: Atty. Reg.#:	Case Number: Division Courtroom

RECEIPT AND RELEASE

Received of _____ , as

☐ personal representative   ☐ conservator   of the estate in:

☐ partial   ☐ full   payment and satisfaction of the following:

    ☐ the devise to me in the will under article(s) _____.

    ☐ my _____ share of the estate in the will under article(s) _____.

    ☐ my _____ share of the estate as heir.

    ☐ other: _____.

☐ Cash in the amount of $ _____.

☐ Tangible personal property described as: * _____

    _____

    _____

    _____

    _____

☐ The following securities: * _____

    _____

    _____

    _____

☐ Other (describe): * _____

    _____

    _____

    _____

☐ I grant a partial release and satisfaction to the fiduciary of the estate as to the above partial distribution.

☐ I grant a full and final release and satisfaction to the estate and to the fiduciary and his or her successors for any liability in connection with my interest in the estate.

DATE: _____

                                     _____
                                     Signature (Type or print name below)

* Attach additional sheets as necessary.

CPC 54   R7/00   RECEIPT AND RELEASE   1

Source: Used by permission of the Supreme Court State of Colorado.

documents contain the signature of the heir or beneficiary. See Colorado's receipt and release in Figure 10-5.

Receipts usually must be filed with the court before it allows closure of the estate and discharge of the personal representative. A New Hampshire statute states:

> Every administrator, upon the payment of a legacy or distributive share of an estate, shall take a receipt and discharge therefore and shall file the same in the probate office, to be there recorded and preserved . . . (N.H. Rev. Stat. Ann. § 561.19).

2. Order for Distribution

distribution:
The process of transferring money or property to a beneficiary or heir in satisfaction of an inheritance.

A state may require a document to be filed with the court indicating the schedule of distribution and approval of it by the court. If the court is agreeing to the distribution, the judge would sign an order of distribution. **Distribution** is the process of transferring property or money to a beneficiary or heir in satisfaction of an inheritance. A state may require a preprinted form or the law firm may create the document. For example, Colorado has a preprinted form (see Figure 10-6), whereas in Illinois the law firm generates the document (see Figure 10-7).

3. Order Discharging the Personal Representative

The final documents filed are those where the personal representative has completed the estate administration process and asks to be discharged, and the court closes the estate. This closure indicates that all work has been completed and the personal representative's authority to act is terminated. Wisconsin law provides the following:

> Upon proof of the recording of the certified copies of the final judgment . . . and upon the filing of receipts from the distributees for all other property assigned in the final judgment, or other evidence of transfer satisfactory to the court, the court shall enter an order finding those facts, discharging the personal representative and canceling the personal representative's bond (Wis. Stat. § 863.47).

Some of these documents may be standard fill-in-the-blank forms. See Wisconsin's order of discharge of personal representative in Figure 10-8. Others may be computer-generated by the law firm. See Illinois's order approving report of distribution and closing the estate in Figure 10-9. The forms contain a caption, information regarding the final account, reference to receipts being on file, and an order from the court discharging the personal representative and canceling bond. The judge or other court personnel sign the document.

The estate is now closed. The decedent's plan has been effectuated. It is up to the new owners of the property to plan its transfer upon their deaths. The cycle will then begin anew.

Will Contests

will contest:
Petitioning the court to declare a will invalid.

Although a **will contest** makes for a very exciting fictional novel or movie screenplay, it rarely occurs in reality. A small number of wills are contested, and of those contested, a smaller percentage yet are invalidated by the court. A will contest is where an individual petitions the court to invalidate a will. A disgruntled,

Figure 10-6 Colorado's schedule of distribution

☐ District Court ☐ Denver Probate Court

_____ County, Colorado

Court Address:

IN THE MATTER OF THE ESTATE OF:

☐ Deceased ☐ Protected Person

▲ **COURT USE ONLY** ▲

Attorney or Party Without Attorney (Name and Address):

Case Number:

Phone Number: E-mail:

FAX Number: Atty. Reg.#:   Division   Courtroom

SCHEDULE OF DISTRIBUTION

Names and Addresses of Distributees	Amount of Money	Description of Personality and Real Estate in Kind

NOTE: This form for use with forms CPC24 and CPC25 (decedent's estates) and forms CPC49 and CPC50 (conservatorship). Previous partial distributions, if any, should not be shown. Use additional sheets if necessary.

CPC 24/25-S   R7/00   SCHEDULE OF DISTRIBUTION   1

Source: Used by permission of the Supreme Court State of Colorado.

Figure 10-7 Illinois's report of distribution

STATE OF ILLINOIS
IN THE CIRCUIT COURT OF THE SEVENTEENTH JUDICIAL CIRCUIT
COUNTY OF WINNEBAGO

IN THE MATTER OF THE ESTATE OF	)	
	)	
Robert A. Benson,	)	
	)	Case No. 06 P 420
Deceased.	)	
	)	

REPORT OF DISTRIBUTION

In accordance with an Order of Distribution entered herein on the 7th day of April 2007, the undersigned acknowledges she made the following distributions to the following persons entitled thereof:

To:		
	Ruth A. Benson	$28,897.18
	Samuel Benson	$14,448.60
	Sarah Hart	$14,448.60
	Timothy Benson	$ 350.00
	TOTAL:	**$58,144.38**

_____
Ruth A. Benson Executrix

Carrie L. Smith
Attorney for the Estate
Attorney No. 5858
8755 Glacier Drive
Byron, Illinois 61010
(815) 555-1212

Figure 10-8   Wisconsin's order of discharge of personal representative

---

STATE OF WISCONSIN, CIRCUIT COURT, _____ COUNTY

	For Official Use

IN THE MATTER OF THE ESTATE OF

**Order of Discharge of
Personal Representative**
(Formal Administration)

_____

_____   Case No. _____

THE COURT FINDS:

1. Final judgment has been entered.

2. A certified copy of the Final Judgment, or Abridgment, has been recorded, if required.

3. Receipts for all other property assigned in the Final Judgment, or other evidence of transfer satisfactory to the court, have been filed.

THE COURTS ORDERS:

1. The personal representative(s) (name) _____
   is discharged.

☐ 2. The bond of the personal representative(s) is cancelled.

BY THE COURT:

Name of Attorney
Address
Telephone Number

_____
Circuit Court Judge/Court Commissioner

_____
Name Printed or Typed

_____
Date

PR-1915, 10/00 Order of Discharge of Personal Representative (Formal Administration)   §§863.29, 863.47, Wisconsin Statutes
This form shall not be modified. It may be supplemented with additional material.

Source: For the most current version of this form, visit www.wicourts.org.

Figure 10-9   Illinois's order approving report of distribution and closing the estate

STATE OF ILLINOIS
IN THE CIRCUIT COURT OF THE SEVENTEENTH JUDICIAL CIRCUIT
COUNTY OF WINNEBAGO

IN THE MATTER OF THE ESTATE OF	)	
	)	
Robert A. Benson,	)	
	)	Case No. 06 P 420
Deceased.	)	
	)	

ORDER APPROVING REPORT OF DISTRIBUTION
AND CLOSING THE ESTATE

THIS MATTER coming on to hearing and the Court fully being advised in the premises, FINDS:

1. That Ruth A. Benson, Executrix of the Estate of Robert A. Benson, Deceased, filed a Final Report in the above matter.

2. That an Order Approving the Final Report and an Order of Distribution was entered herein on the 7th day of April 2007.

3. That a Report of Distribution is on file herein, together with Receipts from the beneficiaries in compliance with the Order of Distribution.

4. That all debts, including taxes, attorney's fees, and court costs have been paid in full, and that due notice was given to all known creditors to file their claims against said estate, and there is not pending in this or any other court, on appeal or otherwise, any claim against said estate.

5. That Robert A. Benson, died testate on the 12th day of August 2006; and that the statutory time required by law has elapsed since the issuance of Testamentary Letters on the 31st day of August 2007.

6. An Inventory setting forth and describing all property of the decedent has heretofore been filed.

7. That proof of heirship was made in the estate.

8. That the estate was not subject to a Federal estate tax, nor to an Illinois estate tax.

9. All interested persons in said estate have entered their appearance, waiving notice of final settlement, and have consented to the entry of an Order closing said estate.

10. That the estate of Robert A. Benson, Deceased, has been fully administered, and there remains nothing further to be done by the Executrix.

(continued)

Figure 10-9   (continued)

WHEREFORE, IT IS HEREBY ORDERED that said Report of Distribution is hereby approved; and IT IS FURTHER ORDERED that all acts of Ruth A. Benson, as Executrix herein, are hereby approved; and that the said Estate of Robert A. Benson, Deceased, is forever closed and terminated; and the individual bond for the aforesaid Executrix is hereby released.

HONORABLE JUDGE MARK WEBER

ENTERED:

PREPARED BY:

Carrie L. Smith
Attorney for the Estate
Attorney No. 5858
8755 Glacier Drive
Byron, Illinois 61010
(815) 555-1212

disinherited relative may plan to contest a will; once three issues are discussed with the relative, however, the plan is usually abandoned. The three issues to consider are the following:

1. The cost of hiring an attorney.

2. The valid grounds for a will contest.

3. The likelihood of success.

1. Cost

The expense of hiring an attorney often changes a potential client's mind about proceeding with the will contest. Once the client hears of the cost to him or her personally, as well as to the estate to defend the claim, he or she often reneges. Another concern is that the estate's cost to defend the suit may then deplete the inheritable assets.

2. Grounds

The fact that an heir is questioning the gifts made in the will does not mean there are valid grounds to contest a will. Some of the valid grounds include:

1. Lack of testamentary capacity, or animus testandi: the testator was not of legal age or mentally competent at the time the will was executed.

2. The will was not properly executed: the testator did not sign the will, or the requisite number of witnesses did not sign the document.

3. Duress on the party (the testator): if the testator does not voluntarily execute the will, it can be invalidated. If David holds a gun to Noel's head and threatens to shoot, the will is not voluntarily executed. If David threatens to kill Noel's children or other family members, duress may be successfully asserted.

4. Undue influence imposed upon the testator: undue influence is similar to duress. If the testator is pressured to act against his will, the will is invalid. Undue influence often arises in special relationships, for example, family or fiduciary situations. Of special interest is the ethical issue for attorneys and paralegals: if a client wishes to leave property to the attorney, the attorney should not draft the will. The idea that the attorney talked the client into the gift or pressured the client could be used. It is best under those circumstances to have the will drafted by another attorney. One exception may be if the attorney is drafting a will for a relative within a third degree of consanguinity. The attorney might still be a beneficiary under the will without creating any undue influence. (See Texas law.)

5. Fraud perpetrated on the testator: the maker does not believe he is signing a will but has been tricked, perhaps by someone claiming the document is another type of writing. For example, Ricco tells Marie she is signing a contract for the purchase of a vacuum cleaner; instead, she is signing her will.

6. The will has been revoked: the will is no longer in existence because it has been cancelled by physical act, later instrument, or operation of law.

7. The testator's signature is forged: someone else fraudulently writes the testator's signature on the document.

If none of the valid grounds allowed by the state apply, then the will contest will not be successful and should not be initiated. Once the grounds are reviewed and discussed with the potential client, the notion of contesting the will is often terminated.

3. Likelihood of Success

The person contesting the will has the burden of proof to prove the aforementioned grounds (see UPC § 3-407). Thus, the presumption is in favor of the will being valid. This makes the likelihood of success even more difficult for the will contestant; for example:

> At the trial, the proponents of the will have the burden of proof of due execution. The contestants of the will have the burden of proof of lack of testamentary intent or capacity, undue influence, fraud, duress, mistake, or revocation. (Cal. Prob. Code § 8252).

Small Estate Administration

Procedures other than formal or informal estate administration exist. These procedures, prescribed by state statute, are to be used for smaller estates. The goal is to save time and money in those instances where there is not much money in the decedent's estate. Less formality is required. State statutes must be consulted to determine under what circumstances these types of procedures may be employed. We will look at two types of small estate administration: summary administration and transfer by affidavit.

1. Summary Administration

Summary administration is typically used when the gross value of the estate does not exceed a certain dollar figure. It often does not require notice to beneficiaries but may require notice to creditors. The personal representative applies for a more expedited and easier method of carrying out the decedent's directions and gifts. The Uniform Probate Code explains summary administration as follows:

> If it appears from the inventory and appraisal that the value of the entire estate, less liens and encumbrances, does not exceed homestead allowance, exempt property, family allowance, costs and expenses of administration, reasonable funeral expenses, and reasonable and necessary medical and hospital expenses of the last illness of the decedent, the personal representative, without giving notice to creditors, may immediately disburse and distribute the estate to the persons entitled thereto and file a closing statement . . . (UPC § 3-1203).

The method of closing an estate through a summary administration is to petition the court for closure. The UPC states the request should contain information regarding the value of the estate, a statement that the personal representative has fully administered the estate, and a statement that the personal representative has sent a copy of the closing statement to all interested persons who are known (UPC § 3-1204). See Wisconsin's summary settlement—petition in Figure 10-10.

The court rules on the petition and signs an order granting it. See Wisconsin's summary settlement—findings and order in Figure 10-11 and North Carolina's order of summary administration in Figure 10-12.

Oklahoma statutes allow the personal representative to move from regular administration to summary administration. Under these circumstances, the personal representative is required to file an application for summary administration and inventory with the court. If the court determines that the value of the decedent's entire estate, both real and personal property, does not exceed one hundred and fifty thousand dollars ($150,000.00), the court dispenses with regular proceedings and allows summary administration. In Oklahoma:

> [T]he court shall order notice to creditors, and issue an order for hearing upon the final accounting and petition for determination of heirship, distribution and discharge (Okla. Stat., tit. 58 § 241).

Once this has been accomplished:

> [T]he matter shall be set for hearing not less than thirty-five (35) days following the first publication of notice to creditors . . . and upon the hearing the court shall, after

Figure 10-10 Wisconsin's summary settlement—petition

STATE OF WISCONSIN, CIRCUIT COURT, _____ COUNTY

| IN THE MATTER OF

_____

_____ | **Summary Settlement -
Petition**
☐ **with Special Administration**

Case No. _____ | *For Official Use* |

UNDER OATH, I STATE THAT:

1. The decedent, whose date of birth was _____, and date of death was _____, died domiciled in _____ County, State of _____, with a post office address of: _____.

2. The petitioner is interested as _____.

3. The estate of the decedent:
☐ qualifies for summary settlement without appointment of a personal representative.
☐ commenced under chapter 856, meets the requirements for termination under summary settlement of small estates.

4. The estate is one properly settled under summary settlement in that: *(Select either a or b below.)*
☐ A. the estate, less the amount of the debts for which any property in the estate is security, does not exceed in value the costs, expenses, allowances, and claims under §859.25(1)(a) to (g), Wis. Stats.
☐ B. the estate, less the amount of the debts for which any property in the estate is security, does not exceed $50,000 (date of death after May 8, 2000) or $30,000 (date of death before May 9, 2000) in value and the decedent is survived by a spouse or one or more minor children or both.

5. A detailed statement of all property subject to administration including any encumbrance, lien, or other charge upon each is as follows: ☐ **See attached.**

Description of Property	**Value of Decedent's Interest at Date of Death**
A. <u>Property Subject to Administration</u>	$
B. <u>Encumbrances, liens or other charges upon each item:</u>	($)
C. <u>Net value of Property Subject to Administration</u> (Total value from Section A above less total from Section B above)	$

PR-1835 01/07   Summary Settlement – Petition   §867.01, Wisconsin Statutes
This form shall not be modified. It may be supplemented with additional material.
Page 1 of 3

(continued)

Figure 10-10   (continued)

Summary Settlement - Petition   Page 2 of 3   Case No. _____

6. The names and addresses of all creditors of the decedent or the decedent's estate of whom the petitioner has knowledge and the amounts of their claims are as follows:

Name of Creditor	Address	Claim Amount

7. The names and post-office addresses of all persons interested (including children of decedent who are not children of the surviving spouse), so far as known to petitioner or ascertainable by the petitioner with reasonable diligence are as follows (indicate persons who are minors or otherwise under disability, and names and post-office addresses of their guardians):

Name	Relationship	Address	Minor's D. O. B.

8. The decedent:

☐ did   ☐ did not   receive medical assistance.
☐ did   ☐ did not   receive family care benefits.
☐ did   ☐ did not   receive benefits from long-term support community options program.
☐ did   ☐ did not   receive aid for treatment of kidney disease.
☐ did   ☐ did not   receive cystic fibrosis aids.
☐ did   ☐ did not   receive hemophilia treatment services.

9. If the decedent was ever married, complete the following: ☐ If more than one spouse, see attached
Name of spouse (☐ living or ☐ deceased): _____.
☐ did   ☐ did not   receive medical assistance.
☐ did   ☐ did not   receive family care benefits.
☐ did   ☐ did not   receive benefits from long-term support community options program.
☐ did   ☐ did not   receive aid for treatment of kidney disease.
☐ did   ☐ did not   receive cystic fibrosis aids.
☐ did   ☐ did not   receive hemophilia treatment services.

PR-1835 01/07   Summary Settlement – Petition   §867.01, Wisconsin Statutes

This form shall not be modified. It may be supplemented with additional material.
Page 2 of 3

(continued)

Figure 10-10   (continued)

Summary Settlement - Petition   Page 3 of 3   Case No. _____

☐ **10.** It is necessary to appoint a special administrator with the following powers:

BASED UPON THESE STATEMENTS, I REQUEST THAT THE COURT:

   1. Assign the property to the persons entitled to it.

   2. Order any person indebted to or holding money or other property of the decedent to pay the indebtedness or deliver the property to the persons found to be entitled to receive it.

   3. Order the transfer of interests in real estate, stocks or bonds registered in the name of the decedent, the title of a licensed motor vehicle, or any other form of property.

   4. Order termination of any life estate.

   5. Certify the right of survivorship of any joint tenant for which a certificate has not been issued.

   6. Certify that any interest of the decedent in survivorship marital property vested in the surviving spouse at death.

   7. Order termination of any estate commenced under Chapter 856, discharge the personal representative and cancel any bond.

☐ **8.** Appoint a special administrator with the powers requested.

Subscribed and sworn to before me
on _____   _____
                                                                          Signature of Petitioner

_____   _____
         Notary Public/Court Official   Name Printed or Typed
My commission expires: _____
                                                            _____
                                                                          Address

                                                            _____

                                                            _____
                                                                          Telephone Number

Name of Attorney	
Address	
Telephone Number	Bar Number

PR-1835 01/07   Summary Settlement – Petition   §867.01, Wisconsin Statutes

This form shall not be modified. It may be supplemented with additional material.
Page 3 of 3

Source: For most current version of this form, visit www.wicourts.org.

Figure 10-11   Wisconsin's summary settlement—findings and order

	For Official Use
STATE OF WISCONSIN, CIRCUIT COURT, _____ COUNTY	
IN THE MATTER OF THE ESTATE OF _____	**Summary Settlement - Findings and Order** ☐ **with Order Appointing Special Administrator**
_____	Case No. _____

A petition for summary settlement having been filed.

THE COURT FINDS THAT:

1. The decedent, whose date of birth was _____, and date of death was _____, died domiciled in _____ County, State of _____, with a post office address of: _____

2. Petitioner is interested as _____.

3. Notice to interested persons: ☐ has been given as required by the court.   ☐ has been waived.   ☐ was not required.

4. Notice, if required, has been given to the Department of Health and Family Services and more than 30 days have elapsed since that notice was given.

5. The estate is one properly settled under summary settlement in that: *(Select either A or B below.)*
   ☐ A. the estate, less the amount of the debts for which any property in the estate is security, does not exceed in value the costs, expenses, allowances, and claims under §859.25(1)(a) to (g), Wis. Stats.
   ☐ B. the estate, less the amount of the debts for which any property in the estate is security, does not exceed $50,000 in value and the decedent is survived by a spouse or one or more minor children or both.

6. A detailed statement of all property subject to administration including any encumbrance, lien, or other charge upon each is as follows: ☐ **See attached.**

Description of Property	**Value of Decedent's Interest at Date of Death**
A. <u>Property Subject to Administration</u>	$
B. <u>Encumbrances, liens or other charges upon each item:</u>	($)
C. <u>Net value of Property Subject to Administration</u> (Total value from Section A above less total from Section B above)	$

(continued)

Figure 10-11 (continued)

Summary Settlement - Findings and Order

---

7. Complete section A or B below.

☐ A. The estate is appropriate to be settled under §867.01(1)(a), Wis. Stats. The priority claims against the estate under §859.25, Wis. Stats., and the persons entitled to payment are:

Persons(s) Entitled to Payment	Amount
(1) Costs and expenses of administration:	
(2) Funeral and burial expenses:	
(3) Provisions for the family of the decedent under §§861.31, 861.33 and 861.35, Wis. Stats.:	
(4) Other priority claims under §859.25, Wis. Stats.:	

☐ B. The estate may be settled under §867.01(1)(b), Wisconsin Statutes. Any property not otherwise assigned shall be assigned as an allowance under §861.31, Wisconsin Statutes to:
　　　　☐ the surviving spouse.
　　　　☐ the minor children.
　　　　☐ both the surviving spouse and the minor children.

8. Any interest of the decedent as joint tenant terminated at death.

9. Any life estate of the decedent terminated at death.

10. Any interest of the decedent in survivorship marital property vested in the surviving spouse at death.

☐ **11.** It is necessary to appoint a special administrator with the following powers:

(continued)

Figure 10-11   (continued)

Summary Settlement - Findings and Order

Page 3 of 3   Case No. _____

THE COURT ORDERS THAT:

1. The property is assigned to the persons entitled to it as stated below.

2. Any person indebted to or holding money or other property of the decedent pay the indebtedness or deliver the property to the persons found to be entitled to receive it as stated below.

3. Interests in real estate, stocks or bonds registered in the name of the decedent, title of licensed motor vehicle(s), or any other form of property are transferred to:

Person(s) Entitled to Receive	Description of Property	Value

4. If the decedent immediately prior to death had an estate for life or an interest as a joint tenant or in survivorship marital property, in any property for which a certificate of termination has not been issued, the court certifies that such interests terminated or vested at death.

☐ **5.** The estate commenced under Chapter 856 is terminated; upon filing receipts, the personal representative is discharged and any bond is cancelled.

☐ **6.** The petitioner shall inform known unsatisfied creditors as to the final disposition of the estate.

☐ **7.** Letters of Special Administration are issued to _____
upon filing a _____ bond of $_____, with the following powers:

BY THE COURT:

Name of Attorney	_____
	Circuit Court Judge/Court Commissioner
Address	_____
	Name Printed or Typed
	_____
Telephone Number	Bar Number	Date

PR-1837, 01/07 Summary Settlement - Findings and Order   §867.01, Wisconsin Statutes
This form shall not be modified. It may be supplemented with additional material.
Page 3 of 3

Source: For the most current version of this form, visit www.wicourts.org.

Figure 10-12 North Carolina's order of summary administration

STATE OF NORTH CAROLINA	*File No.*
	Film No.
_____ County	In The General Court Of Justice Superior Court Division Before The Clerk

IN THE MATTER OF THE ESTATE OF:	
Name Of Decedent	**ORDER** **OF** **SUMMARY ADMINISTRATION** G.S. 28A-28-1 et. seq.
Name And Mailing Address Of Petitioner/Spouse	
Telephone No.	
Legal Residence (County, State)	*County Will Admitted To Probate* / *File No.*
Name And Address Of Attorney, If Any	*Telephone No.*

The Court, in the exercise of its jurisdiction over the probate of wills and the administration of estates, finds that the Petition For Order Of Summary Administration, and supporting evidence, if any, comply with the requirements of G.S. 28A-28-2, and that the above named petitioner/spouse is entitled to summary administration.

Based upon these findings, the Court orders that the estate listed above be administered in accordance with Article 28 of Chapter 28A of the General Statutes of North Carolina, that no further or other administration of the estate is necessary, that the above named petitioner/spouse is fully authorized by the laws of North Carolina to receive, administer, and dispose of all of the assets belonging to the estate, including but not limited to wages and salary of the decedent, accounts and deposits in financial institutions, ownership rights in stocks and securities, the title and license to any motor vehicle registered to the decedent, and the right to convey, lease, sell or mortgage any real estate devised to or inherited by the petitioner from the decedent, and that the above named petitioner/spouse, to the extent of the value of the property received by the petitioner/spouse under the will of the decedent or by intestate succession, assumes all liabilities of the decedent that were not discharged by reason of death, and assumes liability for all taxes and valid claims against decedent or against the estate.

The Court notes that under G.S. 28A-28-5, the person paying, delivering, transferring or issuing property or evidence thereof pursuant to this Order is discharged and released to the same extent as if the person dealt with a duly qualified personal representative of the decedent's estate. If any person to whom the order is presented refuses to pay, deliver, transfer, or issue any property or evidence thereof, the property may be recovered in an action brought for that purpose by the petitioner/spouse, and the court costs and attorney's fees incident to the action shall be taxed against the person whose refusal made the action necessary.

Date
Name Of Presiding Official (Type Or Print)
EX OFFICIO JUDGE OF PROBATE
Signature Of Presiding Official
☐ *Assistant CSC*   ☐ *Clerk Of Superior Court*

SEAL

CERTIFICATION

I certify that this is a true and complete copy of the original Order Of Summary Administration on file in this office.

Date	*Signature*
AOC-E-904M, New 2/96 ©1997 Administrative Office of the Courts	☐ *Deputy CSC* ☐ *Assistant CSC* ☐ *Clerk Of Superior Court*

Source: North Carolina Administrative Office of the Courts.

proof of payment of funeral expenses, payment of last sickness and of administration and allowed claims, issue an order allowing the final accounting, determining heirship and the legatees and devisees, if any, of the decedent, distributing the property of the estate, and discharging the personal representative and surety or sureties on the personal representative's bond . . . (Okla. Stat., tit. 58, § 241).

It is also possible in Oklahoma to commence the estate administration as a summary administration. Okla. Stat., tit. 58, § 245, sets forth the conditions and requirements for petitioning for a summary administration. One condition is that the estate be valued at one hundred seventy-five thousand dollars ($175,000.00) or less. The same statute prescribes the information to be included in the petition, such as a statement of the petitioner's interest; name, age, and date of death of the decedent; county and state of the decedent's domicile at the time of death; the original will or a copy attached (if no will can be found, a statement that the petitioner has diligently searched for one); information regarding heirs, beneficiaries, and executors; information regarding the decedent's creditors; value and character of the property in the estate; and so on. According to the statute, the proposed personal representative becomes the court-appointed personal representative without a hearing, provided certain requirements have been met. Oklahoma goes on to detail notice requirements in Okla. Stat., tit. 58, § 246. It outlines the hearing and the court's final decree in Okla. Stat., tit. 58, § 247.

2. Transfer by Affidavit

Another less formal method of estate administration, done for smaller estates, is transfer by affidavit. State statutes dictate under what circumstances a transfer by affidavit may occur. There is a limit on the amount of the estate's gross value, and this method usually can be used only for the transfer of personal property. In some states, only certain relatives of the decedent, such as a spouse or children who are heirs or beneficiaries, may use this method. An affidavit is prepared and signed by the affiant. An affidavit is a sworn statement of fact, and thus the affiant's signature is notarized. In general, the affidavit states the value of the estate, that a certain time frame from the decedent's date of death has expired, that no personal representative has been appointed, and that the individual is legally entitled to the property. The Uniform Probate Code requires the above in UPC § 3-1201. See Wisconsin's transfer by affidavit in Figure 10-13.

Oregon law provides for a transfer by affidavit procedure. The full procedure is included in Or. Rev. Stat. § 114.505 to Or. Rev. Stat. § 114.560. Oregon allows a transfer by affidavit if

> (a) The fair market value of the estate is $200,000.00 or less; (b) Not more than $50,000.00 of the fair market value of the estate is attributable to personal property; and (c) Not more than $150,000.00 of the fair market value is attributable to real property (Or. Rev. Stat. § 114.515 (2)).

This statute specifies who may file the affidavit and includes "claiming successors of the decedent" or a personal representative named in the decedent's will (Or. Rev. Stat. § 114.515 (1)). The contents of the affidavit are prescribed in Or. Rev. Stat. § 114.525. As with other estate administration applications, similar information is disclosed, including personal information of the decedent, heirs, and beneficiaries; information about creditors; the estate property and fair-market value; a statement explaining if the decedent died testate or intestate; and so on.

Figure 10-13 Wisconsin's transfer by affidavit

STATE OF WISCONSIN, _____ **COUNTY**

IN THE MATTER OF

_____

Decedent

**Transfer by Affidavit
($50,000 and under)**

Register of deeds recording area _____

Name and return address

Note: Use black ink only.

_____

parcel identification number

UNDER OATH, I STATE THAT:

1. The decedent, whose date of birth was _____, and date of death was
   _____, died domiciled in _____ County, State of _____,
   with a post office address of:_____
   _____

2. I am: ☐ an heir, having the following relationship to the decedent:_____.
   ☐ the person who was guardian of the decedent at the time of the decedent's death.
   ☐ trustee of a revocable trust created by the decedent.

3. The total value of the decedent's property subject to administration in Wisconsin on the date of death did not
   exceed $50,000.

4. The total value of the decedent's property subject to administration in Wisconsin at the date of decedent's death
   was $ _____.

5. The decedent:
   ☐ did ☐ did not   receive medical assistance.
   ☐ did ☐ did not   receive family care benefits (through a Care Management Organization – CMO).
   ☐ did ☐ did not   receive benefits from the Community Options Program (COP).
   ☐ did ☐ did not   receive benefits from the Wisconsin Chronic Disease Program.
   ☐ was ☐ was not   patient or inmate of a state or county hospital or institution, or responsible for any
   person owing an obligation to the state or county. If so, explain: _____
   _____

6. If the decedent was ever married, complete the following:
   Name of spouse (☐ living or ☐ deceased): _____.
   The spouse ☐ did ☐ did not   receive benefits from the Community Options Program (COP).
   The spouse ☐ did ☐ did not   receive benefits from the Wisconsin Chronic Disease Program.

PR-1831, 04/07 Transfer by Affidavit ($50,000 and under)   §867.03, Wisconsin Statutes
This form shall not be modified. It may be supplemented with additional material.
Page 1 of 2

(continued)

Figure 10-13   (continued)

Transfer by Affidavit ($50,000 and under)

7. I ask that the following property be transferred to me under §867.03(1g), Wisconsin Statutes:

DESCRIPTION OF REAL ESTATE AND/OR PERSONAL PROPERTY TO BE TRANSFERRED (If real estate, list legal description and tax parcel number. If personal property, specifically describe property including name of financial institutions and account numbers, if any.)	VALUE

8. By accepting the decedent's property under this section, I assume a duty to apply the property transferred for the payment of obligations according to priorities established under §859.25, Wisconsin Statutes, and to distribute any balance to those persons designated in the appropriate governing instrument, as defined in §854.01, Wisconsin Statutes, or if there is no governing instrument, according to the rules of intestate succession under ch. 852, Wisconsin Statutes.

9. If a decedent or decedent's spouse has received any of the benefits that are listed on page 1 of this affidavit, a duplicate affidavit must be sent by certified mail with return receipt requested to the Estate Recovery Program for the State of Wisconsin, Department of Health and Family Services prior to submission of this affidavit for recording. The proof of prior mailed notice should accompany the affidavit for recording, with the delivery date on the mail receipt being at least 10 days prior.

Subscribed and sworn to before me

on _____

_____
Notary Public/Court Official

My commission expires: _____

_____
Signature

_____
Name Printed or Typed

_____
Address

_____

This document was drafted by: _____
Print or Type Name

☐ **Register of Deeds Office viewed the certified mail receipt.**

<u>**ONLY**</u> **if this affidavit describes an interest in or lien on real estate, then a certified copy or duplicate original of this affidavit must be recorded with the register of deeds in each county in Wisconsin where the real estate is located.**

PR-1831, 04/07 Transfer by Affidavit ($50,000 and under)   §867.03, Wisconsin Statutes
This form shall not be modified. It may be supplemented with additional material.
Page 2 of 2

Source: For the most current version of this form, visit www.wicourts.org.

Once the affidavit is delivered to the person holding the property, the property should be transferred to the affiant:

> Any person indebted to the decedent or having possession of personal property belonging to the estate, to whom a certified copy of the affidavit . . . is delivered by the affiant on or after the tenth day following the filing of the affidavit, shall pay, transfer or deliver the personal property to the affiant . . . (Or. Rev. Stat. § 114.535).

Ancillary Administration

ancillary administration:
A probate occurring in a state where the decedent owned property but not in his or her domiciliary state.

domiciliary administration:
A probate occurring in the state where the decedent was domiciled.

When an individual dies, the estate administration is typically done entirely in the state where the decedent was domiciled. Most often, the decedent's property is located in the state of the decedent's domicile, and thus that state has personal jurisdiction over the probate. Sometimes the decedent may own real estate located in another state. Depending on the laws of that state, a secondary proceeding may be instituted, which is called **ancillary administration**. The probate occurring in the state where the decedent was domiciled is called **domiciliary administration**.

An ancillary administration allows the property located in the foreign state to be transferred or sold. The domiciliary state lacks jurisdiction to do this. Usually real estate is the subject of ancillary administration. Most personal property can be transferred or sold in the domiciliary administration. An Ohio statute explains that state's approach to ancillary administration:

> When a nonresident decedent leaves property in Ohio, ancillary administration proceedings may be had upon application of any interested person in any county in Ohio in which is located property of the decedent, or in which a debtor of such decedent resides . . . The ancillary administration first granted shall extend to all the estate of the deceased within the state and shall exclude the jurisdiction of any other court (Ohio Rev. Code Ann. § 2129.04).

State law must be consulted to determine the procedure for ancillary administration. An application or petition is often filed, the will is filed, and letters of appointment are issued. In Ohio, the ancillary administrator is appointed after an authenticated copy of the will is admitted to the record, and a complete record of the grant of the domiciliary letters and other records of the domiciliary administration required by the Ohio court have been filed (Ohio Rev. Code Ann. § 2129.08). After taxes are paid and creditors are satisfied, the property is released. An Ohio statute states under what circumstances the property located in Ohio is distributed to the heirs and beneficiaries:

> When the expenses of the ancillary administration of a nonresident decedent's estate, including such attorney's fee as is allowed by the probate court, all public charges and taxes, all claims of creditors . . . have been paid, and any residue of the personal estate and the proceeds of any real estate sold for payment of debts shall be distributed by the ancillary administrator as follows: (A) with the approval of the court such residue may be delivered to the domiciliary administrator or executor (B) if the court orders, such residue shall be delivered to the persons entitled thereto (Ohio Rev. Code Ann. § 2129.23).

The ancillary proceeding protects creditors of the foreign state. It is also possible that the personal representative from the domiciliary state cannot serve, and a resident of the foreign state must be court-appointed as the personal representative.

Figure 10-14   Connecticut's application for ancillary probate of will

APPLICATION/ANCILLARY
PROBATE OF WILL
PC-201   REV. 7/95

STATE OF CONNECTICUT

RECORDED:

COURT OF PROBATE
*[Type or print in black ink. File in **duplicate**.]*
[Use Second Sheet, PC-180, for additional data.]

TO: COURT OF PROBATE, DISTRICT OF

DISTRICT NO.

ESTATE OF *[Include all names and initials under which any asset was held.]*

SOCIAL SECURITY NO.   DATE OF DEATH

DECEDENT'S RESIDENCE AT TIME OF DEATH *[Include full address.]*

PETITIONER *[Name, address, and zip code.]*

SURVIVING SPOUSE *[Name, address, and zip code. If no surviving spouse, so state.]*

JURISDICTION APPERTAINS TO THIS COURT BASED ON THE FOLLOWING: [C.G.S. §45a-287]

☐ The decedent last resided in this district.

☐ The decedent has real or tangible personal property located in this district.

☐ The decedent has maintained bank accounts or evidence of other tangible property in this district.

☐ An executor or trustee named in the will resides in this district or, in the case of a bank or trust company, has an office in this district.

☐ A cause of action in favor of the decedent arose in this district, or a debtor of the decedent resides or has an office in this district.

HEIRS, NEXT OF KIN, BENEFICIARIES, and TRUSTEES, if any. *[Give names, addresses, zip codes, and relationships.]* **If heir, indicate ancestor through whom heir takes. If beneficiary, indicate paragraph of will where interest is stated or may arise. For all minors listed, give date of birth. Indicate any person who is under legal disability or in the military service. C.G.S. §§45a-436, 438, 439.**

THE PETITIONER REPRESENTS that:

No other application for ancillary probate has been filed in the State of Connecticut.

Decedent, or spouse or children of the decedent, ☐ *did* ☐ *did not* ever receive aid or care from the State of Connecticut.

[If affirmative, check appropriate box(es).] ☐ State of Connecticut (D.A.S) ☐ Department of Veterans' Affairs C.G.S. §45a-355.

THE PETITIONER HEREWITH PRESENTS to the Court the duly authenticated and exemplified copy of the Last Will and Testament and codicils, if any, of the decedent dated _____ and the record of the proceedings proving and establishing the same by a court of competent jurisdiction and REPRESENTS that the time for taking an appeal therefrom ☐ *has* ☐ *has not* expired, and no appeals are presently pending. Attached hereto is a complete statement of the property and estate of the decedent in Connecticut. C.G.S. §45a-288.

WHEREFORE, THE PETITIONER REQUESTS this Court to order that said copies be filed and recorded and that letters ancillary testamentary be issued to the fiduciary named below.

The representations contained herein are made under the penalties of false statement.

Date: ....

....
Petitioner:

PROPOSED FIDUCIARY
IF APPOINTED, I WILL ACCEPT SAID POSITION OF TRUST

Signature ....
[Type or print name under signature.]

....

Address and zip code:

Fiduciary ☐ is ☐ is not a resident of the State of Connecticut.   Fiduciary ☐ is ☐ is not a resident of the State of Connecticut.

Telephone number: Telephone number:

ATTORNEY FOR PROPOSED FIDUCIARY *[Name, address, zip code, telephone number, Conn. Bar Juris No.]*

Each of the undersigned represents that he or she has examined the application and related documents and hereby **WAIVES NOTICE OF HEARING** upon said application and has **NO OBJECTION** to the granting and approval thereof. *[If space is insufficient, use General Waiver, PC-181. Please also type or print name.]*

....

....

APPLICATION/ANCILLARY PROBATE OF WILL
PC-201

Source: Reprinted with the permission of the Office of the Probate Court Administrator.

Here is an example of how ancillary administration works. Amy Woodchuck is domiciled in Iowa. She owns a parcel of real estate in Connecticut, but the remainder of her property is located in Iowa. The domiciliary administration would be done in Iowa, her state of domicile. However, the estate administration of the parcel of land located in Connecticut would need to be done in Connecticut and would be called the ancillary administration. See Connecticut's application for ancillary probate of will in Figure 10-14.

KEY **TERMS**

ancillary administration (p. 230)   domiciliary administration (p. 230)   receipts (p. 210)

distribution (p. 212)   final account (p. 202)   will contest (p. 212)

REVIEW **QUESTIONS**

1. Define final account. List the information contained in it. Why do you think a final account needs to have that information and none other?

2. Name and explain the three common documents used to close the estate.

3. List and explain three valid grounds for a will contest.

4. How does small estate administration differ from formal probate?

5. Compare and contrast summary administration and transfer by affidavit.

6. Compare and contrast domiciliary administration and ancillary administration.

ROLE-PLAYING **ACTIVITIES**

1. With a classmate, debate the pros and cons of formal administration, informal administration, summary administration, and transfer by affidavit.

2. Form groups of four. Two of you act as disgruntled heirs wishing to contest a will. The other two act as lawyers responding to the disgruntled heirs. Determine the likelihood of the lawyers taking the case and under what grounds the contest would be brought.

RESEARCH **ASSIGNMENTS**

1. Research your state's statute regarding information required in the final account. Cite the appropriate statute number. What information is required in the final account?

2. Research your state's requirements and procedure for notice of hearing on the final account.

3. Research your state law and determine what additional documents are required to close an estate.

4. Research the types of small estate administration available in your state. List and briefly explain them.

5. Research your state law regarding ancillary administration.

BUILD YOUR **PORTFOLIO**

1. Using the case example you chose in Chapter 6, draft a final account.

2. Using the case example you chose in Chapter 6, draft a receipt.

3. Using the case example you chose in Chapter 6, draft the document that closes the estate and discharges the personal representative.

Glossary

A

Abatement   A proportional reduction of gifts to beneficiaries because the estate lacks sufficient funds to pay the decedent's debts.

Ademption   A gift by will fails because it is no longer owned by the testator or it is no longer in existence.

Administrator   The court-appointed legal representative, not named in the will, who manages the administration of the decedent's estate.

Ambulatory   Subject to change.

Ancestors   A person's lineal heirs from whom they descend, that is, parent, grandparent, etc.

Ancillary administration   A probate occurring in a state where the decedent owned property but not in his or her domiciliary state.

Anti-lapse statute   A legislative enactment that passes the gift of property to a deceased beneficiary's heirs rather than through the will's residuary clause or intestate succession statute.

Attestation clause   The clause at the end of a will or codicil that states the witnesses certify the document was executed before them.

B

Beneficiary   One who benefits, inherits property from a will (one who benefits from a trust or insurance); the person who receives the benefit of the property placed in a trust.

Bequest   A gift by will of personal property.

Boilerplate   Standard language used in similar documents.

Bond   Promise of a guarantor to pay the estate if the personal representative fails to properly administer the decedent's estate; required by the court to be filed by the personal representative to ensure proper performance of duties.

C

Caption   The top section of a court document.

Cestui que trust   The beneficiary of a trust.

Codicil   A testamentary document that amends a will.

Collateral heirs   People who are not directly related to the decedent, that is, brother, sister, uncle, aunt.

Community property   Property owned by a husband and wife, each having an undivided one-half ownership right because of their marital status.

Constructive trust   An implied trust created by law to prevent fraud or unjust enrichment.

Credits   Amounts subtracted from taxable income to reduce tax liability.

Cy-pres doctrine   As near as possible. If the intention of a settlor cannot be carried out because it would be illegal or impractical, the court will carry out the trust provisions as near as possible to the settlor's initial intention.

D

Deduction   An item allowed to reduce the gross income amount.

Demonstrative bequest   A gift by will of a sum of money from a specified fund or from the sale of particular item.

Descendants   An ancestor's bloodline. Those relatives that descend as lineal heirs from a person, that is, children, grandchildren, etc.

Devise   A gift by will of real property. Today, under the U.P.C., also known as a bequest.

Distribution   The process of transferring money or property to a beneficiary or heir in satisfaction of an inheritance.

Domicile   The place where a person makes his a her permanent home and when absent, plans on returning to it.

Domiciliary administration A probate occurring in the state where the decedent was domiciled.

Durable general power of attorney A power of attorney that does not terminate upon the principal becoming mentally incompetent.

E

Employer identification number (EIN) The number assigned by the Internal Revenue Service to an estate and to be used by the estate when preparing tax returns and paying taxes.

Equitable title The interest a beneficiary has in property contained in a trust. The rights to benefit from the property but not manage it.

Escheat The state inherits the decedent's estate.

Estate administration The process of managing a decedent's property under court supervision; it includes collection of decedent's assets, payment of debts and taxes, and distribution of remaining property.

Estate planning A method of preparing for the administration of a person's property upon death by using documents and other arrangements usually to reduce costs of administration and taxes.

Estate tax A one-time tax imposed on an estate because of the decedent's privilege of transferring property upon death.

Execution The completion of all actions to make a document valid.

Executor A person nominated in the will to carry out the directions and the distribution of gifts contained in the will.

Exordium clause The introductory clause to a will or codicil.

Express trust A trust that is communicated, usually in written terms, and not inferred by the conduct of the parties or by the court to prevent unjust enrichment.

F

Fee simple The highest interest in land. One person has full ownership to the land.

Fiduciary One who acts on behalf of another with trust and confidence.

Final account A financial report to the court and interested persons detailing the income and outflow of an estate's money and property while the estate is pending.

Fixtures Personal property that is securely attached to the land so that it takes on the characteristics of real property and is treated as real property under the law.

Formal probate A proceeding before a judge to determine if the decedent left a valid will.

G

General bequest A gift by will of an amount of money.

Gross income All income from whatever source derived.

Guardian A person who has legal authority and a duty to act on behalf of a minor or mentally incompetent person.

H

Heirs Those persons who inherit from the decedent under the statutes of intestate succession.

Holographic will A will written entirely in the testator's handwriting and not witnessed.

I

Implied trust A trust not expressly communicated but implied based on the conduct of the parties or to prevent unjust enrichment.

Informal probate A process supervised by a court official to probate a will or appoint a personal representative.

Inheritance tax Tax imposed on the privilege of receiving a decedent's property.

Inter vivos trust Also known as a living trust; a trust created to take effect while the person is living, not upon the death of a person.

"In terrorem" clause A provision in a will that states a beneficiary will not receive his or her gift if he or she contests the will.

Intestate Dying without a valid will.

Inventory   A court document that lists all of the decedent's probatable assets and their date-of-death values.

Irrevocable trust   A trust that cannot be terminated or changed by the settlor.

Issue   The stream of progeny of a person, that is, children, grandchildren, etc.

Itemized deduction   A taxpayer expense detailed under an appropriate category to reduce the amount of taxable income.

J

Joint tenancy   A single estate in property held by two or more persons created under one instrument at one time.

Jurat   A clause that states where, when, and whom the notary public is that is certifying the signature.

L

Lapse   A gift by will fails because the beneficiary predeceased the decedent or the beneficiary is unwilling to take the item.

Legacy   A gift by will of personal property.

Legal title   The interest a trustee has in the property contained in a trust. The rights to manage the trust but not benefit from it.

Legatee   A party who receives a gift by will of personal property.

Legator   A person who makes a gift by will of personal property.

Letters of appointment   The appointment of the personal representative is confirmed by court decree and evidenced by this document.

Letters of trust   A document issued by the court confirming the appointment of a trustee to a trust.

Lineal heirs   Those relatives who are in a direct line, either ascending or descending from the decedent, such as a decedent's parent or child, respectively.

Living will   A document where the signer may direct that no artificial measures be employed to postpone his or her death.

Lucid interval   A temporary return to mental capacity.

M

Marital deduction   Property passing to a surviving spouse that is not subject to estate tax.

N

Notary public   A public officer who administers oaths and certifies signatures as genuine.

Nuncupative will   An oral will made by the testator in anticipation of death gifting personal property and made in the presence of a witness.

O

Order   A court ruling on an issue raised during a proceeding.

P

Per capita   All heirs within a class receive equal shares.

Personal representative   Also known as administrator or executor; a legal representative appointed by the court to administer the decedent's estate.

Per stirpes   Also called right of representation. A method of distributing the decedent's estate when the decedent has left behind surviving issue from different generations. A deceased member of one generation who leaves behind surviving issue is represented by them. A living ancestor prevents his issue from inheriting.

Petition   A document that initiates a legal proceeding.

Posthumous child   A child conceived prior to his or her father's death but born after his or her father's death.

Pour-over will   A will that leaves any property owned by the decedent to an already existing inter vivos trust.

Power of attorney health care   A specialized power of attorney where the agent has authority to make health care decisions for the principal.

Power of attorney   A document that authorizes one person (the agent or attorney-in-fact) to act on behalf of another person (principal).

Pretermitted heir   A child or other relative, whether living or not yet born, of the decedent who has been omitted from the will.

Private trust   A trust created to benefit a designated individual or definite class of individuals.

Probate   The process of (a) a court admitting a will as valid, and/or (b) administering a decedent's estate.

Proof of heirship   A court document that lists the decedent's heirs.

Public trust   Also known as charitable trust; a trust created to benefit the public at large.

R

Real property   Land and items securely attached to it.

Receipts   Documents demonstrating that beneficiaries or heirs obtained money or property from the estate.

Residuary bequest   A gift by will of all the remaining property owned by the decedent that has not been gifted in another clause.

Residuary clause   A provision in a will that leaves to a designated beneficiary all remaining property not previously gifted.

Resulting trust   An implied trust based on the circumstances or conduct of the parties.

Revocable trust   A trust that can be terminated by the settlor.

Revocation clause   The clause in the will that cancels an already existing will.

S

Schedule K-1   A tax document informing an estate's beneficiary or heir of the amount of the estate's income and deductions allocated to him or her.

Self-proving will   As prescribed by statute, a will that removes some of the requirements of proof to be admitted to probate. Usually a self-proving affidavit is used.

Separate property   Property that one spouse owns exclusively because it was acquired by the individual prior to marriage or through other methods such that the law deems the property as separate.

Settlor   The creator of the trust who originally owned the property and transferred it to the trust.

Simultaneous death clause   A provision in a will that provides that another person predeceased the decedent if it is unclear who died first.

Slayer's rule or slayer's statute   An heir or beneficiary does not inherit from the decedent if the heir or beneficiary killed the decedent.

Specific bequest   A gift by will of a particular item of personal property.

Spendthrift trust   A trust created to protect the beneficiary from his own inability to spend wisely. The property cannot be reached by creditors.

SS4   The Internal Revenue Service's application used to acquire an employer identification number.

Standard deduction   A percentage amount, set by the Internal Revenue Service, that the taxpayer may use rather than itemized deductions to reduce gross income.

Statutes of descent and distribution   Also called statutes of intestate succession; the statutes that prescribe the pattern of priority to inherit when a person dies intestate.

Supernumerary witness   An extra witness to a will beyond the statutorily required number.

Surety   One who promises to pay money if the personal representative fails to properly administer the decedent's estate.

Survivorship clause or delay clause   A provision of a will that requires a beneficiary to outlive the decedent by a certain specified period of time for the gift to pass to him or her.

T

Taxable income   The income calculated by subtracting deductions and exemptions from gross income, or adjusted gross income, to which tax rates are applied to compute tax liability.

Tenancy by the entirety   Ownership of property by a husband and wife together.

Tenancy in common   An interest held by two or more persons, each having a possessory right in the same piece of property.

Testamentary trust   A trust created to take effect upon the death of a person.

Testamentary   Pertaining to a will or testament.

Testate   Dying with a valid will.

Testator   A man who makes and executes a will.

Testatrix   A woman who makes and executes a will.

Testimonium clause The provision in a will stating that the testator is signing and dating the document.

Totten trust A trust created by one person depositing money (in a bank) in his or her name, which becomes payable to another upon the depositor's death.

Trust Property placed in the care of one person (trustee) for the benefit of another (beneficiary).

Trustee The party who manages and oversees the property placed in trust.

U

Unified credit An amount used to reduce tax liability (credit) that replaces the former lifetime gift tax exemption and estate tax exemption.

Uniform Probate Code (U.P.C.) State legislatures can adopt this body of law relating to all matters in which a probate court has authority.

W

Will contest Petitioning the court to declare a will invalid.

Will A testamentary document that distributes wealth and directs how the estate should be administered.

Index